Why Early A.A. Succeeded

Dick B
2005

Other Titles by Dick B.

Dr. Bob and His Library: A Major A.A. Spiritual Source

Anne Smith's Journal, 1933-1939: A.A.'s Principles of Success

The Oxford Group & Alcoholics Anonymous:
A Design for Living That Works

The Akron Genesis of Alcoholics Anonymous

New Light on Alcoholism: God, Sam Shoemaker, and A.A.

The Books Early AAs Read for Spiritual Growth

Courage to Change:
The Christian Roots of the Twelve-Step Movement

The Good Book and The Big Book: A.A.'s Roots in the Bible

That Amazing Grace:
The Role of Clarence and Grace S. in Alcoholics Anonymous

Good Morning!:
Quiet Time, Morning Watch, Meditation, and Early A.A.

Turning Point:
A History of Early A.A.'s Spiritual Roots and Successes

Hope!: The Story of Geraldine D., Alina Lodge & Recovery

Utilizing Early A.A.'s Spiritual Roots for Recovery Today

The Golden Text of A.A.:
God, the Pioneers, and Real Spirituality

By the Power of God:
A Guide to Early A.A. Groups & Forming Similar Groups Today

Why Early A.A. Succeeded

The Good Book in
Alcoholics Anonymous
Yesterday and Today

(A Bible Study Primer
for AAs and other 12-Steppers)

"We already had the basic ideas, though not in terse and tangible form. We got them . . . as a result of our study of the Good Book."

Dr. Robert Holbrook Smith,
Co-Founder of Alcoholics Anonymous

Dick B.

With a Foreword by Jeffrey H. Boyd, M.D., M.Div., M.P.H.

Paradise Research Publications, Inc.
Kihei, Maui, Hawaii

Paradise Research Publications, Inc., P.O. Box 837, Kihei, HI 96753-0837

This Paradise Research Publications Edition is published by arrangement with Good Book Publishing Co., P.O. Box 837, Kihei, HI 96753-0837

The publication of this volume does not imply affiliation with nor approval or endorsement from Alcoholics Anonymous World Services, Inc. The views expressed herein are solely those of the author. A.A. is a program of recovery from alcoholism—use of the Twelve Steps in connection with programs and activities which are patterned after A.A., but which address other problems, does not imply otherwise.

Note: All Bible verses quoted in this book, unless otherwise noted, are from the Authorized (or "King James") Version. The letters "KJV" are used when necessary to distinguish it from other versions.

Publisher's Cataloging-in-Publication
(Provided by Quality Books, Inc.)

B., Dick.
    Why early A. A. succeeded : the good book in
Alcoholics Anonymous yesterday and tody / Dick B. –
1st ed.
    p. cm.
    Includes bibliographical references and index.
    ISBN 1-885803-31-1
    LCCN 00-093351

    1. Alcoholics–Rehabilitation–Biblical teaching.
2. Alcoholics Anonymous–History. 3. Recovering alcoholics
–Religious life. 4. Twelve-step programs–Religious
aspects–Christianity. 5. Bible–Criticism,
interpretations, etc. I. Title

HV5278.B25 2001   362.292'86
                         QBI00-701365

To Donald Edward Brown

Special thanks to:

Kathryn Mau Trust #1, Manhattan Beach, California
Frederick Robert Johnston, Maui, Hawaii
Mr. and Mrs. Tom W. Shepherd, Hacienda Heights, Calif.

Contents

Foreword

The success rate of early Alcoholics Anonymous in Akron was 75%. In Cleveland, it was 93%. Today, by most accounts, it is less than 10%. How was the effectiveness of A.A. lost? What did the founders know that we don't?

Dick B. is uniquely qualified to answer this question. He has the mind of a lawyer digging up the facts, and the passion of an alcoholic whose life was saved by A.A. It was not until Dick had been an A.A. member four years that he heard that A.A. came from the Bible. As a committed Christian, Dick was fascinated. He spent the next decade researching this issue, publishing 14 titles on the biblical roots of A.A., and amassing the most comprehensive library on the spiritual origins of A.A. that the world has ever seen (more than 23,000 books and other documents). His wisdom is distilled in this volume, which proposes that the decline in A.A.'s effectiveness is directly linked to the loss from A.A. of THE one and only Higher Power who was considered in early A.A. to be THE curative Agent.

Today in A.A., and in most of the 200 other Twelve Step programs that have adopted the A.A. approach, it is commonplace to say that the "Higher Power" mentioned by Step Two could be anything--a light bulb, radiator, the A.A. group itself, New Age spirituality, or whatever the alcoholic wishes to imagine. Anything greater than yourself counts as a "Higher Power" these days. Much, but not all, A.A. literature and many A.A. sponsors are cautious about the Bible and Christianity. Many warn that Bible reading leads directly to drinking, and that church should be avoided. Other historians who write about A.A. (e.g., Ernest Kurtz, William White, Wally P., Charles B., and others) usually omit any mention of Christianity or the Bible from their account of A.A.'s origins. This is astonishing, given that Dr. Bob, the original A.A. groups in Akron, and to some extent even Bill W., were crystal clear that the Bible and the Oxford Group were the primary sources of the spiritual recovery from addiction documented in the Big Book and its Twelve Steps. Such revisionist historians are seeking to please humans rather than pleasing God. They are reading back into A.A. history the distorted assumptions of today's Twelve Step culture. Twelve Steppers have drifted so far from their origins that they no longer know whence they came, and in the process they have lost their effectiveness.

Any Christian interested in how alcoholism or other addictions have been and can be overcome will be fascinated with this book, which balances: (1) readability, and (2) abundant quotes from the original documents, demonstrating beyond any shadow of a doubt that the founding fathers and mothers of A.A. thought that it was the God of the Bible who was delivering them from their slavery to alcohol. The book which was carried into every A.A. meeting before anyone ever thought of writing the "Big Book" was the Bible. The "Good Book" was the textbook out of which A.A. grew.

Jeffrey H. Boyd, M.D., M. Div., M.P.H.
Chairman of Psychiatry, Waterbury Hospital, Waterbury, CT
Ordained Episcopal Minister
Chairman of the New England Evangelical Theological Society

Preface

This book was written in the year 2000 after this author received many requests for information as to how to deal with the Bible when you are in today's A.A. and other 12 Step or Anonymous fellowships.

I felt the best way to start was by seeing how frequently and in what manner the early AAs discussed and used the "Good Book." That was the preliminary approach for this primer and guidebook. I had already done a title on A.A.'s roots in the Bible (*The Good Book and The Big Book*), also on Quiet Time in early A.A.—which always involved Bible study (*Good Morning!*). I had also done several titles on the major contributors to, and sources of, early A.A.'s biblical ideas–Anne Smith (*Anne Smith's Journal, 1933-1939*), the Rev. Sam Shoemaker *(New Light on Alcoholism)*, the Christian literature AAs read (*The Books Early AAs Read for Spiritual Growth*), and the Oxford Group books and practices (*The Oxford Group and Alcoholics Anonymous*). And I wrote several titles on how to use our spiritual roots today, including my last title—*By the Power of God*—which suggested how groups could establish Bible study fellowships in or out of A.A. and still conform to present-day A.A. Traditions. Many have formed such Bible fellowships or Big Book/Bible Study groups. But I discovered that the founders and/or leaders of these groups still were wondering exactly what and how to study in the Bible once the group was formed.

What was needed, it seemed, was a guide to the Bible. A book that would report on those things in the Good Book that the early

AAs had studied. And a book which would, as well, point to exact ideas that either individuals or groups could pursue. The objects were many: (1) Obtaining God's help in curing alcoholism–yes, curing it! (2) Learning first about our Creator, so that people would no longer continue to say that they couldn't understand God (for without understanding Him and all that He provides, it is pretty hard to live according to His will, receive His blessings, and know how to call on Him for help). (3) Accessing the vast amount of information Almighty God has actually made available as to how to become His kids, how to know His will, how to pray and listen to Him, how to receive His forgiveness and deliverance and healing, and what to expect as rewards for coming to Him and obeying Him. (4) Seeing precisely what the Bible is, how it was written, and what our Creator expects us to do with it. (5) Learning that we truly can be released from our prisons, live the abundant life, and be assured of everlasting life if we look to God's Word for the answers. (6) Providing a clear contrast between the self-made religion, absurd names for God, and half-baked prayers that are bewildering newcomers, being settled for by the compromisers, and encouraging the revisionists that are pouring into the scene in an effort to explain away the failures of what's becoming a watered-down "self help" program. (7) Suggesting the straight and dependable path to victory that comes from relying on God, resisting the Devil, and seeking first the kingdom of God in the heavily encumbered "recovery" scene of today.

It is my hope and belief that lives will be saved among those who really want to know and understand our Creator, the accomplishments of His Son Jesus Christ, and the power He made available through the gift of the Holy Spirit. Early AAs knew and understood these things, and talked about them. So can you. And what a message that is–"God has done for me what I could not do for myself." Pass it on!

Dick B.
Kihei, Maui, Hawaii
January, 2001

Acknowledgments

My previous titles have contained long lists of acknowledgments. So it is not necessary to mention again all of the people who have contributed knowledge and information to the work of the past ten years. Most are even specifically mentioned in the text of my books.

Once again, however, it is important to me to mention the help and advice and patience of my son Ken. He's not an alcoholic. He is a wonderful son, a Bible scholar with some 29 years of work under his belt, and now an ordained minister. He has helped me work with drunks, helped offer them the chance to learn of God and His Word, and brought many to fellowship and sonship with God through Jesus Christ. He has helped prove how available today are the resources of our Creator, just as they were in early A.A. He has helped establish today the accuracy of Dr. Bob's statement, "Your Heavenly Father will never let you down!"

There are some new sources of new help. Ozzie and Bonnie at The Wilson House. The many who have attended my seminars there and gone forth to bring God and the Bible back to AAs who want them. Ray G. and Corey F. who helped put the historical message before international A.A. at the Minneapolis Convention of 2000–an event that has not occurred for years. The many who have helped build our collection of historical books and materials to more than 23,000 in number so that we could begin to make these resources accessible, copyable, and known around the United States and the world. Specifically, Dr. Bob's kids, John Seiberling, Jim and Ellie Newton, George Vondermuhll, Jr., Moral Re-Armament, Willard

Hunter, Dennis C., and Danny W. The hundreds who have been visiting our website and then blessing us with phone calls, letters, and emails explaining how much they have wanted to hear about God and the Bible and Jesus Christ in A.A.–newcomers and old-timers alike.

A special word about my sponsee and brother in Christ, Bob J. For the past several years, Bob has been of immeasurable assistance in providing an office, a research center, a number of our resources, some of our historical acquisitions, and lots of enthusiasm. Of late, even filming a good deal of my teaching efforts. In addition, he has traveled with me as I gathered material for this book–to The Wilson House in Vermont, to Dr. Bob's Home and other archives and research spots in Akron, to the International Convention in Minneapolis, to several of the Clarence Snyder retreats, and to many A.A. activities, meetings, and conferences. I needed his help, and he was most generous in providing it.

Robert H., my sponsee and brother in Christ, and Steve C. (a member of our Bible fellowship) have been helpful in assembling materials and making my life easier in the midst of all the work on Maui. And thanks to both my sons, their wives, and my granddaughters who have really shown me the importance of family in sobriety and in life.

1

The Way Out

So, if you think you are standing firm, be careful that you don't fall! No temptation has seized you except what is common to man. And God is faithful; he will not let you be tempted beyond what you can bear. But when you are tempted, he will also provide a way out so that you can stand up under it. (1 Cor. 10:12-13; *New International Version*)

The Beginning

A noble experiment began in Akron, Ohio, on June 10, 1935. There was an attempt by Bill W. and Dr. Bob to solve the seemingly hopeless problem of alcoholism by spiritual means. By 1938, these two founders of the program counted noses and found they had 40 men who had recovered with what A.A. then called "divine aid." Bill W. was commissioned to write a textbook which would describe the steps the pioneers took on their path to a right relationship with our Creator. In the Spring of 1939, Bill's manuscript was ready for publication. But a name was required. Concerning the selection of the name, Bill wrote:

> After endless voting on a title for the new work, we had decided to call it *The Way Out*. But inquiry by Fitz M., our Maryland alcoholic, at the Library of Congress disclosed the fact that

twelve books already bore that title. Surely we couldn't make
our book the thirteenth. So we named it *Alcoholics Anonymous*
instead! Though we didn't know it, our movement then got its
name – a name which because of the implication of humility and
modesty had given us our treasured spiritual principle of
anonymity (*The Language of the Heart*, p. 107).

Hurrah for Bill's mentioning the principles of humility and modesty
and anonymity. They have served a great purpose in A.A. But they
were *not the heart of* "the way out" that A.A.'s pioneers had relied
upon. The "way out" for the real alcoholic did not begin with a
humble, modest, anonymous fellowship. The real way out began
with the Creator they had relied upon. They had relied upon the
power of God Almighty for relief from their alcoholism. They did
that because will-power, self-knowledge, self-reliance, fear, and all
human power had completely failed this afflicted crowd. And the
way–the way out–was found in the Bible, which they affectionately
called "The Good Book." That was their guide!

This book will provide a guide to what they studied, learned,
and applied from the Bible. It will also provide an opportunity for
you to do likewise, should you believe what Dr. Bob said when he
wrote: "Your Heavenly Father will never let you down!"
(*Alcoholics Anonymous*, 3rd ed., p. 181).

A guidebook is not an encyclopedia. It does not purport to
contain *all* the information or answers on a subject. It can, however,
point the way to something one wishes to find or learn. That, then,
is the purpose of this book.

A.A. pioneers wanted something very special. They didn't want
to be just "dry." They didn't want to be "dry" alcoholics who were
merely "on the wagon," yet still wanted to drink, needed to drink,
but had sworn not to drink. They also were looking for much more
than a fellowship of kindred souls who had survived a common
peril; and their basic text said so. Moreover, they wanted something
more than mere sanity when it came to their uncontrolled and
uncontrollable drinking. Believe it or not, they even wanted more
than a "cure" for alcoholism though this was zealously sought.

The Relationship They Sought

A.A.'s founders said quite clearly what they needed, wanted, and sought:

> The central fact of our lives today is the absolute certainty that our Creator has entered into our hearts and lives in a way which is indeed miraculous. He has commenced to accomplish those things for us which we could never do by ourselves (*Alcoholics Anonymous*, 1st ed., 1939, pp, 35-36).

> If what we have learned, and felt, and seen, means anything at all, it means that all of us, whatever our race, creed, or color, are children of a living Creator, with whom we may form a relationship upon simple and understandable terms as soon as we are willing and honest enough to try (*Alcoholics Anonymous*, 1st ed., 1939, p. 39).

> Each individual, in the personal stories, describes in his own language, and from his own point of view the way he established his relationship with God (*Alcoholics Anonymous*, 1st ed., 1939, p. 39).

Early A.A. members wanted, and eagerly sought, a relationship with God, their Creator. Their Big Book said this many times. They wanted to "enter upon a *new* relationship with their Creator . . . [which] would have the elements of a way of living that answered *all [their] problems;*" and their basic text said this as well (*Alcoholics Anonymous*, 1st ed., 1939, p. 23, italics added). These pioneers wanted the Divine power and help that would insure relief from their "cunning, baffling, powerful" foe, which they called alcohol. They specifically indicated they wanted to "find" or "rediscover" God (See the Multilith Copy of the Original Manuscript of the Big Book, p. 13). They wanted a solution that would produce "deep and effective spiritual experiences, which [would revolutionize their] whole attitude toward life, toward [their] fellows, and toward God's universe " (*Alcoholics Anonymous*, 1st ed., 1939, p. 35). And, though many in 12 Step fellowships today would deny the foregoing points, you can readily confirm them by simply reading the first two chapters of *Alcoholics Anonymous*, the First Edition of their text, which was published in 1939.

The alcoholics found their real solution. They found a way out consistent with the promise of 1 Cor. 10:12-13 quoted above. Their Creator provided the way. And their founders said so.

> Suddenly the ceiling went up. We no longer flew blind. A beacon had been lighted. God had shown alcoholics how it might be passed from hand to hand (*RHS*, Memorial Issue of the *AA Grapevine,* issued in January, 1951, on the occasion of Dr. Bob's death, p. 8).

They proposed calling their handbook (their text-book to be) *The Way Out,* though it is not clear whether their favored title's language came from the Bible or from their own deliverance. How strange it is, therefore, that so many addicted and afflicted people today have forgotten that real and early way out. Instead, they have seemingly focused their attention on a fellowship of anonymous well-doers–a fellowship in which the "power" can be that of the "group" or an "it" or just, plain, nothing at all. Many in today's fellowship have followed suit by saying today's A.A. creed is nothing more than: "Just don't drink, and go to meetings." Some add: your "higher power" can be whatever you want "it" to be. In fact, you need not believe in anything at all! You can find this language in many of the pamphlets emanating from A.A. today (See examples quoted in Dick B., *Turning Point*, pp. 5-6).

My People Are Destroyed
for Lack of Knowledge . . .

Let's consider from God's perspective the prevalent trend toward abandoning the original "way out." :

My people are destroyed for lack of knowledge: because thou hast rejected knowledge, I will also reject thee, that thou shalt be no priest to me: seeing thou hast forgotten the law of thy God, I will also forget thy children (Hos. 4:6).

The priests said not, Where *is* the LORD? and they that handle the law knew me not; the pastors also transgressed against me, and the prophets prophesied by Baal, and walked after *things that* do not profit
Hath a nation changed *their* gods, which are yet not gods? but my people have changed their glory for *that which* doth not profit.
Be astonished, O ye heavens at this, and be horribly afraid, be ye very desolate, saith the LORD.
For my people have committed two evils; they have forsaken me the fountain of living waters, and hewed them out cisterns, broken cisterns, that can hold no water (Jer. 2:8, 11-13).

Worse, the abandonment of God's way by some groups has, not surprisingly, spawned a host of new theories about the supposed nature of A.A.'s own spiritual program of recovery. There is today a strong group of revisionists who would change the whole program. To some extent, they already have. Some claim A.A. is no longer about "God;" it is, they say, about "not-god." (See Kurtz, *Not-God*, 1979, p. 109).

Even worse yet, there is an assertion that A.A. *itself* is "not-God" and has, these same analysts believe, now achieved "its profound not-God-ness," whatever that means (See Kurtz, *supra*, pp.135, 159, 185). Others claim A.A. is no longer about the Creator, but about some nebulous "higher power" which, they say, can be a "something," a "lightbulb," some other god (perhaps even a "goddess"), or just plain nothing at all. "Salvation," they insist, "is *accepting reality*," not accepting Christ (Kurtz, *supra*, pp. 184-85). Still others have claimed, and persist in claiming today, that when the word "God" is mentioned in A.A.'s basic text, the three letter word has somehow acquired a manufactured meaning and refers to a "convenient" or "expedient" god (Wally P., *Back to Basics*, pp.38-39). A god which, or who, can be whatever expedience or convenience or sometimes just plain stupidity suggests to you that "it" can be (Compare Dick B., *By the Power of God*, pp. 14-15).

This book is not about any of the foregoing gods, idols, "not-gods," "somethings," or "nothings." It does not accept, describe, endorse, or discuss, as part of its subject matter, the revisionist program–a group of concepts that seeks to "universalize" or "homogenize" the 12 Steps and otherwise "pluralize" the program. Nor does it embrace the idea that 12 Step recovery must somehow satisfy, mollify, and include the theories of each and every religion, of humanism, of agnosticism, of New Age thinking, of pantheism, or of atheism, by changing the Creator to a creature or statue, by admitting all comers, and by virtually reducing the program to a society for entertainment or comfort to any kind of sick newcomer.

Alcoholism is a life or death matter for the real alcoholic. Perhaps even more so for many other varieties of addiction today. The original ideas that A.A. pioneers borrowed from religion have never, ever, been shown to be less valid, less powerful, or any less necessary than they are today. And were yesteryear when a noted physician told early, incurable, real, alcoholics that they were "100% hopeless, apart from Divine help" (*Alcoholics Anonymous*, 1st ed., 1939, p. 55). That precise "Divine help" phrase is still in A.A.'s basic text (See *Alcoholics Anonymous*, 3rd ed., 1976, p. 43). So, it isn't the idea that has been abandoned or sweetened to the taste; it's the writings of those who really don't believe that "Divine help" is the key.

The best answer for them is what Bill Wilson said, in 1943, when he was sharing the platform with Dr. Bob in front of thousands of alcoholics:

> "There is a definite religious element here," Bill said. "I pray and I feel released." He emphasized that Divine Aid was A.A.'s greatest asset, more effective than confinement, environment

changes and dietary experiments (*The Tidings*, March 16, 1943, p. 17).

So, A.A. said in 1939–"100% hopeless, apart from Divine help!" Bill Wilson said in 1943--"Divine Aid was A.A.'s greatest asset!" A.A. still said in 1976–"100% hopeless, apart from Diving help!" The "way out" for anyone who can read is quite clearly "Divine help," "Divine aid!"

Divine Help Doesn't Mean "Idol" Help

The Psalms reminded God's people of the difference between God's help and the "help" that came from self-made religion and self-made "gods":

Not unto us, O LORD, not unto us, but unto thy name give glory, for thy mercy, and for thy truth's sake.
Wherefore should the heathen say, Where is now their God?
But our God is in the heavens: he hath done whatsoever he hath pleased.
Their idols are silver and gold, the work of men's hands.
They have mouths, but they speak not: eyes have they, but they see not:
They have ears, but they hear not: noses have they, but they smell not:
They have hands, but they handle not: feet have they, but they walk not: neither speak they through their throat.
They that make them are like unto them; so is every one that trusteth in them.
O Israel, trust thou in the LORD: he is their help and their shield. (Ps. 115:1-9).

This guide is for those who want the same way out the founders found; who wish to take the same attitude toward the "One with all power" that the founders took; who want to worship and glorify the same Almighty God the pioneers purposed to serve; and who wish

to receive the same guidance and deliverance that the founders
sought and received. Let's therefore see what that was, and look at
a little of what A.A.'s co-founder Bill Wilson said about it:

> As a society we must never become so vain as to suppose that
> we have been the authors and inventors of a new religion. We
> will humbly reflect that each of A.A.'s principles, *every one of
> them,* has been borrowed from ancient sources. . . . Let us
> constantly remind ourselves that the experts in religion are the
> clergymen; that the practice of medicine is for physicians; and
> that we, the recovered alcoholics, are their assistants *(Alcoholics
> Anonymous Comes of Age,* pp. 231-32).

> We are only operating a spiritual kindergarten in which people
> are enabled to get over drinking and find the grace to go on
> living to better effect *(As Bill Sees It,* p. 95).

> While most of us believe profoundly in the principle of
> "guidance," it was soon apparent that to receive it accurately,
> considerable spiritual preparation was necessary *(Pass It On,* p.
> 172).

> [Bill Wilson was addressing the wife of A.A. Number Three,
> and said:] Henrietta, the Lord has been so wonderful to me,
> curing me of this terrible disease that I just want to keep talking
> about it and telling people *(Alcoholics Anonymous,* 3rd ed.
> 1976, p. 191).

Dr. Bob–A.A.'s other co-founder–laid it on the line as follows:

> If you think you are an atheist, an agnostic, a skeptic, or have
> any other form of intellectual pride which keeps you from
> accepting what is in this book, I feel sorry for you.... But if you
> really and truly want to quit drinking liquor for good and all,
> and sincerely feel that you must have some help, we know we
> have an answer for you. Your Heavenly Father will never let
> you down *(Alcoholics Anonymous,* 3rd ed., 1976, p. 181)!

Much has been written, much has been said about the Twelve Steps of AA. These tenets of our faith and practice were not worked out overnight and then presented to our members as an opportunist creed. Born of our early trials and many tribulations, they were and are the result of humble and sincere desire, sought in personal prayer, for divine guidance (Article by Dr. Bob, September, 1948, "The Fundamentals - In Retrospect").

And it has become increasingly clear that the degree of harmonious living which we achieve is in direct ratio to our earnest attempt to follow them [the Twelve Steps] literally under divine guidance to the best of our ability (Article by Dr. Bob, *supra*).

Far better it is for us to fully understand the meaning and practice of "thou good and faithful servant" than to listen to "When 60,000 members, you should have a sixty-stories-high administration headquarters in New York with an assortment of trained "ists" to direct your affairs." We need nothing of the sort. God grant that AA may ever stay that simple. . . . And always, it has been the constructive, personal Twelfth Step work based on an ever-upward-looking faith which has done the job (Article by Dr. Bob, *supra*. For sources of Dr. Bob's biblical reference to "good and faithful servant," see Matt. 25:21; 25:23; Num. 12:7).

Most of us will concede that when it came to the personal showdown of admitting our failures and deciding to surrender our will and our lives to Almighty God, as we understood him, we still had some sneaking ideas of personal justification and excuse. We had to discard them, but the ego of the alcoholic dies a hard death (Article by Dr. Bob, *supra*).

Bill Dotson, who was sponsored by both Bill Wilson and Dr. Bob Smith, and was known as "A.A. Number Three," said this:

Bill [Wilson] was very, very grateful that he had been released
from this terrible thing and he had given God the credit for
having done it, and he's so grateful about it he wants to tell
other people about it. That sentence, "The Lord has been so
wonderful to me, curing me of this terrible disease, that I just
want to keep telling people about it," has been a sort of a golden
text for the A.A. program and for me *(Alcoholics Anonymous,*
3rd ed., 1976, p. 191).

Medical writer Paul de Kruif wrote the following in July, 1991, for
A.A.'s official magazine:

The medicine the AAs use is unique. Though it should be all-
powerful, it has never been tried with any consistent success
against any other major sickness. . . . It is free as air—with this
provision: that the patients it cures have to nearly die before
they can bring themselves to take it. The AAs' medicine is God
and God alone. This is their discovery (*Volume II, Best of the
Grapevine,* pp. 202-03).

All of the foregoing people were talking and writing about our
Creator, Almighty God–and no other!

Our Creator Is in the Deliverance Business

To what, then, is this book a guide? This guide is certainly not the
Bible. Nor does it even discuss the entire Bible. Its author is not a
Bible teacher. It does not cover all of the items that might be studied
in the Bible or that early A.A. members studied in the Bible. It does
not suggest that the following studies are the only studies that can
or should be undertaken.

It *is* a documented guide to what A.A. pioneers said about God
Almighty and what He can do for those suffering from alcoholism
and unmanageable lives. It is a guide to belief that there is a *cure*
for alcoholism–a cure which does not require one to be "in
recovery" for years or "in therapy" for years, or "in meetings" for

years, or without help for *all problems* once alcoholism has been defeated. The process is not interminable. Despite what one part of their basic text says, and what so many propound today about the "disease," early AAs talked about **cure, not illness.**

This book *is* a documented guide to what A.A. pioneers thought about the importance of the Bible, about what to read in it, and about the part it played in their astonishing successes. It is also a guide to the parts they read. It is a guide to what they learned (and you can learn) about bringing the power of God into your life once and for all. Just as the pioneers did.

Think of the verse so frequently quoted in early A.A., and throughout later years by pioneer Clarence Snyder:

> Therefore if any man *be* in Christ, *he is* a new creature: old things are passed away; behold, all things are become new (2 Cor. 5:17; See Dick B., *That Amazing Grace*, pp. 33-34).

This book *is* a guide to the way out--of their alcoholism and other problems--that the early AAs found. In that respect, the pioneers' Good Book itself contains these guides:

> Jesus saith unto him, I am the way, the truth, and the life; no man cometh unto the Father, but by me (John 14:6).

> Search the scriptures; for in them ye think ye have eternal life: and they are they which testify of me (John 5:39).

> Then Jesus said to those Jews which believed on him, If ye continue in my word, *then* are ye my disciples indeed: And ye shall know the truth, and the truth shall make you free (John 8:31-32).

> Stand fast therefore in the liberty wherewith Christ hath made us free, and be not entangled again with the yoke of bondage (Gal. 5:1).

> I have given them thy word; and the world hath hated them,
> because they are not of the world, even as I am not of the
> world.... Sanctify them through thy truth: thy word is truth
> (John 17:17).

> Study to shew thyself approved unto God, a workman that
> needeth not to be ashamed, rightly dividing the word of truth (2
> Tim. 2:15).

Calling All Teachers!

Students need teachers. The disciples of Jesus Christ had Jesus
himself as their teacher.

> And he [Jesus] taught daily in the temple. . . . (Luke 19:47a)

The English verb "taught" in the verse above is a translation of the
Greek verb *didaskō,* "to teach."

> Ye call me [Jesus] Master and Lord: and ye say well; for so I
> am (John 13:13)

The English noun "Master" in the verse above is a translation of the
Greek noun *didaskalos,* "teacher." In fact, the word "disciple," as
it is used in the New Testament, essentially means "student."

> And when he [Jesus] had called unto *him* his twelve disciples,
> he gave them power *against* unclean spirits, to cast them out,
> and to heal all manner of sickness and all manner of disease
> (Matt. 10:1)

The English noun "disciples" in the verse above is a translation of
the Greek noun *mathētēs. Strong's Exhaustive Concordance of the
Bible* defines this word as "a learner, pupil, disciple." *Young's
Analytical Concordance to the Bible* defines it as "taught or trained
one."

The First Century Church had the apostle Peter, the apostle Paul, and others as their teachers. Consider, for example, these verses from the Book of Acts:

> Then the Spirit said unto Philip, Go near, and join thyself to this chariot.
> And Philip ran thither to him, and heard him read the prophet Esaias, and said, Understandest thou what thou readest?
> And he said, How can I, except some man should guide me? And he desired Philip that he would come up and sit with him (Acts 8:29-31)

And consider also this section from Ephesians chapter 4:

> And he gave some, apostles; and some, prophets; and some, evangelists; and some, pastors and teachers;
> For the perfecting of the saints, for the work of the ministry, for the edifying of the body of Christ (Eph. 4:11,12)

We certainly have many trained Bible teachers today who know the Word of God and can give fine instruction to those who want to learn. Most churches conduct Bible studies. Many Bible fellowships teach the Bible. There are video and audio cassette tapes devoted to that end. It may be quite appropriate to seek such instruction either in, or out, of A.A. and 12 Step fellowships.

I was surprised, and even amused, when one of my earlier publishers wrote to the effect that "A.A. has no teachers." I'll leave it to others to ponder the consequences that result from such thinking, particularly in today's A.A. Also, I would remind one and all that A.A. today *does have many* fine "teachers" who conduct "Big Book" seminars and studies. Anyway, the guy was full of prune juice if he was referring to the days when the program was being developed. A couple of verses from Proverbs—which were read by early AAs—provide this answer to the idea that people don't need instruction:

In the lips of him that hath understanding wisdom is found: but
a rod *is* for the back of him that is void of understanding.
Wise *men* lay up knowledge: but the mouth of the foolish *is*
near destruction (Prov. 10:13-14).

Good understanding giveth favour; but the way of transgressors
is hard.
Every prudent *man* dealeth with knowledge: but a fool layeth
open *his* folly (Prov. 13:15-16).

When did some in our great fellowship begin to reject instruction,
knowledge, and understanding! You could say it began when they
stopped reading the Good Book. But the "stinking thinking" of this
particular variety seems to have been a studied theory of scholars:

> "Thirty meetings in thirty days" was its standard prescription
> for newcomers. This maxim asked for investment and
> commitment, but it also expressed a faith that if one brought the
> body, the mind would follow. Another frequent injunction more
> explicitly pointed up both the humanistic tinge of A.A.'s faith
> in human nature and the specific source of this faith in the
> thought of William James. Practices such as attendance at
> meetings, the inventory Steps of its program, and asking for
> help even if one did not believe, were urged under the mandate:
> "Act yourself into a new way of thinking rather than trying to
> think yourself into a new way of acting" (Kurtz, *Not-God*, p.
> 185).

Boy have I heard that stuff in A.A. meetings. But I never read it in
our early history or in the Good Book from which our pioneers got
their ideas!

Early A.A. was a constituent part of the Oxford Group, and the
Oxford Group's Founder, Dr. Frank Buchman, hired teachers such
as Mary Angevine to help Oxford Group people study the Word of
God. Bill Wilson said Rev. Sam Shoemaker's "teachings" were the
well-spring of A.A.'s ideas. And Sam and his circle frequently
taught the Word of God. Rev. Cleve Hicks, Rev. Irving Harris, and

writer Roger Hicks—all of the "Shoemaker group"—taught and wrote about the Bible; and, in the case of Harris and Roger Hicks, even wrote guidebooks on how to study the Bible (see Roger Hicks, *How to Read the Bible*, London: The Oxford Group, 1939):

> The Bible is an essential part of the morning's Quiet Time. It is often helpful daily to follow selected passages such as are provided by the Bible, Reading, Fellowship (Series A) or the *Churchman's Almanack* (Hicks, *How to Read the Bible*, supra, p. 4).

Early A.A. members also learned from qualified teachers such as Dr. Bob, Bob's wife Anne, Henrietta Seiberling, and Mr. And Mrs T. Henry Williams. Pioneers were also encouraged to join churches and have religious affiliations, presumably with the expectation that they would be learning even more from qualified teachers in those places.

Dr. Bob was a prime example, becoming a charter member of Akron's Westside Presbyterian Church in his earliest sobriety, along with his wife. Later, he was to become a communicant at St. Paul's Episcopal Church in Akron. Henrietta, T. Henry, and Clarace were all church members. Bill Wilson sought out Roman Catholic teaching for a time. So there were teachers *aplenty* in the early A.A. days—teachers who were sought and heard. And there are teachers *few* in today's A.A., at least when it comes to helping AAs and 12-Step people understand their program by learning about its spiritual and biblical sources and concepts.

This is not a guide to details. It is a guide to growth. It points the way toward a path that A.A.'s pioneers took and that today's afflicted can also take. It suggests further *work* with teachers and teaching–the same kind of work undertaken by Bill Wilson and Dr. Bob. This is the kind of work the founders did and referred to in the following comments in the Big Book:

> There are many helpful books also. Suggestions about these may be obtained from one's priest, minister, or rabbi. Be quick

to see where religious people are right. Make use of what they have to offer *(Alcoholics Anonymous,* 3rd ed., p. 87).

We think it no concern of ours what religious bodies our members identify themselves with as individuals. This should be an entirely personal affair which each one decides for himself in the light of past associations, or his present choice. Not all of us join religious bodies, but most of us favor such memberships *(Alcoholics Anonymous,* 3rd ed., p. 28).

A Guide to the Way Back and Out!

This guidebook demonstrates that the *fellowship* of Alcoholics Anonymous has headed into a downward spiral. It also shows that a dramatic change has taken place with respect to the zeal of its members for a relationship with God, for coming to Him through Jesus Christ, for study of the Bible, and for establishing or continuing in membership in religious bodies. We will soon see that Bill W. and Dr. Bob regarded Jesus's Sermon on the Mount as the key to A.A.'s philosophy. Dr. Bob studied the Sermon itself (in Matthew chapters 5-7). He also studied some leading writers of the day on that subject. One of those writers was E. Stanley Jones, all of whose books were recommended to AAs by Anne Smith. We now know that Bill Wilson also read Jones, and the author found one of the Jones books in Wilson's library at his Stepping Stones home. Not surprisingly, Jones wrote the following in this book which Dr. Bob studied and circulated--*The Christ of the Mount: A Living Exposition of Jesus' Words as the Only Practical Way of Life* (Nashville: Abingdon, 1st ed, 1931, Festival ed., 1981):

THE WAY OUT *(The Christ of the Mount,* p. 253).

Four years have gone by since I published *Christ at the Round Table.* Have I been compelled to alter the conclusions I recorded there, namely, that by actual experimentation, Christ is proving the Way? After four years more of Round Tables I have no alteration to make except in the way of added emphasis. As I have listened to the finest that the religious East could produce I have been struck with the fact that outside of Christ, men were uncertain, or fumbling. In Christ, they had found God or, rather, God had found them. And with it they had found a working way to live. They were rejoicing. One Moslem lawyer, surprised at this, said. . . "all of you Christians said you had found something, while we Hindus and Moslems all said we had found nothing. Therefore you must have lacked our frankness." I quietly suggested that there was another alternative: Christ is the Way (*The Christ of the Mount*, pp. 326-27)!

An Englishman, high up in the government authority in India, said at the close of an address, "I see no way out of our present difficulties, except as we Englishmen and you Indians both catch the spirit of Christ and live it out in our relationships with each other." . . . In the book of Revelation Jesus says, "I am the Alpha and the Omega"–the first and the last letters of the Greek alphabet. In other words, he is the Christ of the Beginnings and the Christ of the Final Word. The Christ of the Beginnings! Yes, and how amazingly he began! He spoke these great words on the mount and lived them, every one–and more. In the Sermon he taught men to pray, "Our Father. . ." He is the Christ of the Final Word. The Sermon on the Mount is the transcript of his mind and spirit. . . . It is a working philosophy of life–the only one that will work. For the universe backs this way of life (*The Christ of the Mount*, pp. 330-32).

Our guidebook urges that many "in recovery" need to "recover." They need to be delivered. They need to be inspired to change their life to "do God's will"–just as the early AAs were and as the Big Book still encourages. Our guidebook also urges that they know their own early history. They need to know the zeal for God and His Word that existed among our A.A. pioneers. They need a guide to utilizing the power of our Creator in overcoming alcoholism. They need a guide that will assist them in properly relating themselves to Almighty God. They need a guide that will enable them to enjoy the abundant life the Creator promises to those who seek Him through His Son. (See, for example, John 3:16 and John 10:10.) They need truly to be able to call Him their Heavenly Father, just as Jesus did and taught others to do. And just as Dr. Bob so frequently did (Big Book, 3rd ed., p. 181).

For such, this book can be a guide.

2

What Early AAs Said about
Reading the Bible

Do not let any prejudice you may have against spiritual terms deter you from honestly asking yourself what they mean to you. At the start, this was all we [the agnostics to whom these remarks were addressed] needed to commence spiritual growth, to effect our first conscious relation with God as we understood Him (Bill Wilson, *Alcoholics Anonymous*, 3rd ed., p. 47).

Of course the Bible ought to be the main Source Book of all. No day ought to pass without reading it (Anne Ripley Smith, Dr. Bob's wife, quoted in Dick B., *Anne Smith's Journal, 1933-1939*, 3rd ed., p. 82).

There are many in the A.A. Fellowship today, and many outside of it as well, who describe today's A.A. as "spiritual, but not religious." There are also those who believe A.A. is *too* religious. Not surprisingly, there are many clergy and other religious people today who believe A.A. is neither spiritual *nor* religious. Still others claim A.A. is still too "Protestant." And there are those who label it too "Christian."

All could profit by learning what early AAs really did and said, and then comparing that early program—a program far different from today's program—with the Twelve Step programs and fellowships today. There has been too much emphasis on what people *think* A.A. is, rather than upon what early A.A. pioneers, and others who knew it at the beginning, *actually said and reported* it to be. We'll examine the latter statements and reports.

From the Words of A.A.'s Pioneers Themselves . . .

There are plenty of enlightening descriptions of early A.A.'s intimate relationship with religion, the Bible, our Creator, and God's only begotten Son Jesus Christ. The descriptions were uttered by A.A. pioneers themselves. The following are some examples.

A.A. Co-founder Dr. Bob:

> When we started in on Bill D. [who was A.A. Number Three], we had no Twelve Steps... But we were convinced that the answer to our problems was in the Good Book. To some of us older ones, the parts that we found absolutely essential were the Sermon on the Mount, the thirteenth chapter of First Corinthians, and the Book of James (*The Co-founders of Alcoholics Anonymous: Biographical sketches Their last major talks*. New York: Alcoholics Anonymous World Services, Inc., 1972, 1975, pp. 9-10).

> Members of Alcoholics Anonymous begin the day with a prayer for strength and a short period of Bible reading. They find the basic messages they need in the Sermon on the Mount, in Corinthians and the Book of James (From a talk by Dr. Bob in Youngstown, Ohio. See Wally P., *But for the Grace of God,* p. 45).

> [Emphasizing humility, Dr. Bob said in his last major address] Christ said, "Of myself, I am nothing–My strength cometh from My Father in heaven." If He had to say that, how about you and me? (*The Co-Founders, supra,* p. 15).

It is the hope of the King School Group–whose property this is–that this Book may never cease to be a source of wisdom, gratitude, humility, and guidance, as when fulfilled in the life of the Master [Jesus Christ].

The statement above is the inscription in Dr. Bob's Bible which he donated to the King School Group (A.A. Group No. 1). See Dick B., *The Good Book and The Big Book*, p. 5.

A.A.'s Conference-Approved Book, *DR. BOB and the Good Oldtimers:*

"We had much prayer together in those days and began quietly to read Scripture and discuss a practical approach in its application to our lives, " he [Paul S.] said (p. 111).

The Bible was stressed as reading material, of course (p. 151).

Hospitalization was another must in the early days. . . . These patients were allowed only a Bible as reading material (p. 102).

An early Chicago member wrote. . . . "Dr. Bob was the first group leader I heard refer simply and without ostentation to God. He cited the Sermon on the Mount as containing the underlying spiritual philosophy of A.A." (p. 228).

They had the Bible, and they had the precepts of the Oxford Group . . . . They were working, or working out, the A.A. program—the Twelve Steps—without quite knowing how they were doing it (p. 96).

The A.A. members of that time [from 1935 to 1939] did not consider meetings necessary to maintain sobriety. They were simply "desirable." Morning devotion and "quiet time," however, were musts (p. 136).

Sue [Sue Smith Windows, daughter of Dr. Bob and Anne Smith] also remembered the quiet time in the mornings—how they sat around reading the Bible. Later, they also used *The Upper Room*, a Methodist publication that provided a daily inspirational message, interdenominational in its approach [This publication had a Bible verse for each day, and usually contained references to other Bible passages for further study]. Then somebody said a prayer, she recalled. After that, we were supposed to say one ourselves. Then we'd be quiet. Finally, everybody would share what they got, or didn't get. This lasted for at least a half hour and sometimes went as long as an hour (pp. 71-72).

Morning quiet time continued to be an important part of the recovery program in 1938-1939, as did the spiritual reading from which the early members derived a good deal of their inspiration (p. 150).

From the Writing of Dr. Bob's Daughter, Sue Smith Windows:

There was no program. Dad and Mom and Bill were working out the program. At that time I was getting involved with quiet times they had in the morning. The guys would come, and mom would have her quiet time with them. . . . They read the Bible, prayed and listened, and got guidance (Robert Smith and Sue Windows, *Children of the Healer,* pp. 43-44).

From the Remarks of Pioneer Clarence Snyder:

Clarence Snyder was an early A.A. pioneer who got sober in February, 1938, and was sponsored by Dr. Bob. He said:

Everything in this program came from the Bible. . . . A.A. was grounded in the Bible (See Dick B., *That Amazing Grace: The Role of Clarence and Grace S. in Alcoholics Anonymous,* pp. 43, 33.)

"Also, just as Dr. Bob had done, Clarence many times told others that A.A.'s basic ideas had come from Matthew chapters 5-7 (Jesus's Sermon on the Mount), 1 Corinthians13 (the so-called "love" chapter, and the book of James. Grace [Clarence's wife] said Clarence told his babies to read those three segments; and Grace (as one of Clarence's babies) did just that. She said the reading was not recommended reading; it was required" (Dick B., *That Amazing Grace, supra*, p. 34).

"Two years after publication of the book [*Alcoholics Anonymous*, 1ˢᵗ ed., 1939], Clarence made a survey of all of the members in Cleveland. He concluded that, by keeping most of the "old program," including the Four Absolutes and the Bible, ninety-three percent of those surveyed had maintained uninterrupted sobriety" (See Mitchell K., *How It Worked: The Story of Clarence H. Snyder And the Early Days of Alcoholics Anonymous in Cleveland, Ohio*, p. 108).

From the Remarks of Dr. Bob's Son, Robert Smith:

Before there was a Big Book—in the period of "flying blind," God's Big Book was the reference used in our home. The summer of 1935, when Bill lived with us, Dr. Bob had read the Bible completely three times. And the references that seemed consistent with the program goals were the Sermon on the Mount, 1 Corinthians 13, and the Book of James (See Dick B., *The Good Book and The Big Book,* p. ix—the Preface written by Dr. Bob's son "Smitty").

From Early Akron A.A. Pamphlets Commissioned by Dr. Bob:

There is the Bible that you haven't opened for years. Get acquainted with it. Read it with an open mind. You will find things that will amaze you. You will be convinced that certain passages were written with you in mind. Read the Sermon on the Mount (Matthew V, VI, and VII). Read St. Paul's inspired essay on love (I Corinthians XIII). Read the Book of James.

Read the Twenty-third and Ninety-first Psalms. These readings are brief but so important (*A Manual for Alcoholics Anonymous,* 6th rev. ed. Akron, Ohio: AA of Akron).

But, asks the alcoholic, where can I find a simple, step-by-step religious guide? The Ten Commandments give us a set of "Thou Shalt's" and "Thou Shalt Not's"; the Twelve Steps of A.A. give us a program of dynamic action; But what about a spiritual guide? Of course, the answer is, that by following the Ten Commandments and the Twelve Steps to the letter, we automatically lead a spiritual life, whether or not we recognize it (*Spiritual Milestones,* Akron, Ohio, AA of Akron, p. 1).

From Remarks by A.A. Co-founder Bill Wilson:

[Bill Wilson said of his stay with Dr. Bob and Anne for three months in 1935:] Each morning there was devotion. After the long silence Anne [Dr. Bob's wife] would read out of the Good Book. James was our favorite (*RHS.* New York: The AA Grapevine, Inc., 1951, p. 5).

Bill said, "I sort of always felt that something was lost from A.A. when we stopped emphasizing morning meditation." (See *DR. BOB and the Good Oldtimers*, p. 178.)

It should be noted, however, that Bill and Lois themselves continued this practice of morning meditation together until Bill's death, in 1971.

We much favored the Apostle James. The definition of love in Corinthians also played a great part in our discussions (See Kurtz, *Not-God.* Hazelden, 1991, p. 320, n.11).

The Book of James was considered so important, in fact, that some early members even suggested "The James Club" as a name for the Fellowship *(Pass It On.* New York: A.A. World Services, Inc., 1984, p. 147).

[Bill Wilson commented in his December 12, 1954 taped interview of T. Henry and Clarace Williams:] I learned a great deal from you people, from the Smiths themselves, and from Henrietta [Seiberling]. I hadn't looked in the Bible, up to this time, at all [referring to Bill's own brief period of sobriety in New York before staying in Akron during the summer of 1935] (See Dick B., *The Akron Genesis of Alcoholics Anonymous,* p. 64—quoting a tape in A.A.'s General Services Archives).

The Sermon on the Mount [Matthew chapters 5-7] contains the underlying spiritual philosophy of A.A. (See documentation of Bill's statement in Dick B., *The Good Book and The Big Book: A.A.'s Roots in the Bible,* p. 4).

[Of A.A.'s early outspoken atheist and persistent drunkard, Jim Burwell, Bill Wilson said to his Yale audience:] It was his prideful obstinacy. He had thought to himself, "Maybe these fellows have something with their God-business." His hand reached out, in the darkness, and touched something on his bureau. It was a Gideon Bible. Jimmy picked it up and he read from it. I do not know just what he read, and I have always had a queer reluctance to ask him. But Jimmy has not had a drink to this day, and that was five years ago (Lecture 29, "The Fellowship of Alcoholics Anonymous by WW," as given at the Yale School of Alcohol Studies, June, 1945 (*Yale Quarterly Journal, 1945; http://www.historyofaa.com/billw/yale.htm*).

[Speaking to the same Yale audience, Bill remarked as to Bible study:] That experience led us to examine some of the obscure phrases that we sometimes see in our Bibles. For a great many of us have taken to reading the Bible (Lecture 29, *supra,* p. 467).

[In a letter from Bill Wilson to his friend Rev. Sam Shoemaker, dated May 2, 1958, Wilson wrote:] There is no reason why a group of A.A.'s shouldn't get together for Bible study; no reason at all why a group of A.A.'s in a church should not associate themselves into a sort of spiritual kindergarten fellowship, into which anyone might be invited. As a matter of fact, I am anxious to see this sort of thing tried (See Dick B., *Turning Point,* p. 678).

From Dr. Bob's Wife, Anne Ripley Smith, the "Mother of A.A.":

[Anne Ripley Smith, wife of Dr. Bob, wrote in the spiritual journal she shared with early A.A. members and their families:] Of course the Bible ought to be the main Source Book of all. No day ought to pass without reading it (Dick B., *Anne Smith's Journal, 1933-1939,* p. 60).

A maximum experience of Jesus Christ leads to a radical change in personal life, bringing about a selfless relationship to the people about one, which is a challenge to those we come in contact with (Dick B., *Anne Smith's Journal,* p. 120).

[Anne wrote of] Christ's basic principle which he expressed in saying that we must love even the very least of them [and she wrote of] the true way of Jesus Christ (Dick B., *Anne Smith's Journal,* p. 120).

[A.A. pioneer Bob E said of Anne:] She had a quiet, soft way of making you feel at home. I shared a good many of my life problems with her. She read the Bible and counseled with me *(DR. BOB and the Good Oldtimers,* p.116).

[Florence B. of Akron wrote:] Anne was "evangelist, nurse, salesman, employment bureau, all in one. . . ."Anne's personal religion was simple and workable. She never sought to rewrite the Bible nor to explain it. She just accepted it (Dick B., *The Akron Genesis of Alcoholics Anonymous,* pp. 108-09).

From A.A.'s Trustee-to-Be Frank Amos's
Report to John D. Rockefeller, Jr.:

He [the alcoholic] must have devotions every morning—a "quiet time" of prayer and some reading from the Bible and other religious literature. Unless this is faithfully followed, there is grave danger of backsliding (*DR. BOB and the Good Oldtimers*, p. 131).

From Bill Wilson's Secretary
and A.A.'s First Archivist, Nell Wing:

Members gathered there [at the home of Dr. Bob and Anne in the early days] as well as attending the Oxford Group meetings at the home of T. Henry and Clarace Williams.

Early members described how, at their meeting, Bob liked to sit with an open Bible on his lap, out of which a passage would be selected at random and read. A discussion would then follow on its relevance to the personal problems of those present (Nell Wing, *Grateful to Have Been There,* p. 81).

From Dr. Bob Himself on A.A.'s Good Book Source:

If someone asked him [Dr. Bob] a question about the program, his usual response was: "What does it say in the Good Book?" *(DR. BOB and the Good Oldtimers,* p. 144).

I had refreshed my memory of the Good Book, and I had had excellent training in that as a youngster *(The Co-Founders of Alcoholics Anonymous,* pp. 11-12).

I'm somewhat allergic to work, but I felt I should increase my familiarity with the Good Book. . . . *(The Co-Founders of Alcoholics Anonymous,* p. 13).

From Tapes of Early Pioneers That Were Interviewed:

[Pioneer Wally G. said:] I remember the first meeting I attended was led by Dick S. He opened the meeting with a short prayer, read a passage from the Bible which I do not recall, and talked about that in its relationship to the everyday life of those present (Transcript of Wally G.-Bill Wilson interview, located at General Services Archives in New York).

[Pioneer Earl T. said:] I remember most distinctly the first meeting that I attended—Bill D. [A.A. Number Three who got sober in 1935] sat with the Holy Bible in his lap. The meeting had been opened with a prayer. Bill read excerpts from the Bible and translated them into everyday life. After half an hour of this, the meeting was thrown open to everyone in the room and they in turn picked up some of these passages from the Bible that he had discussed and gave their interpretation (Transcript of Earl T.—Bill Wilson interview, located at General Services Archives in New York).

[Early A.A. member Bob E. said concerning weekly regular meetings:] There was a short quote of scripture, next a short prayer, next the short story for the day [from *The Upper Room*] was read. Next if the group was still small enough we would hold hands in a circle and have a short quiet time during which we silently asked God for guidance. (See Dick B., *Turning Point,* p. 138).

[Early A.A. member Alex M., who got sober in 1939, said:] Doc [Dr. Bob Smith] talked much at the regular meetings. He would come just at a regular meeting and speak. About 40 minutes, and he was a simple talker. He had the Bible in front of him and wasn't afraid to read from it. It [that Bible] was at the King School. It was always on the podium (Transcript of Alex M.—Niles P. interview, located at General Services Archives in New York).

[Pioneer William Van Horn said:] So I continued reading the "Upper Room" and the references in the Good Book. The reference one day was to the second book of Corinthians, fifth chapter, and the seventeenth verse. It said there, "Therefore if any man be in Christ, he becomes a new creature, old things are passed away, behold all things are new." I applied that to myself. . . . The Bible, I figured, was my statute now. I immediately got a release from things I thought I would never forget. . . . I tried to attack any books that Doc was reading or that Henrietta [Seiberling] recommended. Henrietta recommended the Twenty-seventh Psalm. Well, I dug that out, and that was very helpful too, because I had a lot of personal trouble (Transcript of William V. H.—Bill Wilson Interview, located at A.A. General Services in New York).

[Toledo pioneer Duke P. said:] When I started, they stressed morning quiet time, daily reading, and daily contact *(DR. BOB and the Good Oldtimers,* pp. 150-51).

From Personal Stories in the First Edition of A.A.'s Basic Text:

No conviction was necessary to establish my status as a miserable failure at managing my own life. I began to read the Bible daily and to go over a simple devotional exercise as a way to begin each day [The Traveler, Editor Story, *Alcoholics Anonymous*, First Edition, p. 263].

They [the pioneers] made it very plain that I had to seek God, that I had to state my case to Him and ask for help. . . . Every morning I read a part of the Bible and ask God to carry me through the day safely [The Salesman Story, *Alcoholics Anonymous*, First Edition, p. 323].

From that day I gave and still give and always will, time everyday to read the word of God and let Him do all the caring. Who am I to try to run myself or anything else? [The Smile With Me Story, *Alcoholics Anonymous*, First Edition, p. 347].

The Foregoing Confirm
the Bible's Critical Role in Early A.A.

For those in Twelve Step Fellowships, and in church recovery groups, who are wondering if it is OK, as a solid and devoted participant in such fellowships, to mention the Bible, study the Bible individually, or read the Bible to chart the way to God's will and deliverance, the foregoing should provide an adequate answer. There are many more substantial pieces of evidence dealing with early A.A. Bible study, prayer, seeking of God's guidance, reading biblical literature, and using Bible devotionals. Much evidence of this can be found in the books about the Oxford Group, of which A.A. was a constituent part in the beginning. Also in the prolific writings of Rev. Sam Shoemaker, whom Bill Wilson credited as the teacher of Twelve Step ideas.

They Mean You Can Study the Good Book Today

The point is that one can, today, and should, start his Bible quest for recovery and deliverance, knowing full-well that the Good Book provided a solid foundation for the early Alcoholics Anonymous recovery program, principles, practices, and fellowship ideas.

3

The Bible and Recovery

Jesus answered, "Go and tell John what you have heard and seen. The blind are now able to see, and the lame can walk. People with leprosy are being healed, and the deaf can hear. The dead are raised to life, and the poor are hearing the good news. God will bless everyone who doesn't reject me because of what I do" (Matt. 11:4-6, *Contemporary English Version*).

If the Bible was a potent factor in early A.A. recovery, can it still be a significant factor today?

Do People Really Want What Early A.A. Had!

You don't have to be a clergyman, a lay priest, or a church deacon to understand the importance of the Bible in *early* A.A.

There probably are several reasons for A.A.'s initial and astonishing successes. Note at the outset that there was a documented 75% success rate in Akron in the initial period from 1935-1939. There was a documented 93% success rate in Cleveland from A.A.'s inception there in1939, and continuing for a few years thereafter. And several facts about these early programs are clear:

- Early A.A.'s basic ideas came from the Bible.

- Early AAs relied on the Bible and studied it.

- Early A.A. meetings were so simple that they consisted of little else but Bible emphasis—there was prayer, Bible reading, seeking of guidance, and discussion of Bible topics.

- Early A.A. surrenders to God were based exclusively on the Bible and in large part on verses in the Book of James.

- People such as Frank Amos were sent to Akron to investigate the ingredients of the program there; and they returned from their investigation reporting Bible emphasis.

- A.A.'s teachers like the Rev. Sam Shoemaker, Henrietta Seiberling, Dr. Bob and Anne Smith, T. Henry and Clarace Williams (and the Oxford Group people who wrote the books that guided old-timers) all spoke in terms of principles and practices that came from the Bible.

- Bill Wilson's own brother-in-law, who was a physician, recommended to Clarence Snyder (one of the early pioneers) that he see the doctor (Dr. Bob) in Akron who was "fixing" drunks. In other words, Bill's own close relative sent Clarence to Dr. Bob for recovery help, rather than to Bill.

- The pioneer A.A. program, according to Bill Wilson, was about establishing a relationship with God, "discovering" God, or "rediscovering" God (Bill used all three descriptions in Big Book drafts and manuscripts).

Now just what could you say was new or unique about the Akron "Program?"

There was nothing new in the medical arena at that time except the frequent admission by physicians as to the seeming hopelessness of alcoholism and the reasons why it appeared to be "medically incurable." Dr. Bob was a physician and certainly knew something about his apparently hopeless situation. The doctor in New York (William D. Silkworth, M.D.) who had frequently treated Bill for alcoholism was frank to admit his own limitations. In fact, in a little-mentioned account of Silkworth's treatment of an alcoholic named "Charles K," as related by Dr. Norman Vincent Peale, Dr. Silkworth strongly recommended the seeking of healing through Jesus Christ, the great "Physician" (See Peale, *The Positive Power of Jesus Christ*, pp. 59-63). Others of that day, who looked at the problem from a medical standpoint, could only highlight the inadequacy of any human power to solve the alcoholic's plight. Such facts merely served to substantiate the thesis of A.A.'s subsequent Step One (admitting powerlessness over alcohol) in the Steps Bill wrote in 1939, purportedly describing the recovery path pioneers had followed.

Just as there was nothing new on the medical scene, there was nothing new about God. People knew plenty about God in 1935. But the alcoholic had never seemed to link up with what the power of God could do, or how to bring it into play for recovery.

There was nothing new about God's Commandments. They had existed for centuries in the Old Testament and in the New. But alcoholics had never seemed to understand, or put much store in, learning and obeying God's will in order to reap the rewards of His love, power, mercy, grace, healing, and deliverance.

There was nothing new about fellowships of believers or fellowships of church people seeking more information about God and His will. But most of the early alcoholics had drifted away from church, from God, and from fellowships of believers. As Bill Wilson appropriately put it, they had often become the "actor" who is revolted by the things he does on his sprees, by certain episodes he vaguely remembers, and by constant fear and tension—all of which made for more drinking and seldom fostered devoted church activity.

As Wilson also added in such striking terms: Real alcoholics became subject to withdrawal from society, to baffling and chilling loneliness, and to "the hideous Four Horsemen—Terror, Bewilderment, Frustration, Despair." He went on to say: "Unhappy drinkers who read this page will understand!" And the author of this guidebook certainly does, where perhaps many others don't or can't. Far therefore were such unhappy alcoholics from the warmth and welcome of a church fellowship or Bible study group.

What *was* new, then? What was different in 1935? For one thing, in Akron, there was a fellowship of altruistic people who—though they did not really know much about the problems of alcoholism—were willing to help in spite of the foibles, fears, and failures of alcoholics. This fellowship sometimes called itself the "alcoholic squad of the Oxford Group." In place of loneliness, they tendered understanding. In place of a dumpster to hide in, they offered the light of a meeting. In place of rejection, condemnation, and pity, they offered the love of God! They offered a relationship with God and fellowship with Him through reading His Word, praying to Him, listening for His voice, and trying to obey His will. "Thy will be done" became their battle cry. "Love thy neighbor as thyself" became part of their code. "Doing unto others" became another part of this code founded on Jesus' sermon on the mount. These all meant the avoidance of judging, grudging, and selfish objectives.

These ideas themselves *were, of course,* as old as the Bible. But there was a new group willing to apply them. There was a group of sober Christians and sick drunks (not necessarily exclusive terms) who were willing to meet together, learn the biblical ideas, practice trying to live them, witness to others, and fellowship together, dedicating themselves to obeying God's will. *This was new.* This was, perhaps, a first for drunks, as a group, and for an ongoing program.

The Bible, of course, spoke clearly about God, God's power, God's will, loving God and loving others, obedience to God, and what God could and would do as to healing, forgiveness, and deliverance if and when He was sought and obeyed. And Akron's Christian fellowship–dedicated to including in its ranks, and focusing on deliverance of, drunks--*was* new. At least it was new in 1935 as America emerged from the Prohibition era.

The key, then, was not in an instruction group for alcoholics. It was not in life-change alone. It was not in fellowship alone. It was not in Bible-study alone. It was in a life-changing, Bible fellowship--devoted to God, willing to seek Him through prayer and listening, and strongly desiring to learn about and understand our Creator through *study* of His Word.

Missions had long offered sermons, Bible verses, Christian hymns, altar calls, beds, coffee, blankets, and meals. But Akron's Christian fellowship (consisting of believers helping alcoholics to become, or live as, believers) practicing God's will--and then witnessing to other drunks outside of a mission--presented a new approach. To the end that those alcoholics, for whom God had done the seemingly impossible, could help others obtain that very same deliverance–and do it by something other than meetings and testimonials alone.

It worked!

What's up with Anonymous Fellowships and the Bible Today?

Are people in Twelve Step programs today really hostile to the Bible? To God? To Jesus Christ? Let's look at today's scene and let the facts speak for themselves. Let's remember too that what people say and do at any given point in time depends a great deal on how much they know or have been given the opportunity to know before or at the time of their statements. Thus, while author Ken Ragge seems totally unaware of A.A.'s roots in the Bible, seems determined to attack A.A. as if it were an Oxford Group subsidiary, and burdens his title with sarcastic characterizations, the following statements he made *do* perhaps reflect the language and attitude of many in today's A.A.:

God–A supernatural being more powerful than Devil Drink.
Giver of the Twelve Steps, a guide to living in accordance with
His will. Unlikely to save alcoholics who are too willful to work
a spiritual program. All evidence indicates that God is unlikely
to help those whose willfulness causes them to depend on a
religious instead of a purely spiritual program (Ragge: *The Real
AA: Behind the Myth of 12-Step Recovery*, p. 102).

Although Ragge heavily and cynically loads a lot of A.A.
shortcomings into one purported definition of God, I have to say
myself that I have personally been exposed to the foregoing kind of
misguided "spiritual" thinking within the rooms of A.A. Ragge then
continues, at a later point:

The reason one's "Higher Power" need not be "God" becomes
clear: "Isn't it true that in all matters touching upon alcohol,
each of them has decided to turn his or her life over to the care,
protection, and guidance of Alcoholics Anonymous. . . Now if
this is not turning one's will and life over to a newfound
providence, then what is it?" *There is no distinction made
between Alcoholics Anonymous and God in A.A. theology. . .
turning one's "will and life" over to Alcoholics Anonymous is
the same as turning it over to God*" (Ragge, *The Real A.A.,
supra*, pp. 121-22).

The foregoing generalizations certainly will not apply or hold up in
a fellowship that contains one to two million members (at any given
point of time)–all of widely diverse races, creeds, and origins.
Assuredly, also, Ragge far overstates the situation as far as pioneer
A.A. goes. Yet beware: Ragge's remarks may not be too far afield
when it comes to Bill's Wilson's tortured and ever-expanding
theories about the nature of a "higher power." Moreover, Ragge's
reasoning is commanding when it comes to religion and the Bible in
today's A.A. Much of the opposition to the word "religion" today,
many of the worshipful references to a "higher power,"many of the
emphases on "spiritual" and "spirituality," and many of the

objections to the word "God," stem from thinking closely resembling that described in Ragge's statements.

That's why this guide speaks a good deal about today's "revisionists." There has been too much emphasis on the supposed faults of the Oxford Group, the supposed frailties and views of Oxford Group founder Frank Buchman, and the supposed obeisance of A.A. to Oxford Group principles. There has been too much print-space given to the New Age and other "new religion" writers whose theories appear in today's Conference Approved literature, but do not in any way correlate with A.A.'s original Bible-based program or even the recovery path described in the First Edition of its Big Book.

And why?

The Facts about Early A.A. Are Basically Unknown Today

Have today's Twelve Step fellowships been provided with such a limited number of historical facts that they just plain don't know that:

- A.A.'s basic ideas were taken from the Bible?

- When asked a question about the pioneer "Program," A.A.'s co-founder Dr. Bob would reply: "What does the Good Book say?"

- Reading the Bible was very much stressed in early A.A?

- The A.A. pioneers read the Bible at almost every early meeting in Akron, in group quiet times at Dr. Bob's home, and in their own, individual quiet times?

Do Twelve Step fellowships today really know these facts? It's for sure, that I never heard any of them in the hundreds of meetings I attended in early sobriety. If Ragge ever participated in A.A. or any other 12-Step fellowship, he probably didn't hear them either.

I never saw the facts in the Big Book that I read so earnestly in
A.A. I know of no A.A. "Conference Approved" publication today
that gives specifics or details about what A.A.'s pioneers studied in,
or borrowed from, the Bible. And even though there is general
information available today in A.A. literature that *early* AAs put
great store in the contents of Matthew, James, and Corinthians, such
information is little mentioned, never fleshed-out, and seldom
analyzed. People just don't know the specifics.

One interesting fact stands out: If you go to Akron, Ohio,
during its annual Founders Day, as thousands do each year, you will
see virtually nothing substantial about the Bible itself. At the
archives at Dr. Bob's Home (the birthplace of A.A.), there is lots
of history you will *not* see. What you *can* see is under glass. Most
important of all, there is nothing in that excellent historical display
that shows the great emphasis Dr. Bob placed on the Bible. And
there is nothing at all about Anne Smith's Spiritual Journal, even
though it was read at that very house every single morning to AAs
and their families during Anne's morning Quiet Times. This dearth
of facts about A.A.'s Bible origins also prevails at the otherwise
excellent displays at Akron's Intergroup Office. You would learn
nothing there about the Bible's real and central place in early A.A.
even though there are good historical displays on the walls and a
good number of early A.A.'s spiritual books locked in a room and
in glass cases.

Then there's the matter of Dr. Bob's Bible and A.A. Group
Number One–the King School Group–which still meets in Akron
today. Even Dr. Bob's own Bible, which used to be taken to the
podium at the beginning of every meeting of A.A. Group Number
One, is no longer given that prominence and honor. This, though
that very Good Book has inscriptions in it by Dr. Bob, Bill Wilson,
and Bill Dotson (A.A. Number Three).

Except for the opportunity I was given at Archives 2000, a
historical meeting, whose A.A. sponsors had to convene *outside*
A.A.'s International Convention environs, I don't recall ever
hearing someone present *details* about A.A. and the Bible at any

A.A. group, meeting, or conference I have attended. And there have been more than 2,000 of these!

A.A.'s "In-house" Teachers Are Long Gone

Without having available to them early A.A.'s non-alcoholic teachers such as Anne Smith, Henrietta Seiberling, T. Henry and Clarace Williams (and certainly Rev. Sam Shoemaker and his assistant minister Irving Harris), and without Dr. Bob's stern emphasis on the Bible as absolutely essential, today's Twelve Step people often simply don't know where to begin when Bible study is suggested. They may ask what they are supposed to *do* with the Good Book, what the Bible really *is*, where to *start* their reading, *what parts* would be particularly helpful in overcoming their own problems, and what the Bible will actually *disclose* to them. Disclose to them about the Creator upon whom early AAs placed such tremendous reliance. About prayer. About healing. About forgiveness. About overcoming fear, anxiety, guilt, despair, confusion, self-destructive ideas, frustration, and depressed mental states. About the healing and cure of alcoholism itself. Today, instead of receiving information and instruction from the Bible on these things, they are frequently warned to steer clear of the Bible.

Today's Emphasis on Simplicity Encourages Ignorance

"Keep it simple" is an expression heard all too frequently in today's "self-help" fellowships. Sometimes, that phrase is reshaped and replayed as KISS: "Keep it simple, stupid." AAs and other addicts may be (and in fact are) often very very sick; but they certainly are not stupid. They simply need information, guidance, and discipline. They do *not* need "simple," self-made religion, half-baked prayers, or absurd names for Almighty God. In fact, their "co-founder" Sam Shoemaker told them so in his books and in his talks at A.A.'s own International Convention.

This guide may not seem itself to be simple. It may, in fact, seem to challenge alcoholics and addicts to much further study. And does! But it will, right here and now, provide a positive, guided *approach* for alcoholics and other afflicted people to the best-selling book of all times—a book that can and will point the way to deliverance for those today who are suffering from life-controlling problems and really want permanent freedom.

A.A. should never have become known, or be known, as America's repository for stupidity or ignorance. Commonly heard phrases like "Take the cotton out of your ears and put it in your mouth" often suggest to the newcomer that he knows nothing and will hear great pearls of wisdom from others. Yet he doesn't–not when it comes to our Creator or the Bible, these days! Perhaps an appropriate admonition for today's self-appointed bleeding deacons of "simplicity" was uttered by Jesus in a somewhat different context:

> Jesus answered and said unto him, Ye do err, not knowing the scriptures, nor the power of God (Matt. 22:29).

AAs are told by some oldltimers today (and they *often* are told) that they must not mention God or read the Bible because it might scare away the newcomers or get them drunk. But the author strongly believes they need to know sooner or later that such language and warnings were not present when A.A.'s success rate was highest. Failure to know the Bible and failure to know the power of God can be, and certainly was, fatal for the alcoholic who, according to A.A.'s own basic text, is 100% hopeless apart from Divine help. Certainly fatal if the newcomer is to make something out of the present-day basic text guiding him to establishing a relationship with God in A.A.

Long ago, A.A.'s Bill Wilson wrote the following in the First Edition of A.A.'s Big Book:

Remember it was agreed at the beginning *we would go to any lengths for victory over alcohol* (pp. 88-89).

Our real purpose is to fit ourselves to be of maximum service to God and the people about us (p. 89).

We have entered the world of Spirit. Our next function is to grow in understanding and effectiveness. This is not an overnight matter. It should continue for our life time (p. 97).

Every day is a day when we must carry the vision of God's will into all of our activities. "How can I best serve Thee—Thy will (not mine) be done." These are thoughts which must go with us constantly (p. 98).

What Pioneer A.A. Was About

It Was about "Finding" God

God, the Creator of the heavens and the earth, is not lost. But alcoholics and other addicts have often lost or forgotten or rejected all fellowship with Him.

Bill Wilson was, by his own declaration, a conservative atheist. From his first spiritual teacher, the Reverend Sam Shoemaker, rector of Calvary Episcopal Church in New York, Bill no doubt heard many times that he had been estranged from God. That he suffered from a spiritual malady. That he needed to "find God." And that there was a *way to find God.* In fact, in the very first year of Wilson's sobriety, Shoemaker published in his parish journal an article, "The Way to Find God." It was often reprinted and was frequently the subject of Shoemaker's writings, sermons, and books—both before and after Sam began teaching Bill..

God, of course, has never been, and is not, lost. Bill Wilson, however, certainly *was* lost, in late November of 1934. He *was* lost—in alcoholic stupor and a pointless life. And going down hill fast. Almighty God was, at that point, not only available, but easy

to "find," when "sought." As Sam Shoemaker wrote, in his very
first book, *Realizing Religion:*

> Now the thing which is striking about much of the misery one
> sees is that it is spiritual misery.... For the root of the malady
> is estrangement from God-estrangement from Him in people
> that were made to be His companions. . . . Something is
> lacking. Somehow we have missed the way. . . . The trouble is
> within, not without. . . . What you want is simply a vital
> religious experience. You need to find God. You need Jesus
> Christ (pp. 4-5, 8-9).

Find God? Vital religious experience? Well, that is exactly what Bill
Wilson also heard "prescribed" by his "sponsor" Ebby Thacher,
and by Bill and Ebby's friend Rowland Hazard. And both Ebby and
Rowland had heard these expressions from the lips of Sam
Shoemaker himself. Rowland had been told by his psychiatrist, Dr.
Carl Jung, in Switzerland, that (to be cured of alcoholism) he
needed union with God, a religious association, and a conversion by
which Rowland could be transformed. Rowland sought this
conversion experience by joining A First Century Christian
Fellowship (also known as the Oxford Group). He followed its
precepts and was healed of alcoholism. Rowland passed along to
Ebby Thacher, and later to Bill Wilson himself, the principles and
practices of that Christian fellowship (the Oxford Group).

Here, therefore, is what Bill Wilson wrote in the First Edition
of A.A.'s basic text, *Alcoholics Anonymous,* as Bill sought to
describe the solution to alcoholism as Bill saw it:

> The great fact is just this, and nothing less: that we have had
> deep and effective spiritual experiences, which have
> revolutionized our whole attitude toward life, toward our
> fellows, and toward God's universe. The central fact of our
> lives today is the absolute certainty that our Creator has entered
> into our hearts and lives in a way which is indeed miraculous
> (pp. 35-36).

A certain American business man [Rowland Hazard] . . . had gone to Europe placing himself in the care of a celebrated physician [Dr. Carl Jung]. . . . Nevertheless he was drunk in a short time. . . . So he returned to this doctor, whom he admired, and asked him point-blank why he could not recover.... The doctor said: "You have the mind of a chronic alcoholic. I have never seen one single case recover, where that state of mind existed to the extent that it does in you. . . . [But] Here and there, once in a while, alcoholics have had what are called vital spiritual experiences. . . ." Here was the terrible dilemma in which our friend found himself when he had the extraordinary experience, which as we have told you, made him a free man. . . . What seemed at first a flimsy reed, has proved to be the loving and powerful hand of God (pp. 36-38).

In a letter Dr. Carl Jung wrote from Switzerland to Bill Wilson in1961 (long after the founding of A.A. and long after the writing of its Big Book), Dr. Jung wrote forcefully about the conversion. This conversion was the solution he had recommended to Rowland Hazard. Jung said he had been speaking of "union with God." Jung cited the following from the Bible:

As the hart panteth after the water brooks, so panteth my soul after thee, O God. Psalm 42:1 [For the Jung-Wilson correspondence, see *Pass It On*, pp. 381-86].

Bill Wilson claimed to have had what Wilson chose to describe [in Oxford Group terms] as a vital spiritual or religious experience himself while a patient at Towns Hospital in New York in December, 1934. Bill picked up on this theme in his introductions to the Twelve Steps. First, he told of a disillusioned alcoholic [John Henry Fitzhugh Mayo] who had said, "WHO ARE YOU TO SAY THERE IS NO GOD?" Bill recounted what then had followed:

[Fitz] "tumbled out of bed to his knees. In a few seconds he was overwhelmed by a conviction of the Presence of God. . . . Save for a few brief moments of temptation the thought of drink has never returned; and at such times a great revulsion has risen in him. Seemingly he could not drink even if he would. God had restored his sanity. . . . He has come to all who have honestly sought Him. When we drew near to Him, He disclosed Himself to us!" (*Alcoholics Anonymous*, 1ˢᵗ ed., pp. 68-69).

Then Bill gathered together the common experiences of Rowland, of other recovered Oxford Group people, of Ebby (who had sobered up before there was an AA), of Fitz in New York, and then from the remarkable recoveries in Akron. Bill wrote the words now known to almost every A.A. member today:

Remember that we deal with alcohol—cunning, baffling, powerful. Without help it is too much for us. But there is One who has all power—That One is God. May you find Him now! Half measures availed us nothing. We stood at the turning point. We asked His protection and care with complete abandon. Here are the steps we took, which are suggested as a Program of Recovery (*Alcoholics Anonymous*, 1ˢᵗ ed.,pp. 70-71).

With that backdrop provided by Bill Wilson, we can proceed to the biblical steps the early A.A. pioneers *really took*–Took with Bible in hand. Prayers in their hearts. Ears tuned for guidance from their Creator. And joined together in common fellowship with Quiet Times at home, Quiet Times each morning with Dr. Bob's wife Anne at the Smith home, and Quiet Times in the early meetings as well.

A.A. Was Really about Seeking God

A.A.'s other co-founder, Dr. Bob, was not an atheist, nor did he have trouble 'finding" God. Dr. Bob had believed in God from his earliest youth in St. Johnsbury, Vermont. Bob Smith had confessed Jesus Christ as his Lord and Saviour, and had studied the Bible extensively as a youngster, in St. Johnsbury's North Congregational

Church. Also in Christian Endeavor, and then during his later years in Akron.

As with Bill Wilson, Dr. Bob's later and very serious problem was alcoholism. Bob–like Bill--was a "real" alcoholic. Just before Bill met Dr. Bob in Akron, Dr. Bob, his wife, and their Oxford Group friends had joined him in prayer on their knees at the home of T. Henry and Clarace Williams. They asked for Bob's healing by God. In no time at all, Bill Wilson appeared in Akron seemingly out of nowhere. He was put in touch with Bob by Henrietta Seiberling. After that, Dr. Bob and Bill Wilson learned that one drunk could help another "find" or "rediscover" God and become free. That's how Wilson described the individual experiences in an early draft of the Big Book— He said the pioneers had "found" or "rediscovered" God.

After one relapse, Dr. Bob decided to quit for good. Bill Wilson moved in with the Smiths in Akron. Study of the Bible, and the development of A.A.'s program, began in earnest. Dr. Bob's wife read the Bible to the two men daily. Bob and Bill discussed the Bible till the wee hours of the morning. Dr. Bob thus again returned to God, to the Bible, and to deliverance through the accomplishments of Jesus Christ. Also, to the new task of helping others to do likewise.

Dr. Bob said, about his studies, about Bill and himself, and about the Good Book itself:

We [Bill and Bob] had been associated with the Oxford Group, Bill in New York for five months, and I in Akron for two and a half years. Bill had acquired their idea of service. I had not, but I had done an immense amount of reading they had recommended. I had refreshed my memory of the Good Book, and I had had excellent training in that as a youngster (*The Co-founders of Alcoholics Anonymous*, 1972, p. 7).

There was hardly a night [during the three months of Bill Wilson's stay at the Smith home in the summer of 1935] that we didn't sit up until two or three o'clock talking. It would be hard for me to say that, during these nightly discussions around our kitchen table, nothing was said that influenced the writing of the Twelve Steps. We already had the basic ideas, though not in terse and tangible form. We got them . . . as a result of our study of the Good Book *(The Co-Founders of Alcoholics Anonymous,* p. 14).

We [the A.A. pioneers] were convinced that the answer to our problems was in the Good Book. To some of us older ones, the parts we found absolutely essential were the Sermon on the Mount [Matthew chapters 5-7], the 13th chapter of First Corinthians, and the Book of James. *(The Co-Founders of Alcoholics Anonymous*, p. 13).

In Los Angeles, California, in 1943, before an audience of more than 4,500 alcoholics and their families, when Bill and Bob were both on stage together, Dr. Bob said:

"Read religious literature. Resume church attendance. Cultivate the habit of prayer, and transmit the desires and principles of Alcoholics Anonymous to others." [He particularly emphasized reading the Bible, said the reporter who covered the talk.].

So just what can AAs, their families, and Twelve Step groups read in the Bible today that will give them a chance at the same spiritual understanding of God, the same relationship with God, and the same willingness to learn and obey God's Will? The same objective A.A. pioneers had?

How do you *seek* God? Our founders frequently and strongly suggested reading the Bible, reading religious literature, resuming church attendance, and cultivating the habit of prayer. Then they urged witnessing to the principles and practices of Alcoholics Anonymous in order that others might also find God.

4

Begin Your Bible Study by Learning about God

See, I am Yahweh, the God of all mankind: is anything impossible to me? [Jer. 32:27 Jerusalem Bible (JB)]

Learn *and* Understand

As we approach this subject of how to study the Bible—the "Good Book" of early Alcoholics Anonymous—please remember that this book is a guide. It will not quote the Bible in toto or even large parts of it. It will not tell you how to interpret the Bible or where to go to be taught about it. It will *suggest some approaches*. Many of these approaches have now been documented as those used by the A.A. pioneers. They may help you in graduating from A.A.'s "spiritual kindergarten," as Bill Wilson called it, and in moving on to a greater understanding of God (the Creator our pioneers relied upon), the Bible (the "Good Book" they read for spiritual truths), and the spiritual principles (which they borrowed from the Bible and Bible-related literature, and used as their guide to loving and serving God and doing His will).

We will depart here from what might have been the starting point for early A.A. Bible study. Dr. Bob and others said repeatedly that the parts of the Bible the pioneers considered absolutely essential were the Sermon on the Mount, 1 Corinthians 13, and the Book of James. Dr. Bob and Bill both said many times that the Sermon on the Mount contained the underlying philosophy of A.A. Although it is unlikely that early AAs simply opened their Bible and began reading the Sermon on the Mount, 1 Corinthians 13, and James, that is certainly a possibility. If Anne Smith's journal is any guide, they did not *start* with the three segments. If Dr. Bob's own reading of the entire Bible three times is any example, once again the three segments do not necessarily constitute the starting point. Finally, Dr. Bob read the Bible to the pioneers frequently in meetings. He often quoted the Bible when explaining some idea. And he often suggested that a newcomer answer his own question by looking in the Good Book. Anne Smith said the Bible should be the main sourcebook of all and suggested a number of books to be read. However, to make sure we don't omit and don't fail to highlight the "absolutely essential" parts mentioned by Dr. Bob, we have included in this title Appendix 2 which contains a revised and enlarged study of the Sermon on the Mount, 1 Corinthians 13, and James.

It may well be that you wish to start your own A.A.-related Bible study with the Sermon on the Mount, 1 Corinthians, and James. If so, Appendix 2 should be very helpful. We have, however, a far more basic and simple approach.

Where and how should you start reading the Bible if you are one who wants learn what the Word of God has to say about recovery, about deliverance, about God, and about spiritual growth in A.A. or other 12-Step Fellowships today? Well, why not start at the beginning! Necessarily, we start with the existence of God.

God Exists

Here is what Bill Wilson wrote in the Third Edition of A.A.'s Big Book:

> When we became alcoholics, crushed by a self-imposed crisis we could not postpone or evade, we had to fearlessly face the proposition that either God is everything or else He is nothing. God either is, or He isn't. What was our choice to be? Arrived at this point, we were squarely confronted with the question of faith. We couldn't duck the issue (p. 53).

Wilson's spiritual teacher, the Reverend Sam Shoemaker, frequently addressed this same point. Shoemaker wrote:

> I shall be at pains to show you that it makes a difference whether a man believes in God, and what it will do to transform the whole course of his subsequent existence if he catches a genuine vision of the reality of God in this universe. Here, let me say, I am not using "vision" in the technical sense of spiritual experience to the eye of the inward soul: I mean rather some experience, of hearing, seeing, feeling or discovering which causes a man to acquire an absolute faith "that God is, and that he is a rewarder of them that seek him" (Shoemaker, *Religion That Works*, p. 88).

> God is, or He isn't (Shoemaker, *Confident Faith*, p. 187).

For additional points Shoemaker made on these ideas from Heb. 11:6, see Dick B., *New Light on Alcoholism: God, Sam Shoemaker, and A.A.*, pp. 46-49, 161.

The Bible contains an important declaration, upon which the foregoing statements are based:

> But without faith, *it is* impossible to please *him*: for he that cometh to God must believe that he is and *that* he is a rewarder of them that diligently seek him (Heb. 11:6).

And to see that God "is" (i.e., "exists"), we merely need to turn to the first verse in the Bible.

In the beginning God created the heaven and the earth (Gen. 1:1)

The existence of God is not explicitly stated or debated. It is implicit and obvious in the statement that God "created the heaven and the earth." God is the subject of the powerful verb "create."
Psalm 14 states the matter of God's existence this way:

The fool hath said in his heart, There is no God (Ps. 14:1a).

Dr. Bob said in the Big Book:

If you think you are an atheist, an agnostic, a skeptic, or have any other form of intellectual pride which keeps you from accepting what is in this book [*Alcoholics Anonymous*], I feel sorry for you. . . .
Your Heavenly Father will never let you down! (3d ed., p. 181.)

Enough said!

God Is the Creator of the Heavens and the Earth

Genesis 1:1 presents the great truth that God **created** "the heaven and earth." He has more power, by far, than any other living being in the heavens or on earth. The Hebrew word translated "heaven" in the KJV is always plural throughout the Hebrew Old Testament. Modern versions such as the New International Version (NIV) and the New American Standard Version (NASV) translate it "heavens" in Genesis 1:1.

In the beginning God created the heavens and the earth (NIV)

In the beginning God created the heavens and the earth (NASV)

As we have seen, Gen. 1:1—the first verse in the Bible—declares that God created the heavens and the earth. Perhaps this explains why the first 164 pages of A.A.'s Big Book text refer to God as "Creator" 12 times (*Alcoholics Anonymous,* 3rd ed., pp. 13, 25, 28, 56, 68, 72, 75, 76, 80, 83, 158, 161). And the Bible certainly declares, confirms, and reiterates that God is our Creator, saying:

> Remember now thy Creator in the days of thy youth. . . . (Eccles. 12:1).

> Hast thou not known? Has thou not heard, *that* the everlasting God, the LORD, the Creator of the ends of the earth, fainteth not, neither is weary? *there is* no searching of his understanding (Isa. 40:28).

> Thus saith God the LORD, he that created the heavens, and stretched them out; he that spread forth the earth, and that which cometh out of it; he that giveth breath unto the people upon it, and spirit to them that walk therein (Isa. 42:5).

> Wherefore let them that suffer according to the will of God commit the keeping of their souls to *him* in well doing, as unto a faithful Creator (1 Pet. 4:19).

Establishing a Relationship with God, the Creator

A.A.'s Big Book many times refers to the necessity for *establishing a relationship* with God, the Creator. If you are to establish a relationship with the Creator, it behooves you to learn all you can about Him.

The Bible describes man's possible relationship with God in a number of ways. Here are three important descriptions:

1. God offered to the children of Israel the opportunity to have Him as their God and for them to be His people:

And I will take you to me for a people, and I will be to you a
God: and ye shall know that I [am] the LORD your God, which
bringeth you out from under the burdens of the Egyptians
(Exod. 6:7)

2. Beginning with the Day of Pentecost (Acts 2:1ff.), God offered
to every human being the opportunity to become His son via the
new birth:

That if thou shalt confess with thy mouth the Lord Jesus, and
shalt believe in thine heart that God hath raised him from the
dead, thou shalt be saved.
For with the heart man believeth unto righteousness; and with
the mouth confession is made unto salvation (Rom. 10:9, 10).

But when the fulness of the time was come, God sent forth his
Son, made of a woman, made under the law,
To redeem them that were under the law, that we might receive
the adoption of sons.
And because ye are sons, God hath sent forth the Spirit of his
Son into your hearts, crying, Abba, Father.
Wherefore thou art no more a servant, but a son; and if a son,
then an heir of God through Christ (Gal. 4:4-7)

3. And God offers His born-again children the opportunity to have
fellowship with each other, with God, and with His Son, Jesus
Christ:

That which we have seen and heard declare we unto you, that
ye also may have fellowship with us: and truly our fellowship
is with the Father, and with his Son Jesus Christ.
And these things write we unto you, that your joy may be full.
This then is the message which we have heard of him, and
declare unto you, that God is light, and in him is no darkness at
all.
If we say that we have fellowship with him, and walk in
darkness, we lie, and do not the truth:

> But if we walk in the light, as he is in the light, we have fellowship one with another, and the blood of Jesus Christ his Son cleanseth us from all sin (1 John 1:3-7)

There is no doubt about A.A.'s emphasis on the importance of the relationship with God. The reader may notice that the Bible's descriptions of a relationship with God do not necessarily coincide with the descriptions Bill Wilson used in A.A.'s basic text. The third edition of the Big Book says:

> My friend promised when these things were done I would enter upon a new **relationship** with my Creator; that I would have the elements of a way of living which answered all my problems (p. 13, emphasis added).

> If what we have learned and felt and seen means anything at all, it means that all of us, whatever our race, creed, or color are the children of a living Creator with whom we may form a **relationship** upon simple and understandable terms as soon as we are willing and honest enough to try (p. 28, emphasis added).

> Each individual, in the personal stories, describes in his own language and from his own point of view the way he established his **relationship** with God (p. 29, emphasis added).

> We have been trying to get a new attitude, a new **relationship** with our Creator, and to discover the obstacles in our path (p. 72, emphasis added).

> It is dependent upon his **relationship** with God (p. 100, emphasis added).

> See to it that your **relationship** with Him is right, and great events will come to pass for you and countless others (p. 164, emphasis added).

When A.A.'s Big Book speaks—as did Bill W.'s spiritual mentor Rev. Sam Shoemaker—about "finding" God, it also speaks about a *path*. It directs the reader to that path and then refers to "the steps we took." These are the steps to establishing the desired relationship with God, as A.A. viewed the solution both in the beginning *and* now.

Sam Shoemaker wrote often about establishing a relationship with God and about the blocks which stood in the way of doing so. He said, for example:

> Whatever keeps us from a living, loving relation with other people–or from a vital and open relationship with God–is sin (Shoemaker, *How to Become a Christian*, p. 56).

> Only God, therefore, can deal with sin. He must contrive to do for us what we have lost the power to do for ourselves (Shoemaker, *If I Be Lifted Up*, p. 133).

> Conversion is the only means by which a radically bad person can be changed into a radically good person. It is thus a breach, a breaking off, a turning, a change (Shoemaker, *Realizing Religion*, p. 22).

> The heart of surrender does not lie in asking God to take our problems and solve them for us because we have been unable to do so: it lies in giving ourselves to Him for the doing of His will (Shoemaker, *The Gospel According to You*, p. 86).

> All subsequent life is a development of the relationship with God which conversion opened (Shoemaker, *Children of the Second Birth*, p. 16).

So AAs were to establish a relationship with God, the Creator of the heavens and the earth. They were to turn from sin, be converted, and have their sins taken away. Compare, for example, these verses from the Book of Acts:

> Then Peter said unto them, Repent, and be baptized every one
> of you in the name of Jesus Christ for the remission of sins, and
> ye shall receive the gift of the Holy Ghost (Acts 2:38)

> Repent ye therefore, and be converted, that your sins may be
> blotted out, when the times of refreshing shall come from the
> presence of the Lord (Acts 3:19)

This they were to do by a new birth, by conversion. And their new way of life—a life of doing the will of the Creator—was to be a process of *continuing development* of the relationship with God which their conversion began. They were not to be struck blind by a white light and wander aimlessly thereafter. They were to establish a relationship, develop that relationship, and move into having fellowship: (1) with God, the Creator; (2) with His Son, Jesus Christ; and (3) with each other.

> That which we have seen and heard declare we unto you, that
> ye also may have fellowship with us: and truly our fellowship
> is with the Father, and with his Son Jesus Christ (1 John 1:3)

The Name of the Creator

The subject of the name of the Creator of the heavens and the earth is one of the most important and exciting topics in the Bible. Your investment of time in studying this section carefully will be well worth every moment.

The A.A. Backdrop and Why the Particulars about the Creator's Name Are Vital

"God," *with* a capital "G," is specifically called "God" 277 times in the Third Edition of A.A.'s Big Book. That Big Book also contains 107 specific pronouns—he, him, his, and himself—which are similarly capitalized and hence unquestionably refer to "God." Counting the additional places where A.A.'s Big Book contains references to our Creator—calling Him "Creator," "Maker," "Father," "Father of Light," and "Spirit"—the Creator is thus specifically mentioned in the Big Book more than 400 times. (See Dick B., *The Good Book and The Big Book*, pp. 49-50.) Not surprisingly, but certainly unfortunately, the Big Book nowhere calls the Creator by His proper name. Nonetheless, the Big Book distinguishes the Creator from any other "god" or kind of "god."

Bill Wilson, author of almost every word in the Big Book's basic text, can quickly be seen as articulate and careful in his grammatical usages. Especially when dealing with, and capitalizing, certain words! In the "Handbook of Style" section of the *Merriam-Webster's Collegiate Dictionary, Tenth Edition*, the following is stated about capitalized words:

> Capitals are used with almost all proper nouns–that is, nouns that name particular persons, places, or things (including abstract entities), distinguishing them from others of the same class. . . . The essential distinction in the use of capitals and lowercase letters at the beginnings of words lies in this individualizing significance of capitals as against the generalizing significance of lowercase. . . . (pp. 1541-42)

In the sub-subsection titled "Religious Terms," the following is also stated in the "Handbook of Style" section of *Merriam-Webster's Collegiate Dictionary, Tenth Edition*:

> 28. Words designating the Deity are capitalized.
> 29. Personal pronouns referring to the Deity are usually capitalized, even when they closely follow their antecedent (p. 1544).

The Creator's Name Is Important to Us

Note first:

> For God is not *the author* of confusion, but of peace, as in all churches of the saints (1 Cor. 14:33)

> As concerning therefore the eating of those things that are offered in sacrifice unto idols, we know that an idol *is* nothing in the world, and that *there is* none other God but one.
> For though there be that are called gods, whether in heaven or in earth, (as there be gods many, and lords many,)
> But to us *there is but* one God, the Father, of whom *are* all things, and we in him; and one Lord Jesus Christ, by whom *are* all things, and we by him (1 Cor. 8:4-6)

There is therefore no doubt, considering the many references by Bill and Bob to the Bible, that Bill was, in the Big Book and his other early writings, specifically talking about the "Deity" of the Bible. His capitalized references to God, the Creator, Maker, and Father, were not referring and did not refer to a "group," a "doorknob," a "lightbulb," "the Big Dipper," or some other vague "higher power" of Bill's own making. Bill's intent to designate our Creator is further evident from the frequent mention by Bill (and Bob) of his "Heavenly Father," just as Jesus did in the "Sermon on the Mount" (Matthew chapters 5 to 7). In other specific, biblical references to the Creator, Bill spoke of Him as the "living God," as "God Almighty," and as "God our Father"– all terms in and from the Bible. A Bible which refers to false gods, but never to the Creator as one of these false gods, or as a group, as a lightbulb, or as a "higher power."

Again, not surprisingly, but certainly regrettably, the Big Book did not refer to the Creator by his personal name. We will see in a moment that the Creator Himself made it possible to identify Him with exactness and clarity. That identification comes with the use of His proper, personal name.

There are many reasons for getting Bill's biblical references to "God" and our "Creator" straight. They start with the need for identifying our Creator's *actual name*. First, as will be discussed below, in the Bible, God specifically declares what His name is—many times. He indicates the importance of that very name to Himself. He states clearly that *His* name is "my holy name." Second, there is endless confusion today in A.A. talk about strange new gods, higher powers, and inanimate objects such as chairs and bulldozers.

Our Creator long ago explicitly distinguished the difference between Himself and the kind of phoney idols that are proliferating today. Psalm 115 says:

> Not unto us, O LORD, not unto us, but unto thy name give glory, for thy mercy, *and* for thy truth's sake.
> Wherefore should the heathen say, Where *is* now their God?
> But our God *is* in the heavens; he hath done whatsoever he hath pleased.
> Their idols *are* silver and gold, the work of men's hands.
> They have mouths, but they speak not: eyes have they, but they see not:
> They have ears, but they hear not: noses have they, but they smell not:
> They have hands, but they handle not: feet have they, but they walk not: neither speak they through their throat.
> They that make them are like unto them; so *is* everyone that trusteth in them.
> O Israel, trust thou in the LORD: he *is* their help and their shield. (Ps. 115:1-9)

Psalm 115 makes obvious the absurdity of trusting in a lightbulb, as some AAs declare today that *you* can do. And a word to the wise is sufficient.

Reverend Sam Shoemaker spoke to AAs at their international convention and decried the use of "absurd names for God." Such absurdities, of course, can be eliminated in a moment by referring to the Creator of the heavens and the earth by His proper name which He Himself sets forth in the Bible. And He makes clear in the Ten Commandments that there are to be no other "gods" before Him–no gods, graven images, or substitutes.

There follow therefore specific references in the Bible to the Creator's holy name and explanations of what the Creator has said about His name in the Good Book.

The Creator's Name Is Important to Him!

When you want to get to know someone, one of the first things you usually want to know is his or her name. And peoples' names tend to be very important to them. The Bible indicates in many ways that the name of the Creator of the heavens and the earth is very important to Him also.

> Thou shalt not take **the name of the LORD thy God** in vain; for the LORD will not hold him guiltless that taketh **his name** in vain (Exod. 20:7, emphasis added)

> And ye shall not swear by **my name** falsely, neither shalt thou profane **the name of thy God**: I *am* the LORD (Lev. 19:12, emphasis added)

> Because he hath set his love upon me [i.e., the LORD], therefore will I deliver him: I will set him on high, because he hath known **my name**. (Ps. 91:14, emphasis added)

> Glory ye in **his holy name**: let the heart of them rejoice that seek the LORD (Ps. 105:3, emphasis added).

> He sent redemption unto his people: he hath commanded his covenant for ever: **holy and reverend is his name** (Ps. 111:9, emphasis added).

And I will sanctify **my great name**, which was profaned among the heathen, which ye have profaned in the midst of them; and the heathen shall know that I *am* the LORD, saith the Lord GOD, when I shall be sanctified in you before their eyes (Ezek. 36:23, emphasis added)

So will I make **my holy name** known in the midst of my people Israel; and I will not let them pollute **my holy name** any more: and the heathen shall know that I am the LORD, the Holy One of Israel (Ezek. 39:7, emphasis).

The Creator's Name is Yahweh

Somewhere between the fifth and the second centuries bce a tragic accident befell God: he lost his name. More exactly, Jews gave up using God's personal name Yahweh, and began to refer to Yahweh by various periphrases: God, the Lord, the Name, the Holy One, the Presence, even the Place. Even where Yahweh was written in the biblical text, readers pronounced the name as Adonai. With the final fall of the temple, even the rare liturgical occasions when the name was used ceased, and even the knowledge of the pronunciation of the name was forgotten [David J. A. Clines, "Yahweh and the God of Christian Theology," *Theology* 83 (1980), pp. 323-30].

In the Bible, the Creator of the heavens and the earth specifically tells us His name many times. That name in the Hebrew Old Testament is represented by four Hebrew letters—*Yud-Heh-Vav-Heh* (or *YHWH*)—and these four letters are sometimes called the tetragrammaton ("four-letter writing"). *YHWH*, Strong's number 3068, occurs 6,519 times in the Hebrew Old Testament underlying the KJV [according to the *Blue Letter Bible* (BLB) on the Internet (www.blueletterbible.org/)], and 6,828 times in the Hebrew Old Testament from which the NIV was translated [*The Hebrew-English Concordance to the Old Testament* (HECOT, p. 630)]. In fact, *YHWH* is one of the 35 most frequently occurring terms in the Hebrew Old Testament!

As to the *pronunciation* of the four Hebrew letters *YHWH*, Kenneth L. Barker states:

There is almost universal consensus among scholars today that the sacred Tetragrammaton (YHWH) is to be vocalized and pronounced **Yahweh**. [Barker, "YHWH Sabaoth: 'The Lord Almighty,'" *The NIV: The Making of a Contemporary Translation* http://www.gospelcom.net/ibs/niv/mct/9.php, emphasis added]

And the *Encyclopaedia Britannica* adds:

Although Christian scholars after the Renaissance and Reformation periods used the term Jehovah for YHWH, in the 19th and 20th centuries biblical scholars again began to use the form **Yahweh**. Early Christian writers, such as Clement of Alexandria in the 2nd century, had used a form like Yahweh, and this pronunciation of the tetragrammaton was never really lost. Other Greek transcriptions also indicated that YHWH should be pronounced **Yahweh** [*Encyclopædia Britannica* (http://www.britannica.com/eb/article?eu=79806&tocid=0), "Yahweh," emphasis added]

As to the *meaning* of the Creator's name *YHWH*, "Yahweh," Exodus chapter three provides important information:

[11] And Moses said unto God, Who *am* I, that I should go unto Pharaoh, and that I should bring forth the children of Israel out of Egypt?
[12] And he said, Certainly **I will be** [*ehyeh*] with thee; and this *shall be* a token unto thee, that I have sent thee: When thou hast brought forth the people out of Egypt, ye shall serve God upon this mountain.
[13] And Moses said unto God, Behold, *when* I come unto the children of Israel, and shall say unto them, The God of your fathers hath sent me unto you; and they shall say to me, What *is* his name? what shall I say unto them?

[14] And God said unto Moses, **I AM THAT I AM** [*ehyeh asher ehyeh*]: and he said, Thus shalt thou say unto the children of Israel, **I AM** [*ehyeh*] hath sent me unto you.
[15] And God said moreover unto Moses, Thus shalt thou say unto the children of Israel, **the LORD** [*YHWH*, Yahweh] God of your fathers, the God of Abraham, the God of Isaac, and the God of Jacob, hath sent me unto you: this *is* my name for ever, and this *is* my memorial unto all generations.
[16] Go, and gather the elders of Israel together, and say unto them, The LORD [*YHWH*, Yahweh] God of your fathers, the God of Abraham, of Isaac, and of Jacob, appeared unto me, saying, I have surely visited you, and seen that which is done to you in Egypt (Exod. 3:11-16, KJV, emphasis added).

The best known modern Bibles [such as the NIV, NASV, and the Revised Standard Version (RSV)] all differ from the KJV and agree with each other in their translation of the Hebrew words underlying "I AM THAT I AM" in Exodus 3:14:

God said to Moses, "I AM WHO I AM.[f] This is what you are to say to the Israelites: 'I AM has sent me to you.'" (NIV)

God said to Moses, "'I AM WHO [c]I AM"; and He said, "Thus you shall say to the sons of Israel, "'I AM has sent me to you." (NASV)

God said to Moses, "I AM WHO I AM."[e] And he said, "Say this to the people of Israel, 'I AM has sent me to you.'" (RSV)

The NIV and RSV also offer alternative translations in their footnotes relating to verse 14:

Or *I WILL BE WHAT I WILL BE* (NIV, footnote "f")

Or I AM WHAT I AM or I WILL BE WHAT I WILL BE (RSV, footnote "e")

And the NIV and NASV provide information concerning the relationship between the term "I AM" which occurs three times in verse 14 and the term "the LORD" [*YHWH*] in verse 15:

> The Hebrew for *LORD* [in verse 15] sounds like and may be derived from the Hebrew for *I AM* in verse 14 (NIV, footnote "g")

> ["I AM" in verse 14 is] Related to the name of God, *YHWH*, rendered *LORD*, which is derived from the verb *HAYAH, to be* (NASV, footnote "c").

In the chapter titled "YHWH Sabaoth" quoted earlier, Barker points out the importance of Exodus chapter 3 relative to the meaning of "Yahweh":

> In my opinion this verse [i.e., Exod. 3:14] is a divine commentary on—or exposition of—the meaning of the name Yahweh (v.15).

Scott Grant, in his article "Being Involved" which is posted on the Internet [http://www.pbc.org/dp/grant/exodus/exo003.html], states:

> God seems to indicate that his name is "I AM" (or "I WILL BE"), for he tells Moses to tell the people that "I AM" has sent him [verse 14]. This is the first-person singular form of the verb "to be." God has used it elsewhere already in this passage in conveying his nature. In Exodus 3:12, he says, "I will be with you." Although in the New American Standard translation, the name "I AM" and the verb "I will be" appear to be different tenses, they appear in the same Hebrew tense, and they are one and the same word. . . .
>
>   . . . God twice identifies his name with a word translated "the Lord" (3:15, 16) [i.e., *YHWH*, Yahweh]. This word is likely the third-person singular form of the verb "to be" and **means** . . . "HE IS" or "HE WILL BE." **The transliteration**

from Hebrew into English, near as we can tell, **is** "Yahweh" (emphasis added).

And the New English Translation's discussion of Exod. 3:14 in note 47 states:

> The verb form used here [for "I am" in verse 14] is . . . ('ehyeh), the Qal imperfect, 1csg, of the verb "to be," hyh (haya). It forms an excellent paronomasia with the name [Yahweh]. So when God used the verb to express his name, he used this form saying, "I AM." When his people refer to him as Yahweh, which is the 3msg form of the same verb, it actually means "he is." Some commentators argue for a future tense translation, "I will be who I will be," because the verb has an active quality about it, and the Israelites lived in the light of the promises for the future. The Greek translation [of the Hebrew Old Testament known as the Septuagint or "LXX" (for the supposed 70 translators)] used a participle to capture the idea [i.e., *ego eimi ho on*, "I am he who is"]; . . . The simplest meaning is the English present tense, which embraces the future promises. The point is that Yahweh is sovereignly independent of all creation and that his presence guarantees the fulfillment of the covenant. Others argue for a causative Hiphil translation of "I will cause to be," but nowhere in the Bible does this verb appear in Hiphil or Piel (http://www.bible.org/).

The meaning of God's holy name *Yahweh* has been frequently discussed in scholarly literature through the years. If the reader would like to pursue this matter further, here are several additional sources for consideration: (1) "Yahweh," *Encyclopædia Britannica Article* (http://www.britannica.com); (2) "Jehovah (Yahweh)," Catholic Encyclopedia (http://www.newadvent.org/cathen/); and (3) our Appendix 1, The Creator's Name is Yahweh![1]

---

[1]See also: G. H. Park-Taylor, hwhy , Yahweh, the Divine Name in the Bible (Waterloo, Ontario, 1975); B. Beitzel, "Exodus 3:14 and the Divine Name: A Case of
(continued...)

Here are some key verses in which the Creator's name Yahweh occurs:

Abraham planted a tamarisk at Beersheba and there he invoked Yahweh, the everlasting God. [Gen. 21:33 Jerusalem Bible (JB)]

The KJV translates "there he invoked" as "called there on the name of" in verse 33 because the Hebrew Old Testament contains the word *shem*, "name."

And God also said to Moses, "You are to say to the sons of Israel: 'Yahweh, the God of your fathers, the God of Abraham, the God of Isaac, and the God of Jacob, has sent me to you'. This is my name for all time; by this name I shall be invoked for all generations to come (Exod. 3:15 JB)

(Note Bill Wilson's usage of the phrase "God of our fathers" in *Twelve Steps and Twelve Traditions*, AAWS, 1987, p. 29.)

God spoke to Moses and said to him, "I am Yahweh. To Abraham and Isaac and Jacob I appeared as El Shaddai; I did not make myself known to them by my name Yahweh." (Exod. 6:2, 3 JB)

And let them know this: you alone bear the name Yahweh, Most High over the whole world (Ps. 83:18 JB).

My name is Yahweh, I will not yield my glory to another, nor my honour to idols. (Isa. 42:8 JB)

---

[1](...continued)
Biblical Paronomasia," TJ 1 (1980): 5-20; C. D. Isbell, "The Divine Name ehyeh as a Symbol of Presence in Israelite Tradition," HAR 2 (1978): 101-18; J. G. Janzen, "What's in a Name? Yahweh in Exodus 3 and the Wider Biblical Context," Int 33 (1979): 227-39; J. R. Lundbom, "God's Use of the Idem per idem to Terminate Debate," HTR 71 (1978): 193-201; A. R. Millard, "Yw and Yhw Names," VT 30 (1980): 208-12; and R. Youngblood, "A New Occurrence of the Divine Name 'I AM,'" JETS 15 (1972): 144-52.

Now listen, I am going to make them acknowledge, this time I am
going to make them acknowledge my hand and my might; and then
they will know that Yahweh is my name. (Jer. 16:21 JB)

Learn What the Bible Says about the Creator

The Creator of the heavens and the earth has revealed a great deal
to us about Himself in His Word, the Bible (known in early A.A.
as "the Good Book"). For example:

God Is Almighty

And when Abram was ninety years old and nine, the LORD
[Yahweh] appeared to Abram, and said unto him, I *am* the
Almighty God; walk before me, and be thou perfect (Gen.
17:1).

And God said unto him [Jacob]. I *am* God Almighty: be fruitful
and multiply. . . . (Gen. 35:11).

(Compare Bill Wilson's statement that only God Almighty could
cure the alcoholic's form of lunacy: Dick B., *The Akron Genesis of
Alcoholics Anonymous*, pp. 12-13):

God Is Our Maker

Shall mortal man be more just than God? shall a man be more
pure than his maker? (Job 4:17)

Thus saith the LORD [Yahweh], the Holy One of Israel, and his
Maker, Ask me of things to come concerning my sons, and
concerning the work of my hands command ye me. I have made
the earth, and created man upon it: I, *even* my hands, have
stretched out the heavens, and all their host have I commanded
(Isa. 45:11-12).

[Note the references in *Alcoholics Anonymous,* to our Maker, God (3rd ed., pp. 57, 63).]

God Is in Heaven

> After this manner therefore pray ye: Our Father which art in heaven, . . . (Matt. 6:9).

> But whosoever shall deny me before men [said Jesus], him will I also deny before my Father which is in heaven (Matt. 10:33).

> So then after the Lord [Jesus] had spoken unto them, he was received up into heaven, and sat on the right hand of God (Mark 16:19).

> Be not rash with thy mouth, and let not thine heart be hasty to utter *any* thing before God: for God *is* in heaven, and thou upon earth: therefore let thy words be few (Eccles. 5:2).

> The fool hath said in his heart, *There is* no God. Corrupt are they, and have done abominable iniquity: *there is* none that doeth good. God looked down from heaven upon the children of men, to see if there were *any* that did understand, that did seek God (Ps. 53:1-2).

> The LORD [Yahweh] looked down from heaven upon the children of men, to see if there were any that did understand, *and* seek God (Ps. 14:2).

[Note the references to our Father which is in heaven in the last line of Dr. Bob's story (*Alcoholics Anonymous,* 3rd ed., p. 181), and in *Alcoholics Anonymous Comes of Age,* (p. 234).]

God Is Spirit

> God *is* a Spirit: and they that worship him must worship him in spirit and in truth (John 4:24).

God Is Not a Man

God *is* not a man, that he should lie; neither the son of man, that he should repent: hath he said, and shall he not do *it?* Or hath he spoken, and shall not make it good? (Num. 23:19).

And also the Strength of Israel [i.e., the Creator] will not lie nor repent: for he *is* not a man, that he should repent (1 Sam. 15:29).

For *he* [the Creator] *is* not a man, as I *am, that* I should answer him, *and* we should come together in judgment (Job 9:32).

I will not execute the fierceness of mine anger, I will not return to destroy Ephraim: for I *am* God, and not man; the Holy One in the midst of thee: and I will not enter into the city (Hos. 11:9).

God Is Invisible

Now unto the King eternal, immortal, invisible, the only wise God, *be* honour and glory for ever and ever. Amen (1 Tim. 1:17).

Who [the Father's dear Son] is the image of the invisible God, the firstborn of every creature (Col. 1:15).

No man hath seen God at any time; the only begotten Son, which is in the bosom of the Father, he hath declared *him* (John 1:18).

God Is Love

He that loveth not knoweth not God; for God is love (1 John 4:8).

And we have known and believed the love that God hath to us. God is love; and he that dwelleth in love dwelleth in God, and God in him (1 John 4:16).

God Is Light

This then is the message which we have heard of him, and declare unto you that God is light, and in him is no darkness at all (1 John 1:5).

Some Other Things God Is

- The eternal God (Deut. 33:27)
- The everlasting God (Gen. 21:33; Isa. 40:28; Rom. 16:26)
- The living God (Deut. 5:26; Josh. 3:10; 1 Sam. 17:26, 36; 2 Ki. 19:4, 16; Ps. 42:2; Ps. 84:2; Isa. 37:4, 17; Jer. 10:10; Jer. 23:36; Dan. 6:20, 26; Hos. 1:10; Matt. 16:16; Matt. 26:63; John 6:69; Acts 14:15; Rom. 9:26; 2 Cor. 3:3; 2 Cor. 6:16; 1 Tim. 3:15; 1 Tim. 4:10; Heb. 3:12; Heb. 9:14; Heb. 10:31; Heb. 12:32; Rev. 7:2)
- The true God (2 Chron. 15:3; Jer. 10:10; John 17:3; 1 John 5:20)
- The living and true God (1 Thess. 1:9)
- An holy God (Josh. 24:19; cp. Lev. 11:44, 45; 1 Sam. 2:2)
- The God of peace (Rom. 15:33; Rom. 16:20; Phil. 4:9; 1 Thess. 5:23; Heb. 13:20)
- The God of hope (Rom. 15:13)
- The God of patience and consolation (Rom. 15:5)
- The God of all grace (1 Pet. 5:10)
- The God of all comfort (2 Cor. 1:3)
- The God of our Lord Jesus Christ (Eph. 1:17; cp. Matt. 27:46; Mark 15:34; Rev. 3:12)
- The Father of our Lord Jesus Christ (Rom. 15:6; 2 Cor. 1:3; Col. 1:3)
- The God and Father of our Lord Jesus Christ (2 Cor. 11:31; Eph. 1:3; 1 Pet. 1:3)
- The Father of mercies (2 Cor. 1:3)

- The Father of lights (James 1:17)
- The living Father (John 6:57)
- The Saviour of all men (1 Tim. 4:10)

There Is Only One God

Hear, O Israel: The LORD [Yahweh] our God *is* one LORD
[Yahweh]: And thou shalt love the LORD [Yahweh] thy God
with all thine heart, and with all thy soul, and with all thy might
(Deut. 6:4, 5).

And one of the scribes came, and having heard them reasoning
together, and perceiving that he had answered them well, asked
him, Which is the first commandment of all?
And Jesus answered him, The first of all the commandments is,
Hear, O Israel; The Lord our God is one Lord:
And thou shalt love the Lord thy God with all thy heart, and
with all thy soul, and with all thy mind, and with all thy
strength: this is the first commandment.
And the second is like, namely this, Thou shalt love thy
neighbour as thyself. There is none other commandment greater
than these.
And the scribe said unto him, Well, Master, thou hast said the
truth: for there is one God; and there is none other but he (Mark
12:28-32)

But to us *there is but* one God, the Father, of whom *are* all
things, and we in him; and one Lord [,] Jesus Christ, by whom
are all things, and we by him (1 Cor. 8:6)

One God and Father of all, who *is* above all, and through all,
and in you all (Eph. 4:6).

For *there is* one God, and one mediator between God and men,
the man Christ Jesus (1 Tim. 2:5).

Thou believest that there is one God; thou doest well: the devils also believe, and tremble (Jam. 2:19).

There Is No Other "God" Like Yahweh

And [Solomon] said, O LORD [Yahweh] God of Israel, *there is* no God like thee in the heaven, nor in the earth; which keepest covenant, and *shewest* mercy unto thy servants, that walk before thee with all their hearts (2 Chron. 6:14)

Thus saith the LORD [Yahweh] the King of Israel, and his redeemer the LORD [Yahweh] of hosts; I *am* the first, and I *am* the last; and beside me *there is* no God (Isa. 44:6)

I *am* the LORD [Yahweh], and *there is* none else, *there is* no God beside me: I girded thee, though thou hast not known me (Isa. 45:5)

Tell ye, and bring *them* near; yea, let them take counsel together: who hath declared this from ancient time? *who* hath told it from that time? *have* not I the LORD [Yahweh]? and *there is* no God else beside me; a just God and a Saviour; *there is* none beside me (Isa. 45:21)

Yet I *am* the LORD [Yahweh] thy God from the land of Egypt, and thou shalt know no god but me: for *there is* no saviour beside me (Hos. 13:4)

And God spake all these words, saying,
I *am* the LORD [Yahweh] thy God, which have brought thee out of the land of Egypt, out of the house of bondage.
Thou shalt have no other gods before me.
Thou shalt not make unto thee any graven image, or any *likeness of any* thing that *is* in heaven above, or that *is* in the earth beneath, or that *is* in the water under the earth:
Thou shalt not bow down thyself to them, nor serve them: for I the LORD [Yahweh] thy God *am* a jealous God, visiting the

iniquity of the fathers upon the children unto the third and
fourth *generation* of them that hate me;
And shewing mercy unto thousands of them that love me, and
keep my commandments (Exod. 20:1-6)

Don't Mention the Name of Other Gods

And in all things that I have said unto you be circumspect: and
make no mention of the name of other gods, neither let it be
heard out of thy mouth (Exod. 23:13)

That ye come not among these nations, these that remain among
you: neither make mention of the name of their gods, nor cause
to swear by them, neither serve them, nor bow yourselves unto
them (Josh. 23:7)

5

Learning about God's Word, the Bible

These were more noble than those in Thessalonica, in that they received the word with all readiness of mind, and searched the scriptures daily, whether those things were so.
Therefore many of them believed; . . . (Acts 17:11, 12a)

Dr. Bob and Anne Urged the Bible's Importance

We have already documented that Dr. Bob studied the Good Book and talked about it with other AAs. We have also shown that he stressed to AAs the importance of reading it; and, in fact, even read it to AAs. It is equally important to review what his wife Anne Smith said. Anne recorded her thoughts about the Good Book in her journal and shared her ideas with AAs and their families most every day at the Quiet Time on Ardmore Avenue (the Smith home in Akron where A.A. was founded). She said:

Of course the Bible ought to be the main Source Book of all. No day ought to pass without reading it. Read until some passage comes that "hits" you. Then pause and meditate over its meaning for your life. Begin reading the Bible with the Book of Acts and follow up with the Gospels and then the Epistles of Paul. Let "Revelation" alone for a while. The Psalms ought to

73

be read and the Prophets (Dick B., *Anne Smith's Journal*, 3rd ed., p. 82).

Yes, the Bible was important in early A.A. Yes, A.A.'s basic ideas were taken from the Bible. And, yes, Bible study was stressed by the pioneers. Let's remember why! Establishing a new and right relationship with the Creator of the heavens and the earth was the objective. The end of Bible study was to learn truths about, and from, our Heavenly Father, God.

God Communicates His Will
to Human Beings in Many Ways

Hebrews chapter 1 touches upon the important topic of how God makes His will known to people:

> God, who at sundry times and in divers manners spake in time past unto the fathers by the prophets,
> Hath in these last days spoken unto us by his Son, . . . (Heb. 1:1, 2a)

Over the centuries, God has used many means to communicate with humanity. The Bible is one. Here are some of the others.

God Himself Speaks to People Directly

> And the LORD [Yahweh] God commanded the man [Adam], saying, Of every tree of the garden thou mayest freely eat (Gen. 2:16).

> And when Abram was ninety years old and nine, the LORD [*Yahweh*] appeared to Abram, and said unto him, I am the Almighty God; walk before me, and be thou perfect. (Gen. 17:1).

And God said unto him [Jacob], I *am* God Almighty: be fruitful and multiply. . . (Gen. 35:11).

And the LORD [Yahweh] said unto Moses, Pharaoh shall not hearken unto you; that my wonders may be multiplied in the land of Egypt. (Exod. 11:9).

Now after the death of Moses the servant of the LORD [Yahweh] it came to pass, that the LORD [Yahweh] spake unto Joshua the son of Nun, Moses' minister, saying,
Moses my servant is dead; now therefore arise, go over this Jordan, thou, and all this people, unto the land which I do give to them, even to the children of Israel (Josh. 1:1, 2)

[Jesus said:] Father, glorify thy name. Then came there a voice from heaven, saying, I have both glorified it, and will glorify it again (John 12:28)

God Speaks through Angels:

And the angel of God spake unto me in a dream, saying, Jacob: And I said, Here am I.
And he said, Lift up now thine eyes, and see, all the rams which leap upon the cattle are ringstraked, speckled, and grisled: for I have seen all that Laban doeth unto thee.
I am the God of Bethel, where thou anointedst the pillar, and where thou vowedst a vow unto me: now arise, get thee out from this land, and return unto the land of thy kindred (Gen. 31:11-13)

Now Moses kept the flock of Jethro his father in law, the priest of Midian: and he led the flock to the backside of the desert, and came to the mountain of God, even to Horeb.
And the angel of the LORD [Yahweh] appeared unto him in a flame of fire out of the midst of a bush: and he looked, and, behold, the bush burned with fire, and the bush was not consumed.

And Moses said, I will now turn aside, and see this great sight, why the bush is not burnt.

And when the LORD [Yahweh] saw that he turned aside to see, God called unto him out of the midst of the bush, and said, Moses, Moses. And he said, Here am I.

And he said, Draw not nigh hither: put off thy shoes from off thy feet, for the place whereon thou standest is holy ground.

Moreover he said, I am the God of thy father, the God of Abraham, the God of Isaac, and the God of Jacob. And Moses hid his face; for he was afraid to look upon God.

God Speaks through Prophets

And the LORD [Yahweh] said unto Moses, . . .

. . . thou shalt say unto Pharaoh, Thus saith the LORD [Yahweh], Israel is my son, even my firstborn (Exod. 4:21a, 22)

And the LORD [Yahweh] said unto Moses, See, I have made thee a god to Pharaoh: and Aaron thy brother shall be thy prophet.

Thou shalt speak all that I command thee: and Aaron thy brother shall speak unto Pharaoh, that he send the children of Israel out of his land (Exod. 7:1, 2)

And it came to pass that night, that the word of the LORD [Yahweh] came unto Nathan, saying,

Now therefore so shalt thou [Nathan] say unto my servant David, Thus saith the LORD [Yahweh] of hosts, I took thee from the sheepcote, from following the sheep, to be ruler over my people, over Israel (2 Sam. 7:4, 8)

Then came the word of the LORD [Yahweh] by Haggai the prophet, saying,

Is it time for you, O ye, to dwell in your cieled houses, and this house lie waste?

Now therefore thus saith the LORD [Yahweh] of hosts; Consider your ways (Hag. 1:3-5)

In the eighth month, in the second year of Darius, came the word of the LORD [Yahweh] unto Zechariah, the son of Berechiah, the son of Iddo the prophet, saying,
The LORD [Yahweh] hath been sore displeased with your fathers.
Therefore say thou unto them, Thus saith the LORD [Yahweh] of hosts; Turn ye unto me, saith the LORD [Yahweh] of hosts, and I will turn unto you, saith the LORD [Yahweh] of hosts (Zech. 1:1-3)

And as we tarried there many days, there came down from Judaea a certain prophet, named Agabus.
And when he was come unto us, he took Paul's girdle, and bound his own hands and feet, and said, Thus saith the Holy Ghost, So shall the Jews at Jerusalem bind the man that owneth this girdle, and shall deliver him into the hands of the Gentiles.
And when we heard these things, both we, and they of that place, besought him not to go up to Jerusalem (Acts 21:10-12)

God Speaks through His Son, Jesus Christ

God, who at sundry times and in divers manners spake in time past unto the fathers by the prophets,
Hath in these last days spoken unto us by his Son, . . . (Heb. 1:1, 2a)

Jesus answered them, and said, My doctrine is not mine, but his that sent me.
If any man will do his will, he shall know of the doctrine, whether it be of God, or *whether* I speak of myself (John 7:16-17)

Then said Jesus unto them, When ye have lifted up the Son of man, then shall ye know that I am *he*, and *that* I do nothing of myself; but as my Father hath taught me, I speak these things (John 8:28)

For I have not spoken of myself; but the Father which sent me, he gave me a commandment, what I should say, and what I should speak.
And I know that his commandment is life everlasting: whatsoever I speak therefore, even as the Father said unto me, so I speak. (John 12:49-50)

God Speaks by Revelation to Born-again Believers:

But as it is written, Eye hath not seen, nor ear heard, neither have entered into the heart of man, the things which God hath prepared for them that love him.
But God hath revealed them unto us by his Spirit: for the Spirit searcheth all things, yea, the deep things of God (1 Cor. 2:9, 10)

But the manifestation of the Spirit is given to every man to profit withal.
For to one is given by the Spirit the word of wisdom; to another the word of knowledge by the same Spirit;
To another faith by the same Spirit; to another the gifts of healing by the same Spirit;
To another the working of miracles; to another prophecy; to another discerning of spirits; to another divers kinds of tongues; to another the interpretation of tongues:
But all these worketh that one and the selfsame Spirit, dividing to every man severally as he will (1 Cor. 12:7-11)

Note specifically "word of wisdom," "word of knowledge," and "discerning of spirits" above, which could be called the "revelation manifestations" of the gift of the Holy Spirit.

Brethren, I count not myself to have apprehended: but this one thing I do, forgetting those things which are behind, and reaching forth unto those things which are before,
I press toward the mark for the prize of the high calling of God in Christ Jesus.

Let us therefore, as many as be perfect, be thus minded: and if in any thing ye be otherwise minded, God shall reveal even this unto you (Phil. 3:13-15)

For this cause I Paul, the prisoner of Jesus Christ for you Gentiles,
If ye have heard of the dispensation of the grace of God which is given me to you-ward:
How that by revelation he made known unto me the mystery; (as I wrote afore in few words,
Whereby, when ye read, ye may understand my knowledge in the mystery of Christ)
Which in other ages was not made known unto the sons of men, as it is now revealed unto his holy apostles and prophets by the Spirit;
That the Gentiles should be fellowheirs, and of the same body, and partakers of his promise in Christ by the gospel (Eph. 3:1-6)

God Speaks by Way of the Bible:

All scripture *is* given by inspiration of God, and is profitable for doctrine, for reproof, for correction, for instruction in righteousness: That the man of God may be perfect, throughly furnished unto all good works (2 Tim. 3:15-16)

Knowing this first, that no prophecy of the scripture is of any private interpretation.
For the prophecy came not in old time by the will of man: but holy men of God spake as they were moved by the Holy Ghost (2 Pet. 1:20, 21)

Paul, a servant of Jesus Christ, called to be an apostle, separated unto the gospel of God,
(Which he had promised afore by his prophets in the holy scriptures,) [Rom. 1:1, 2]

If thou shalt hearken unto the voice of the LORD [Yahweh] thy God, to keep his commandments and his statutes which are written in this book of the law, and if thou turn unto the LORD [Yahweh] thy God with all thine heart, and with all thy soul (Deuteronomy 30:10)

. . . according unto that which is written in the book of the law of Moses, wherein the LORD [Yahweh] commanded, saying, . . . (2 Kings 14:6b)

. . . Hilkiah the priest found a book of the law of the LORD [Yahweh] given by Moses (2 Chron. 34:14b)

. . . they spake unto Ezra the scribe to bring the book of the law of Moses, which the LORD [Yahweh] had commanded to Israel (Nehemiah 8:1b)

And they stood up in their place, and read in the book of the law of the LORD [Yahweh] their God one fourth part of the day; and another fourth part they confessed, and worshipped the LORD [Yahweh] their God (Nehemiah 9:3)

Seek ye out of the book of the LORD [Yahweh], and read: . . . (Isaiah 34:16)

Thus speaketh the LORD [Yahweh] God of Israel, saying, Write thee all the words that I have spoken unto thee in a book (Jeremiah 30:2)

And it came to pass in the fourth year of Jehoiakim the son of Josiah king of Judah, that this word came unto Jeremiah from the LORD [Yahweh], saying,
Take thee a roll of a book, and write therein all the words that I have spoken unto thee against Israel, and against Judah, and against all the nations, from the day I spake unto thee, from the days of Josiah, even unto this day.

It may be that the house of Judah will hear all the evil which I purpose to do unto them; that they may return every man from his evil way; that I may forgive their iniquity and their sin.

Then Jeremiah called Baruch the son of Neriah: and Baruch wrote from the mouth of Jeremiah all the words of the LORD [Yahweh], which he had spoken unto him, upon a roll of a book.

And Jeremiah commanded Baruch, saying, I am shut up; I cannot go into the house of the LORD [Yahweh]:

Therefore go thou, and read in the roll, which thou hast written from my mouth, the words of the LORD [Yahweh] in the ears of the people in the LORD's [Yahweh's] house upon the fasting day: and also thou shalt read them in the ears of all Judah that come out of their cities.

It may be they will present their supplication before the LORD [Yahweh], and will return every one from his evil way: for great is the anger and the fury that the LORD [Yahweh] hath pronounced against this people.

And Baruch the son of Neriah did according to all that Jeremiah the prophet commanded him, reading in the book the words of the LORD [Yahweh] in the LORD's [Yahweh's] house.

Learning What the "Bible" Is

Back in early 1970s, the author was president of a Christian church in Mill Valley, California. He had seen his mother studying the Bible for years. He had heard the minister teach in Bible classes and quote the Bible in sermons. His son was intensely studying the Bible in a Bible fellowship. And the thought suddenly occurred to him: I don't know what the Bible *is*. A question about this was then tendered to the Assistant Minister, David. And David prepared and sent a letter which the author still has. The gist of the letter was that the various translations and versions of the Bible as we know it today represent the efforts of individuals and teams of scholars to present their reconstructions of what the original "Word of God" said. They based their reconstructions on their study of numerous manuscripts and fragments of manuscripts of the books of the Bible written in Hebrew, Aramaic, Greek, Latin, and other languages. And many scholars also consulted quotations from, and allusions to, the Bible found in the writings of Bible commentators living within a few hundred years of the birth of Christ.

This information sent the author on a quest to the Holy Land, and to Great Britain and Ireland, to see some of these existing early biblical manuscripts for himself. While in the Sinai Peninsula, he learned of the discovery there of most of the *Codex Sinaiticus* (a nearly complete manuscript of the Bible written in Greek and dated to about 350 A.D.), and how it eventually wound up in the British Museum in London. At the British Museum, he saw before him, fully displayed, the *Codex Sinaiticus* and the *Codex Alexandrinus* (a nearly complete manuscript of the Bible written in Greek and dated to about 450 A.D.). He also learned that the *Codex Vaticanus* (a nearly complete Bible written in Greek and dated to about 300 A.D.) was located in the Vatican library in Rome.

Before long, the author and his son went to the John S. Rylands Library in Manchester, England, and there saw the very early New Testament Greek papyrus manuscript fragment known as Papyrus 52 or p^{52} (John Rylands Papyrus 458) dated to about 125 A.D. And the next trip took them to Dublin, Ireland. There they visited the Chester Beatty Library and saw the almost complete papyri containing the Gospels and the Pauline Epistles. These were dated to about 200 A.D.; and the author and his son have picture copies of the latter. Many of the foregoing biblical treasures can now be seen, in part, on the internet. [For an interesting summary, see *The Dead Sea Scrolls Bible*, 1999, pp. vii-xx. On the Internet, see "Dating the Oldest New Testament Manuscripts," Peter van Minnen (http://scriptorium.lib.duke.edu/papyrus/texts/manuscripts.html)]

There are today no publicly known *original* manuscripts of the "Word of God" produced when "holy men of God spake *as they were* moved by the Holy Ghost" (2 Pet. 1:21). However, with respect to the New Testament:

> There are some 8,000 manuscripts of the Latin Vulgate and at least 1,000 for the other early versions. Add over 4,000 Greek manuscripts and we have 13,000 manuscript copies of portions of the New Testament. Besides all this, much of the New Testament can be reproduced from the quotations of the early Christian writers (*Evidence That Demands a Verdict* by Josh McDowell, p. 21)

And since the information quoted above was written, the number of Greek New Testament manuscripts has grown to well over 5,000. [On the Internet, see "The Oldest New Testament Copies" (http://thegreatestpuzzle.com/oldest.htm).] In addition, nearly the entire New Testament may be reconstructed from quotations found in the writings of various ancient authors (commonly known as the "Church Fathers") who cite the New Testament. [See the article "The Church Fathers and Patristic Citations" by Robert Waltz (http://www.skypoint.com/ ~ waltzmn/Fathers.html)]. Lectionaries [i.e., books or lists of lections (liturgical lessons for a particular day) for the church year] and other sources also preserve sections of the New Testament.

The following information is enlightening as to the preservation of the Hebrew text of the Old Testament:

> Jews preserved it as no other manuscript has ever been preserved. With their *massora* (*parva*, *magna*, and *finalis*) they kept tabs on every letter, syllable, word and paragraph. They had special classes of men within their culture whose sole duty was to preserve and transmit these documents with practically perfect fidelity—scribes, lawyers, massoretes (*Evidence That Demands a Verdict* by Josh McDowell, p. 22).

Today, there are hundreds of Bibles translations and versions. The author has examined and used the KJV (Protestant in origin), the NIV (Protestant in origin), the JB (Roman Catholic in origin), *The Shocken Bible* (Jewish in origin), *The Dead Sea Scrolls Bible*, and such parallel New Testaments and Bibles as *The Contemporary*

Parallel New Testament (1995) and the *Comparative Study Bible* (1999). Even *The Living Bible*. And learning how the Word of God was transmitted and preserved through the centuries represents a very exciting line of study.

The Word of God

The important phrase "word of God" occurs 48 times in the KJV according to the BLB (http://www.blueletterbible.org/). Of the four occurrences of that phrase in the Old Testament, the English term "word" is the translation of the Hebrew word *dabar* [Strong's number 1697 (pronounced "daw-baw'")] in each of the three occurrences which include the word "the" in the phrase (i.e., "the word of God"):

> *And* as they were going down to the end of the city, Samuel said to Saul, Bid the servant pass on before us, (and he passed on), but stand thou still a while, that I may shew thee the word [*dabar*] of God (1 Sam. 9:27)

> But the word [*dabar*] of God came unto Shemaiah the man of God, saying (1 Ki. 12:22)

> And it came to pass the same night, that the word [*dabar*] of God came to Nathan, saying (1 Chron. 17:3)

In almost all of the 44 occurrences of that phrase in the New Testament, the English term "word" is the translation of the Greek word *logos* [Strong's number 3056 (pronounced "log'-os)"]. Here are several examples:

> But he [Jesus] said, Yea rather, blessed *are* they that hear the word [*logos*] of God, and keep it (Luke 11:28)

> And when they had prayed, the place was shaken where they were assembled together; and they were all filled with the Holy

Ghost, and they spake the word [*logos*] of God with boldness (Acts 4:31)

For we are not as many, which corrupt the word [*logos*] of God: but as of sincerity, but as of God, in the sight of God speak we in Christ (2 Cor. 2:17)

For this cause also thank we God without ceasing, because, when ye received the word [*logos*] of God which ye heard of us, ye received *it* not *as* the word [*logos*] of men, but as it is in truth, the word [*logos*] of God, which effectually worketh also in you that believe (1 Thess. 2:13)

There are a number of different translations of, opinions about, and possible usages of, the underlying Hebrew term *dabar* and Greek term *logos* as they are used in connection with the phrases "word(s) of God" and "word(s) of the LORD (Yahweh)." But time spent studying the occurrences of the term "word(s)" as used in these phrases would be very rewarding. Here are some additional verses to help you get started:

The words of the LORD [Yahweh] *are* pure words: *as* silver tried in a furnace of earth, purified seven times (Ps. 12:6)

Thy word *is* a lamp unto my feet, a light unto my path (Ps. 119:105).

Now in the first year of Cyrus king Persia, that the word of the LORD [Yahweh] by the mouth of Jeremiah might be fulfilled, . . . (Ezra 1:1).

The words of Jeremiah the son of Hilkiah, . . .
To whom the word of the LORD [Yahweh] came in the days of Josiah . . . (Jer. 1:1-2)

The word of the LORD [Yahweh] that came to Micah the Morasthite . . . (Mic. 1:1).

The burden of the word of the LORD [Yahweh] to Israel by Malachi (Mal. 1:1).

So then faith *cometh* by hearing, and hearing by the word of God (Rom. 10:17).

For the word of God *is* quick, and powerful, and sharper than any twoedged sword. . . . (Heb. 4:12).

But be ye doers of the word, and not hearers only, deceiving your own selves (James 1:22).

(For scholarly discussions of the term "word" in the Bible, see, for example, F. F. Bruce, *The Gospel of John*, 1983, p. 29; John Lightfoot, *A Commentary on the New Testament from the Talmud and Hebraica*, 1989, vol. 3., p. 238; Thorlief Boman, *Hebrew Thought Compared with Greek,* 1960, p. 58; J. N. Birdsall, *New Bible Dictionary*, "Language of the New Testament," 1975, p. 715).

How We Got the Word of God

Another profitable avenue of study is the matter of how God's message got from God into writing. In the case of the ten commandments, the Bible states that Yahweh wrote them Himself!

And the LORD [Yahweh] said unto Moses, Come up to me into the mount, and be there: and I will give thee tables of stone, and a law, and commandments which I have written; that thou mayest teach them (Exod. 24:12)

And he [verse 12: the LORD (Yahweh)] gave unto Moses, when he had made an end of communing with him upon mount Sinai, two tables of testimony, tables of stone, written with the finger of God (Exod. 31:18)

And he [verse 12: the LORD (Yahweh)] declared unto you his covenant, which he commanded you to perform, *even* ten commandments [*dabar*, words]; and he wrote them upon two tables of stone (Deut. 4:13).

And the LORD [Yahweh] delivered unto me two tables of stone written with the finger of God; and on them *was written* according to all the words, which the LORD [Yahweh] spake with you in the mount out of the midst of the fire in the day of the assembly.
And it came to pass at the end of forty days and forty nights, *that* the LORD [Yahweh] gave me the two tables of stone, *even* the tables of the covenant (Deut. 9:10, 11)

At that time the LORD [Yahweh] said unto me, Hew thee two tables of stone like unto the first, and come up unto me into the mount, and make thee an ark of wood.
And I will write on the tables the words that were in the first tables which thou brakest, and thou shalt put them in the ark.
And I made an ark of shittim wood, and hewed two tables of stone like unto the first, and went up into the mount, having the two tables in mine hand.
And he wrote on the tables, according to the first writing, the ten commandments, which the LORD [Yahweh] spake unto you in the mount out of the midst of the fire in the day of the assembly: and the LORD [Yahweh] gave them unto me (Deut. 10:1-4)

In Jeremiah chapter 36, we see precisely how the "word" (*dabar*) that "came unto Jeremiah from the LORD [Yahweh]" was then written on a "roll" (i.e., scroll) by Baruch.

And it came to pass in the fourth year of Jehoiakim the son of Josiah king of Judah, that this word came unto Jeremiah from the LORD [Yahweh], saying,
Take thee a roll of a book, and write therein all the words that I have spoken unto thee against Israel, and against Judah, and

against all the nations, from the day I spake unto thee, from the days of Josiah, even unto this day.

It may be that the house of Judah will hear all the evil which I purpose to do unto them; that they may return every man from his evil way; that I may forgive their iniquity and their sin.

Then Jeremiah called Baruch the son of Neriah: and Baruch wrote from the mouth of Jeremiah all the words of the LORD [Yahweh], which he had spoken unto him, upon a roll of a book.

And Jeremiah commanded Baruch, saying, I am shut up; I cannot go into the house of the LORD [Yahweh]:

Therefore go thou, and read in the roll, which thou hast written from my mouth, the words of the LORD [Yahweh] in the ears of the people in the LORD's [Yahweh's] house upon the fasting day: and also thou shalt read them in the ears of all Judah that come out of their cities.

It may be they will present their supplication before the LORD [Yahweh], and will return every one from his evil way: for great is the anger and the fury that the LORD [Yahweh] hath pronounced against this people.

And Baruch the son of Neriah did according to all that Jeremiah the prophet commanded him, reading in the book the words of the LORD [Yahweh] in the LORD's [Yahweh's] house.

And it came to pass in the fifth year of Jehoiakim the son of Josiah king of Judah, in the ninth month, that they proclaimed a fast before the LORD [Yahweh] to all the people in Jerusalem, and to all the people that came from the cities of Judah unto Jerusalem.

Then read Baruch in the book the words of Jeremiah in the house of the LORD [Yahweh], in the chamber of Gemariah the son of Shaphan the scribe, in the higher court, at the entry of the new gate of the LORD's [Yahweh's] house, in the ears of all the people.

When Michaiah the son of Gemariah, the son of Shaphan, had heard out of the book all the words of the LORD [Yahweh],

Then he went down into the king's house, into the scribe's chamber: and, lo, all the princes sat there, even Elishama the scribe, and Delaiah the son of Shemaiah, and Elnathan the son of Achbor, and Gemariah the son of Shaphan, and Zedekiah the son of Hananiah, and all the princes.

Then Michaiah declared unto them all the words that he had heard, when Baruch read the book in the ears of the people.

Therefore all the princes sent Jehudi the son of Nethaniah, the son of Shelemiah, the son of Cushi, unto Baruch, saying, Take in thine hand the roll wherein thou hast read in the ears of the people, and come. So Baruch the son of Neriah took the roll in his hand, and came unto them.

And they said unto him, Sit down now, and read it in our ears. So Baruch read it in their ears.

Now it came to pass, when they had heard all the words, they were afraid both one and other, and said unto Baruch, We will surely tell the king of all these words.

And they asked Baruch, saying, Tell us now, How didst thou write all these words at his mouth?

Then Baruch answered them, He pronounced all these words unto me with his mouth, and I wrote them with ink in the book.

Then said the princes unto Baruch, Go, hide thee, thou and Jeremiah; and let no man know where ye be.

And they went in to the king into the court, but they laid up the roll in the chamber of Elishama the scribe, and told all the words in the ears of the king.

So the king sent Jehudi to fetch the roll: and he took it out of Elishama the scribe's chamber. And Jehudi read it in the ears of the king, and in the ears of all the princes which stood beside the king.

Now the king sat in the winterhouse in the ninth month: and there was a fire on the hearth burning before him.

And it came to pass, that when Jehudi had read three or four leaves, he cut it with the penknife, and cast it into the fire that was on the hearth, until all the roll was consumed in the fire that was on the hearth.

Yet they were not afraid, nor rent their garments, neither the king, nor any of his servants that heard all these words.

Nevertheless Elnathan and Delaiah and Gemariah had made intercession to the king that he would not burn the roll: but he would not hear them.

But the king commanded Jerahmeel the son of Hammelech, and Seraiah the son of Azriel, and Shelemiah the son of Abdeel, to take Baruch the scribe and Jeremiah the prophet: but the LORD [Yahweh] hid them.

Then the word of the LORD [Yahweh] came to Jeremiah, after that the king had burned the roll, and the words which Baruch wrote at the mouth of Jeremiah, saying,

Take thee again another roll, and write in it all the former words that were in the first roll, which Jehoiakim the king of Judah hath burned.

And thou shalt say to Jehoiakim king of Judah, Thus saith the LORD [Yahweh]; Thou hast burned this roll, saying, Why hast thou written therein, saying, The king of Babylon shall certainly come and destroy this land, and shall cause to cease from thence man and beast?

Therefore thus saith the LORD [Yahweh] of Jehoiakim king of Judah; He shall have none to sit upon the throne of David: and his dead body shall be cast out in the day to the heat, and in the night to the frost.

And I will punish him and his seed and his servants for their iniquity; and I will bring upon them, and upon the inhabitants of Jerusalem, and upon the men of Judah, all the evil that I have pronounced against them; but they hearkened not.

Then took Jeremiah another roll, and gave it to Baruch the scribe, the son of Neriah; who wrote therein from the mouth of Jeremiah all the words of the book which Jehoiakim king of Judah had burned in the fire: and there were added besides unto them many like words (Jer. 36:1-32)

After seeing how the ten commandments (or "words") were written, and how Yahweh's word was revealed to Jeremiah and then recorded on a roll (or "scroll"), a verse like the following takes on a much greater meaning:

All scripture *is* given by inspiration of God, and *is* profitable for doctrine, for reproof, for correction, for instruction in righteousness (2 Tim. 3:16)

The five English words "given by inspiration of God" in the verse above are the translation of one word in the Greek New Testament. That Greek word, *theopneustos*, Strong's number 2315, comes from *theos*, "God," and *pneō*, "to breathe," and is translated "God-breathed" in the NIV. The Bible is the Word of God.

The Word of God and the Will of God

In his titles on the Oxford Group and the teachings of Rev. Sam Shoemaker, the author has pointed out that the Oxford Group progenitors, the Oxford Group's writers, and Sam Shoemaker himself all spoke of the Bible (the Word of God) as containing and setting forth God's "universal" or "general" will. In the Bible itself, Jesus explained the principle that the Word of God is the will of God. In three different statements, using as a reference, his mother and his siblings, Jesus declared:

> While he yet talked to the people, behold, his mother and his brethren stood without, desiring to speak with him.
> Then one said unto him, Behold, thy mother and thy brethren stand without, desiring to speak with thee.
> But he answered and said unto him that told him, Who is my mother? and who are my brethren?
> And he stretched forth his hand toward his disciples, and said, Behold my mother and my brethren!
> For **whosoever shall do the will of my Father which is in heaven**, the same is my brother, and sister, and mother (Matt. 12:46-50, emphasis added)

> There came then his brethren and his mother, and, standing without, sent unto him, calling him.
> And the multitude sat about him, and they said unto him, Behold, thy mother and thy brethren without seek for thee.
> And he answered them, saying, Who is my mother, or my brethren?

> And he looked round about on them which sat about him, and said, Behold my mother and my brethren!
> For **whosoever shall do the will of God**, the same is my brother, and my sister, and mother. (Mark 3:31-35, emphasis added).

> Then came to him his mother and his brethren, and could not come at him for the press.
> And it was told him by certain which said, Thy mother and thy brethren stand without, desiring to see thee.
> And he answered and said unto them, My mother and my brethren are **these which hear the word of God, and do it** (Luke 8:19-21, emphasis added).

One can see from the verses above that Jesus is equating the "the word of God" with "the will of God" and "the will of my Father which is in heaven." And from these verses and many others dealing with the word(s) and commandments of God, one can see that the Bible sets forth the will of God.

The Word of God: Truth

Jesus said several profoundly important things about truth in the Gospel of John. First, we see that Jesus told the Jews which believed on him that they would know the truth if they continued in his word.

> Then said Jesus to those Jews which believed on him, If ye continue in my word, *then* are ye my disciples indeed; And ye shall know the truth, and the truth shall make you free (John 8:31-32).

A few verses later, Jesus went on to say that the truth he had told them he had heard from God.

But now ye seek to kill me, a man that hath told you the truth,
which I have heard of God: this did not Abraham (John 8:40)

Then, in his prayer to God in John chapter 17, Jesus says explicitly
that God's word is truth.

I have given them thy [i.e., God's] word; . . .
Sanctify them through thy truth: thy word is truth (John 17:14a,
17).

The Good Book Offers Far More Than Sobriety

Jesus answered and said unto him, Verily, verily, I say unto
thee, Except a man be born again, he cannot see the kingdom
of God (John 3:3).

For God so loved the world that he gave his only begotten Son,
that whosoever believeth in him should not perish, but have
everlasting life (John 3:16).

The thief cometh not, but for to steal, and to kill, and to
destroy: I am come that they might have life, and that they
might have *it* more abundantly (John 10:10).

But ye shall receive power, after that the Holy Ghost is come
upon you: . . . (Acts 1:8).

Verily, verily, I say unto you, He that believeth on me, the
works that I do shall he do also; and greater *works* than these
shall he do; because I go unto my Father (John 14:12).

And these signs shall follow them that believe: In my name shall
they cast out devils; they shall speak with new tongues. They
shall take up serpents; and if they drink any deadly thing, it
shall not hurt them; they shall lay hands on the sick, and they
shall recover (Mark 16:17-18).

Who *shall* separate us from the love of Christ? Shall tribulation, or distress, or persecution, or famine, or nakedness, or peril, or sword? . . . . Nay, in all these things we are more than conquerors through him that loved us, For I am persuaded that neither death, nor life, nor angels, nor principalities, nor powers, nor things present, nor things to come, Nor height, nor depth, nor any other creature, shall be able to separate us from the love of God, which is in Christ Jesus our Lord (Rom. 8:35, 37-39).

Finally, my brethren, be strong in the Lord and in the power of his might. Put on the whole armour of God, that ye may be able to stand against the wiles of the devil (Eph. 6:10).

It Offers Victory

It is not surprising that various clergy and A.A. old-timers have established groups that are not necessarily competitive with A.A., but do confirm their aim of victory–not just abstinence or sobriety or senses-knowledge existence. Thus today we have Alcoholics Victorious; Overcomers; Overcomers Outreach, Inc.; Alcoholics for Christ; and so on. Note the emphasis of victory and on overcoming in the following verses:

Now thanks *be* unto God, which always causeth us to triumph in Christ, and maketh manifest the savour of his knowledge by us in every place (2 Cor. 2:14).

But thanks *be* to God, which giveth us the victory through our Lord Jesus Christ.
Therefore, my beloved brethren, be ye stedfast, unmoveable, always abounding in the work of the Lord, forasmuch as ye know that your labour is not in vain in the Lord (1 Cor. 15:57, 58).

Ye are of God, little children, and have overcome them: because greater is he that is in you, than he that is in the world (1 John 4:4).

For whosoever is born of God overcometh the world: and this is the victory that overcometh the world, *even* our faith.
Who is he that overcometh the world, but he that believeth that Jesus is the Son of God (1 John 5:4-5).

It Speaks of Future Rewards

For we are labourers together with God: ye are God's husbandry, *ye are* God's building.
According to the grace of God which is given unto me, as a wise masterbuilder, I have laid the foundation, and another buildeth thereon. But let every man take heed how he buildeth thereupon.
For other foundation can no man lay than that is laid, which is Jesus Christ.
Now if any man build upon this foundation gold, silver, precious stones, wood, hay, stubble;
Every man's work shall be made manifest: for the day shall declare it, because it shall be revealed by fire; and the fire shall try every man's work of what sort it is.
If any man's work abide which he hath built thereupon, he shall receive a reward.
If any man's work shall be burned, he shall suffer loss: but he himself shall be saved; yet so as by fire. (1 Cor. 3:9-15).

For though I preach the gospel, I have nothing to glory of: for necessity is laid upon me; yea, woe is unto me, if I preach not the gospel!
For if I do this thing willingly, I have a reward: but if it is against my will, a dispensation *of the gospel* is committed unto me.
What is my reward then? *Verily,* that when I preach the gospel, I may make the gospel of Christ without charge, that I abuse not my power in the gospel.

For though I be free from all *men*, yet have I made myself servant unto all, that I might gain the more.
And this I do for the gospel's sake, that I might be partaker thereof with *you*.
Know ye not that they which run in a race run all, but one receiveth the prize? So run, that ye may obtain.
And every man that striveth for the mastery is temperate in all things. Now they *do it* to obtain a corruptible crown; but we an incorruptible. (1 Cor. 9:16-19, 23-25).

And this is love, that we walk after his commandments. This is the commandment, That, as ye have heard from the beginning, ye should walk in it.
For many deceivers are entered into the world, who confess not that Jesus Christ is come in the flesh. This is a deceiver and an antichrist.
Look to yourselves, that we lose not those things which we have wrought, but that we receive a full reward.
Whosoever transgresseth, and abideth not in the doctrine of Christ, hath not God. He that abideth in the doctrine of Christ, he hath both the Father and the Son. (2 John 6-9).

It Enables One to Discern Truth from Error

The Good Book speaks of knowing the truth that will make one free. God provides the means (through the gift of the Holy Spirit) for His children to learn that truth.

For this *is* good and acceptable in the sight of God our Saviour;
Who will have all men to be saved, and to come unto the knowledge of the truth (1 Tim. 2:3-4).

Henrietta Seiberling frequently quoted the following verses to illustrate the need for receiving God's gift of holy spirit in order to understand spiritual matters:

But as it is written, Eye hath not seen, nor ear heard, neither have entered into the heart of man, the things which God hath prepared for them that love him.

But God hath revealed *them* unto us by his Spirit: for the Spirit searcheth all things, yea, the deep things of God.

For what man knoweth the things of a man, save the spirit of man which is in him? even so the things of God knoweth no man, but the Spirit of God.

Now we have received, not the spirit of the world, but the spirit which is of God; that we might know the things that are freely given to us of God.

Which things also we speak, not in the words which man's wisdom teacheth, but which the Holy Ghost teacheth; comparing spiritual things with spiritual.

But the natural man receiveth not the things of the Spirit of God: for they are foolishness unto him: neither can he know *them*, because they are spiritually discerned.

But he that is spiritual judgeth all things, yet he himself is judged of no man.

For who hath known the mind of the Lord, that he may instruct him? but we have the mind of Christ. (1 Cor. 2:9-16).

"Wise" and "Wisdom" in Proverbs

Note that Anne Smith specifically recommended, in her journal that Psalms and Proverbs be read. So did some of the early A.A. pamphlets. And note the place of wisdom and understanding in the following verses. No great applause is given to those who talk, but don't listen; to those who turn from wisdom, and don't understand; or to those who reject instruction and spurn increase in learning.

A wise man will hear, and will increase learning; and a man of understanding shall attain unto wise counsels: (Prov. 1:5)

Hear instruction, and be wise, and refuse it not (Prov. 8:33)

Give instruction to a wise man, and he will be yet wiser: teach a just man, and he will increase in learning(Prov. 9:9)

The wise in heart will receive commandments: but a prating fool shall fall (Prov. 10:8)

The way of a fool is right in his own eyes: but he that hearkeneth unto counsel is wise (Prov. 12:15)

A wise man feareth, and departeth from evil: but the fool rageth, and is confident (Prov. 14:16)

The heart of the prudent getteth knowledge; and the ear of the wise seeketh knowledge (Prov. 18:15)

To know wisdom and instruction; to perceive the words of understanding (Prov. 1:2)

The fear of the LORD is the beginning of knowledge: but fools despise wisdom and instruction (Prov. 1:7)

For the LORD giveth wisdom: out of his mouth cometh knowledge and understanding (Prov. 2:6)

Wisdom is the principal thing; therefore get wisdom: and with all thy getting get understanding (Prov. 4:7)

He that getteth wisdom loveth his own soul; he that keepeth understanding shall find good (Prov. 19:8)

Speak not in the ears of a fool: for he will despise the wisdom of thy words (Prov. 23:9)

The Vital Importance of God's Guidance

There is, in the words of the Bible itself, much more to studying and learning from the Bible than just the reading of it. For believers, there should be prayer. There must be God's guidance.

> Trust in the LORD [Yahweh] with all thine heart; and lean not unto thine own understanding. In all thy ways acknowledge him, and he shall direct thy paths (Prov. 3:5-6).

> Howbeit when he, the Spirit of truth is come, he will guide you into all truth: for he shall not speak of himself; but whatsoever he shall hear, *that* shall he speak: and he will shew you things to come (John 16:13).

> But the anointing which ye have received of him abideth in you, and ye need not that any man teach you: but as the same anointing teacheth you of all things, and is truth, and is no lie, and even as it hath taught you, ye shall abide in him (1 John 2:27).

Therefore, Study the Good Book

> Blessed is the man that walketh not in the counsel of the ungodly, nor standeth in the way of sinners, nor sitteth in the seat of the scornful, But his delight is in the law of the LORD [Yahweh]; and in his law doeth he meditate day and night. And he shall be like a tree planted by the rivers of water, that bringeth forth his fruit in his season; his leaf also shall not wither; and whatsoever he doeth shall prosper (Ps. 1:1-3).

> My son, if thou wilt receive my words, and hide my commandments with thee; So that thou incline thine ear unto wisdom, *and* apply thine heart to understanding; Yea, if thou criest after knowledge, *and* liftest up thy voice for understanding; If thou seeketh her as silver, and searchest for her as *for* hid treasures; Then shalt thou understand the fear of

the LORD [Yahweh], and find the knowledge of God. For the LORD [Yahweh] giveth wisdom: out of his mouth *cometh* knowledge and understanding (Prov. 2:1-6).

Search the scriptures; for in them ye think ye have eternal life: and they are they which testify of me (John 5:39).

These [i.e., the people in Berea] were more noble than those in Thessalonica, in that they received the word with all readiness of mind, and searched the scriptures daily, whether those things were so. Therefore many of them believed; also of honourable women which were Greeks, and of men, not a few (Acts 17:11-12).

Study to shew thyself approved unto God, a workman that needeth not to be ashamed, rightly dividing the word of truth. But shun profane *and* vain babblings: for they will increase unto more ungodliness (2 Tim. 2:15-16).

I will worship toward thy holy temple, and praise thy name for thy lovingkindness and for thy truth: for thou hast magnified thy word above all thy name (Ps. 138:2).

6

Learning about
God's Son, Jesus Christ!

Say ye of him, whom the Father hath sanctified, and sent into
the world, Thou blasphemest; because I said, I am the Son of
God? (John 10:36)

And many other signs truly did Jesus in the presence of his
disciples, which are not written in this book: But these are
written, that ye might believe that Jesus is the Christ, the Son of
God; and that believing ye might have life through his name
(John 20:30-31)

This guide is not about A.A. and Christianity. It *is* about what early
AAs studied in the Bible and what you can study today. It *is* about
how early AAs who were "lost" were able to "find" or
"rediscover" God. It *is* about the importance the pioneers assigned
to Jesus Christ as they sought also to "establish a relationship with
God;" to be delivered from the power of darkness; to be healed of
alcoholism; to be forgiven for their sins; and to receive and utilize
the power of God in their lives. This guide will introduce you to
what early AAs had spiritually if you decide that you really want
what they had.

Early AAs certainly knew that God was not a lightbulb or a
chair. They certainly had a substantial understanding of God from

the Good Book itself. But they also studied about Jesus Christ, established a relationship with God through Jesus Christ, and called themselves a Christian Fellowship.

They also studied, and were urged to study, *in the Bible*, a great deal of material about Jesus Christ. In addition, they studied about Jesus Christ in other well-known books of that day. Anne recommended reading E. Stanley Jones's *The Christ of the Mount*–a book owned and studied by Dr. Bob. Anne recommended Harry Emerson Fosdick's *The Manhood of the Master*, which was also read and circulated by Dr. Bob. Anne specifically said: "One should by all means read at least one book on the life of Christ a year for a while. More would be better" (Dick B., *Anne Smith's Journal*, p. 84). To that end, Anne then specifically recommended James Stalker's *The Life of Jesus Christ*; George A. Barton's *Jesus of Nazareth*; T. R. Glover's *The Jesus of History*; and Robert E. Speer's *The Man Christ Jesus*.

Other books that were studied and recommended were Oswald Chambers' *Studies in the Sermon on the Mount* and Emmet Fox's *The Sermon on the Mount*. There were still others about the teachings and principles of Jesus–titles that were authored by Glenn Clark, E. Stanley Jones, Robert E. Speer, Samuel M. Shoemaker, Jr., and so on. (See Dick B., *The Books Early AAs Read for Spiritual Growth*, 7th ed.; and *New Light on Alcoholism: God, Sam Shoemaker, and A.A.*)

"Jesus Is the Christ, the Son of God"

In the New Testament, Jesus Christ is referred to as "the Son of God" many times. Your time will be well spent in looking up the many occurrences of this phrase and studying the contexts in which the phrase occurs. Here are some important verses to get you started.

As we noted at the beginning of this chapter, the purpose for the Gospel of John is declared to be:

But these are written, that ye might believe that Jesus is the Christ, the Son of God; and that believing ye might have life through his name (John 20:31).

The Creator of the heavens and the earth said:

And lo a voice from heaven, saying, This is my beloved Son, in whom I am well pleased (Matt. 3:17).

And there was a cloud that overshadowed them: and a voice came out of the cloud, saying, This is my beloved Son: hear him (Mark 9:7).

Jesus himself said he was the Son of God:

He trusted in God; let him deliver him now, if he will have him: for he said, I am the Son of God (Matt. 27:43).

(See also John 3:16-18, John 5:25, John 9:35 and 37, and John 10:36.)

The writer of the Gospel of Mark stated:

The beginning of the gospel of Jesus Christ, the Son of God (Mark 1:1).

The writer of the Gospel of John declared:

No man hath seen God at any time; the only begotten Son, which is in the bosom of the Father, he hath declared *him* (John 1:18).

The writer of the First Epistle of John stated:

That which we have seen and heard declare *we* unto you, that *ye* also may have fellowship with us: and truly our fellowship *is* with the Father, and with his Son Jesus Christ (1 John 1:3).

Here are several of the Apostle Paul's statements concerning Jesus Christ's being the Son of God:

> And straightway he [the Apostle Paul] preached Christ in the synagogues, that he is the Son of God (Acts 9:20).

> For if, when we were enemies, we were reconciled to God by the death of his Son, much more, being reconciled, we shall be saved by his life (Rom. 5:10).

> For the Son of God, Jesus Christ, who was preached among you by us, *even* by me and Silvanus and Timotheus, was not yea and nay, but in him was yea (2 Cor. 1:19)

> But when the fulness of the time was come, God sent forth his Son, made of a woman, made under the law (Gal. 4:4).

The Gospel of Luke records the following concerning the Angel of God's visit to Mary, Jesus's mother:

> And the angel answered and said unto her [Mary, the mother of Jesus], The Holy Ghost shall come upon thee, and the power of the Highest shall overshadow thee: therefore also that holy thing which shall be born of thee shall be called the Son of God (Luke 1:35).

John the Baptist declared that Jesus was the Son of God:

> And John bare record, saying, I saw the Spirit descending from heaven like a dove, and it abode upon him [Jesus].
> And I knew him not: but he that sent me to baptize with water, the same said unto me, Upon whom thou shalt see the Spirit descending, and remaining on him, the same is he which baptizeth with the Holy Ghost.
> And I saw, and bare record that this is the Son of God (John 1:32-34).

And here is Simon Peter's great statement concerning Jesus:

> And Simon Peter answered [Jesus] and said, Thou art the Christ, the Son of the living God (Matt. 6:16).

Here are some others who declared that Jesus was the Son of God:

- Martha (John 11:27);

- The man who was born blind (John 9:35-38);

- The disciples in the ship (Matt. 14:33);

- Philip and the Ethiopian eunuch (Acts 8:37);

- The Roman centurion (Matt. 27:54);

- Evil spirits (Matt. 8:29; Mark 3:11; Luke 4:41).

It should hardly be surprising, therefore, that early AAs were learning about Jesus, the Son of God, and for a variety of reasons.

Anne Smith's Journal and Your Path

Anne Ripley Smith becomes our primary guide. Her statements provide a starting point for understanding the role of Jesus Christ in A.A.. This was the role that gave rise to the surrenders to Jesus Christ that were required of every early AA in Akron. This was the role that led them to their relationship with God. And this was the role that led them to the power they so desperately sought in order to be relieved of their alcoholism and have new lives. We have very clear statements by three early AAs about the necessity in early A.A. for the acceptance of Jesus Christ as Lord and Savior.

The author personally heard the recorded telephone message of Ed Andy, the A.A. old-timer from Lorain, Ohio, who founded and maintained the "First AA Museum" and said on the phone to Danny W. in Lancaster, California, on January 9, 1994:

> They would not let you in unless you surrendered to Jesus Christ on your knees.

Larry B. was an old-timer from Cleveland, Ohio. He wrote the author in a letter dated September 18, 1992, that he was in and out of the A.A. fellowship between 1939 and 1944. Larry said in the letter and then told the author on the telephone:

> They took me upstairs to be a born again human being and be God's helper to alcoholics.

Clarence Snyder got sober on February 11, 1938. He was sponsored by A.A. co-founder Dr. Bob. Though the author never heard it from Clarence, he heard directly from Clarence's wife Grace and also from several of the men Clarence sponsored that Clarence had surrendered to Jesus Christ and described that surrender as follows:

> He went upstairs to T. Henry Williams's master bedroom with Dr. Bob, T. Henry Williams, and an Oxford Group member. These men told Clarence to get on his knees, and they joined him on their knees around T. Henry's bed. These three men led Clarence through a "Sinner's Prayer." Clarence said that prayer was the very one that Dr. Bob had used from the beginning of A.A. surrenders in Akron.

And following are some pertinent remarks about and from Anne Smith's Journal.

About the "Surrenders":

Surrenders were required in New York and Akron A.A. at the beginning. **They were not biblical**. They seem to have stemmed from Professor William James and his "self-surrender" ideas and

Rev. Sam Shoemaker's teaching of these ideas. In New York, Sam Shoemaker was famous for getting people on their knees on their first meeting with him. And here's what Anne Smith wrote in the journal she shared almost every morning with the pioneer AAs and their families:

> Try to bring a person to a decision to "surrender as much of himself as he knows to as much of God as he knows." Stay with him until he makes a decision and says it aloud (Dick B., *Anne Smith's Journal*, p. 25).

> Surrender is a complete handing over of our wills to God, a reckless abandon of ourselves, all that we have, all that we think, that we are, everything we hold dear, to God to do what he likes with (*Anne Smith's Journal*, supra, p. 29).

> Surrender . . . 1st step the life & will. Surrender–fears–sins–most of all their wills–putting God 's will ahead of everything (*Anne Smith's Journal*, supra, p. 29).

> Release–surrender–conversion. William James defines it as "that process, gradual or sudden, by which a self divided, inferior, unhappy, and consciously wrong, becomes united, superior, happy, and consciously right." We usually have both sudden and gradual elements in our surrender (*Anne Smith's Journal*, supra, p.28).

To As Much of God As You Understand or Know

Anne adopted the Oxford Group idea and the explicit Sam Shoemaker teaching that you didn't need a complete understanding or knowledge of God in order to surrender your "will" to Him. You simply surrendered as much of yourself as you understood to as much of God as you understood.

This concept, regularly followed in the Oxford Group (of which A.A. was a constituent part) and in the practices of Rev. Sam Shoemaker (whom Bill Wilson called an A.A. "Co-founder"), has

been much bashed, warped, and modified in today's A.A. This, for
the simple reason that today's Twelve Step people don't know it's
origin. Many take the "God as we understood Him" phrase as a
license to make up their own "god.":

> Our concepts of a Higher Power and God–as we understand
> Him–afford everyone a nearly unlimited choice of spiritual
> belief and action (*Came to Believe*, p. 77).

> I couldn't accept the concept of a Higher Power because I
> believed God was cruel and unloving. In desperation I chose a
> table, a tree, then my A.A. group, as my Higher Power (*Daily
> Reflections*, p. 175).

> However, everyone defines this power as he or she wishes.
> Many people call it God, others think it is the A.A. group, still
> others don't believe in it at all (*a Newcomer asks. . .*, p. 4).

> "It doesn't matter what your Higher Power is, as long as it
> works to keep you sober. It could even be that light bulb over
> there." This concept of Higher Power was introduced at a
> recent AA meeting by the speaker for the evening (Webb, *Tree
> of Renewed Life*, pp. 116-17).

The author of this guidebook has heard all of the above and many
many more. The "higher power" can be Ralph, Gertrude, the Big
Dipper, a bulldozer, Santa Claus, the "group conscience," a door
knob, and so on.

But that nonsensical language was certainly not that of early
A.A., nor the early AA way. A.A. pioneers "surrendered to as
much of God as they understood" to gain a relationship with Him
through Christ, and studied the *Bible to grow in understanding* and
knowledge.

To get clear on this point, you need to know what Bill Wilson
was saying before he invented a "higher power" that could be the
"group." In a thirty-four page document, that the author located at
Bill's Stepping Stones home, Bill wrote:

This is what my friend [Ebby Thacher] suggested I do: Turn my
face to God as I understand Him and say to Him with
earnestness–complete honesty and abandon–that I henceforth
place my life at His disposal and Direction forever (Bill Wilson,
Original Story, p.30).

Bill told his audience at Yale much the same thing concerning what
Ebby Thacher had told him to do. Bill said:

[Ebby told him] So, call on God as you understand God. Try
prayer (See *Yale Quarterly Journal of Studies on Alcohol*, 1945,
pp. 461-73).

Neither Anne Smith, nor Dr. Bob, nor Ebby Thacher, nor Bill
Wilson invented "God" or a "god" or a "group" or a high chair.
From the beginning of A.A., they were talking about surrender to
the Creator, as far as they comprehended Him at the outset of their
search for Him.

You Came to Him through Believing on His Son:

We will get to Jesus as the "Way" in a moment. But there was no
doubt in the founders' minds that they were to establish their
relationship with God by accepting His Son Jesus Christ as their
Lord and Savior. The three statements by pioneers that are quoted
above should establish that point. Anne Smith elaborated in her
journal as follows:

We must be in such relationship with God that He *can* guide us
(*Anne Smith's Journal*, supra, p. 24).

2nd step. To get in right relationship with God (*Anne Smith's
Journal*, supra, p. 24).

Paul speaks of a wish toward good, but the power to carry it out
is lacking. A stronger power than his was needed. God provided

that power through Christ, so that we could find a new kind of relationship with God. Christ gives the power, we appropriate it. It is not anything that we do ourselves; but it is the appropriation of a power that comes from God that saves us from sin and sets us free (*Anne Smith's Journal*, supra, p. 22).

Note also these two statements by Bill Wilson:

[The patent lawyer from Cleveland said:] One evening I had gone out after dinner to take on a couple of double-headers and stayed a little later than usual, and when I came home Clarence [Snyder] was sitting on the davenport with Bill W. [Bill Wilson]. I do not recollect the specific conversation that went on but I believe I did challenge Bill to tell me something about A.A. and I do recall one other thing: I wanted to know what this was that worked so many wonders, and hanging over the mantel was a picture of Gethsemane [See Matt. 26:36-64] and Bill pointed to it and said, "There it is," which didn't make much sense to me (Big Book, 3rd ed., pp. 216-17).

[A.A. Number Three Bill Dotson said:] Bill looked across at my wife, and said to her, "Henrietta, the Lord [See Acts 2:22-36; 3:1-19; 4:7-12] has been so wonderful to me, curing me of this terrible disease, that I just want to keep talking about it and telling people (Big Book, 3rd ed., p. 191).

Perhaps you are one of those cynical people who will turn away when I say that the root of this new discovery is religion (said Wilson, as quoted in *Liberty Magazine*, September, 1939).

Even though the man [the newcomer] might be an atheist or agnostic; he will almost always admit there is some sort of force operating in the world–some cosmic power weaving a design. And his new friend [the A.A. veteran] will say: "I don't care what you call this "Somebody Else." We call it God" (said Wilson, as quoted in *Liberty Magazine, supra*).

Power after Confession and Belief

Bill Wilson wrote in the Big Book:

> Lack of power, that was our dilemma. We had to find a power
> by which we could live, and it had to be a Power greater than
> ourselves. . . . And it means, of course, that we are going to
> talk about God (Big Book 3rd ed., p. 45).

Sam Shoemaker had written in books very popular with early AAs:

> It [sin] makes a gap between myself and the Ideal which I am
> powerless to bridge. It distances me from the All-Holy God.
> And I cannot climb or crawl back across that distance. . . .
> Only God, therefore, can deal with sin. He must contrive to do
> for us what we have lost the power to do for ourselves
> (Shoemaker, *If I Be Lifted Up*, pp. 131, 133).

> We believe entirely that conversion is the experience which
> initiates the new life [See Acts 2:37-41]. But we are not fools
> enough to think that the beginning is the end! All subsequent life
> is a development of the relationship with God which conversion
> opened [See Acts 2:41-47; 4:29-37; 6:2-8; 10:33-48; 13:26-49]
> (Shoemaker, *Children of the Second Birth*, p. 16).

> Except a man be born again, he cannot see the kingdom of God
> [See John: 3:1-8]. . . . A man is born again when the control of
> his life, its center and its direction pass from himself to God
> (Shoemaker, *National Awakening*, p. 57).

In his very first book, Sam wrote:

> What you want is simply a vital religious experience. You need
> to find God. You need Jesus Christ (Shoemaker, *Realizing
> Religion*, p. 9).

Anne Smith faithfully picked up on such ideas to guide the early AAs. She said in her journal:

> Takes whole power of Christ to help us do the smallest thing. Step that puts man in position to receive the grace of God who alone commands. Surrender sins and wills putting God's will ahead. Whole thing begins to work (*Anne Smith's Journal*, supra, p. 24).

Learn How Jesus Fits in the Picture

The foregoing represent the statements of A.A. founders and their teachers. These ideas impacted heavily on A.A. But none of these teachers was so lacking in humility that he or she did not want to know what the Bible itself said. So let's provide some more guides to the Good Book.

Jesus: The Only Way to the Only True God

> Jesus saith unto him [Thomas], I am the way, the truth, and the life; no man cometh unto the Father, but by me (John 14:6).

> Be it known unto you all [said the Apostle Peter], and to all the people of Israel, that by the name of Jesus Christ of Nazareth, whom ye crucified, whom God raised from the dead, *even* by him doth this man stand here before you whole. . . .
> Neither is there salvation in any other; for there is none other name under heaven given among men whereby we must be saved (Acts 4:10, 12).

> For *there is* one God, and one mediator between God and men, the man Christ Jesus;
> who gave himself a ransom for all, to be testified in due time (1 Tim. 2:5-6).

> And this is life eternal, that they might know thee the only true God, and Jesus Christ, whom thou hast sent (John 17:3)

Becoming God's Kids

For God so loved the world, that he gave his only begotten Son, that whosoever believeth in him should not perish, but have everlasting life.
For God sent not his Son into the world to condemn the world; but that the world through him might be saved (John 3:16-17).

Then Peter, filled with the Holy Ghost, said unto them, Ye rulers of the people, and elders of Israel,
If we this day be examined of the good deed done to the impotent man, by what means he is made whole;
Be it known unto you all, and to all the people of Israel, that by the name of Jesus Christ of Nazareth, whom ye crucified, whom God raised from the dead, even by him doth this man stand here before you whole.
This is the stone which was set at nought of you builders, which is become the head of the corner.
Neither is there salvation in any other: for there is none other name under heaven given among men, whereby we must be saved (Acts 4:8-12)

Then Peter opened his mouth, and said, Of a truth I perceive that God is no respecter of persons:
But in every nation he that feareth him, and worketh righteousness, is accepted with him.
The word which God sent unto the children of Israel, preaching peace by Jesus Christ: (he is Lord of all:)
That word, I say, ye know, which was published throughout all Judaea, and began from Galilee after the baptism which John preached;
How God anointed Jesus of Nazareth with the Holy Ghost and with power: who went about doing good, and healing all that were oppressed of the devil; for God was with him.
And we are witnesses of all things which he did both in the land of the Jews, and in Jerusalem; whom they slew and hanged on a tree;

Him God raised up the third day, and shewed him openly. Not to all the people, but unto witnesses chosen before God, even to us, who did eat and drink with him after he rose from the dead. And he commanded us to preach unto the people, and to testify that it is he which was ordained of God to be the Judge of quick and dead.
To him give all the prophets witness, that through his name whosoever believeth in him shall receive remission of sins. (Acts 10:34-43).

Then he [the keeper of the prison] called for a light, and sprang in, and came trembling, and fell down before Paul and Silas,
And brought them out, and said, Sirs, what must I do to be saved?
And they said, Believe on the Lord Jesus Christ, and thou shalt be saved, and thy house.
And they spake unto him the word of the Lord, and to all that were in his house (Acts 16:29-32)

. . . The word is nigh thee, *even* in thy mouth, and in thy heart: that is, the word of faith, which we preach;
That if thou shalt confess with thy mouth the Lord Jesus, and shalt believe in thine heart that God hath raised him from the dead, thou shalt be saved.
For with the heart man believeth unto righteousness; and with the mouth confession is made unto salvation.
For the scripture saith, Whosoever believeth on him shall not be ashamed.
For there is no difference between the Jew and the Greek: for the same Lord over all is rich unto all that call upon him.
For whosoever shall call upon the name of the Lord shall be saved (Rom. 10:8-13).

For ye are all the children of God by faith in Christ Jesus (Galatians 3:26)

Whosoever believeth that Jesus is the Christ is born of God: and every one that loveth him that begat loveth him also that is begotten of him (1 John 5:1).

Holy Spirit, Power, and the Love of God by God's Grace

For by grace [the unearned, unmerited favor of God] are ye saved through faith; and that not of yourselves: *it is* the gift of God: Not of works, lest any man should boast (Eph. 2:8-9).

In whom ye also *trusted*, after that ye heard the word of truth, the gospel of your salvation: in whom also after that ye believed, ye were sealed with that holy Spirit of promise (Eph. 1:13).

But when the fulness of the time was come, God sent forth his Son, made of a woman, made under the law, To redeem them that were under the law, that we might receive the adoption of sons. And because ye are sons, God hath sent forth the Spirit of his Son into your hearts, crying, Abba, Father. Wherefore thou art no more a servant, but a son; and if a son, then an heir of God through Christ (Gal. 4:4-7).

But ye shall receive power, after that the Holy Ghost is come upon you: and ye shall be witnesses unto me both in Jerusalem, and in all Judaea, and in Samaria, and unto the uttermost part of the earth (Acts 2:8).

We are of God: he that knoweth God heareth us; he that is not of God heareth not us. Hereby know we the spirit of truth, and the spirit of error. Beloved, let us love one another; for love is of God; and every one that loveth is born of God, and knoweth God. He that loveth not knoweth not God; for God is love (1 John 4:6-8).

For God hath not given us the spirit of fear; but of power, and of love, and of a sound mind (2 Tim. 1:7).

Fellowship with God, His Son, and Each Other

> That which we have seen and heard declare we unto you, that
> ye also may have fellowship with us: and truly our fellowship
> *is* with the Father, and with his Son Jesus Christ (1 John 1:3).

Necessity for Obeying God's Commandments

> And hereby we do know that we know him, if we keep his
> commandments. He that saith, I know him, and keepeth not his
> commandments, is a liar, and the truth is not in him. But whoso
> keepeth his word, in him verily is the love of God perfected:
> hereby know we that we are in him. He that saith he abideth in
> him ought himself so to walk, even as he walked (1 John 2:3-6).

> By this we know that we love the children of God, when we
> love God, and keep his commandments. For this is the love of
> God, that we keep his commandments: and his commandments
> are not grievous (1 John 5:2-3).

> Grace be with you, mercy, and peace from God the Father,
> and from the Lord Jesus Christ, the Son of the Father, in truth
> and love. I rejoiced greatly that I found thy children walking
> in truth, as we have received a commandment from the
> Father. . . . And this is love, that we walk after his
> commandments. This is the commandment, That, as ye have
> heard from the beginning, ye should walk in it (2 John 3-4, 6).

Knowing and Understanding God through Christ

There is a myth today in A.A. and elsewhere that you can't know
or understand God. That belief is just plain hogwash. The Bible is
about knowing and understanding God. It's also about knowing and
understanding God *better* through communicating to and hearing
from Him. And the myth of lack of knowledge arises only if you
steer clear of the Bible.

Jesus Christ Declared God

No man hath seen God at any time; the only begotten Son, which is in the bosom of the Father, he hath declared *him* (John 1:18).

For the Father loveth the Son, and sheweth him all things that himself doeth: and he will shew him greater works than these, that ye may marvel (John 5:20).

Jesus answered them, and said, My doctrine is not mine, but his that sent me. If any man will do his will, he shall know of the doctrine, whether it be of God, or *whether* I speak of myself. He that speaketh of himself seeketh his own glory; but he that seeketh his glory that sent him, the same is true, and no unrighteousness is in him (John 7:16-18).

Jesus Christ Came to Destroy the Devil and His Works

Forasmuch then as the children are partakers of flesh and blood, he [Jesus Christ] also himself likewise took part of the same; that through death he might destroy him that had the power of death, that is, the devil (Heb. 2:14)

He that commiteth sin is of the devil; for the devil sinneth from the beginning. For this purpose the Son of God was manifested, that he might destroy the works of the devil (1 John 3:8)

Jesus Christ and the Will of God

Not everyone that saith unto me, Lord, Lord, shall enter into the kingdom of heaven; but he that doeth the will of my Father which is in heaven (Matt. 7:21).

For I came down from heaven, not to do mine own will, but the will of him that sent me (John 6:38).

Jesus cried and said, He that believeth on me, believeth not on me, but on him that sent me. And he that seeth me seeth him that sent me. I am come a light into the world, that whosoever believeth on me should not abide in darkness. And if any man hear my words, and believe not, I judge him not: for I came not to judge the world, but to save the world. He that rejecteth me, and receiveth not my words, hath one that judgeth him: the word that I have spoken, the same shall judge him in the last day. For I have not spoken of myself; but the Father which sent me, he gave me a commandment, what I should say, and what I should speak (John 12:44-49).

And he that sent me is with me; the Father hath not left me alone; for I do always those things that please him. . . . If ye continue in my word, *then* are ye my disciples indeed; And ye shall know the truth, and the truth shall make you free. . . . (John 8:29, 31-32).

I have given them thy word. . . . Sanctify them through thy truth; thy word is truth (John 17:14, 17).

Jesus Christ and His Accomplishments

1. *Everlasting life for believers*:

He that believeth on the Son hath everlasting life; and he that believeth not the Son shall not see life; but the wrath of God abideth on him (John 3:36).

2. *Abundant life for believers*:

I am the door; by me if any man enter in, he shall be saved, and shall go in and out, and find pasture. The thief cometh not, but for to steal, and to kill, and to destroy: I am come that they might have life, and that they might have *it* more abundantly (John 10:9-10).

3. *Remission of believers' past sins*

Being justified freely by his grace through the redemption that
is in Christ Jesus: Whom God hath set forth *to be* a propitiation
through faith in his blood, to declare his righteousness for the
remission of sins that are past, through the forbearance of God
(Rom. 3:24-25).

4. *Forgiveness of believers' present and future sins*

If we confess our sins, he is faithful and just to forgive us *our*
sins, and to cleanse us from all unrighteousness. . . . My little
children, these things write I unto you, that ye sin not. And if
any man sin, we have an advocate with the Father, Jesus Christ
the righteous (1 John 1:9; 2:1).

5. *Sending to believers the gift of the Holy Spirit—the power of
   God*

And I will pray the Father, and he shall give you another
Comforter, that he may abide with you for ever; *Even* the Spirit
of truth; whom the world cannot receive, because it seeth him
not, neither knoweth him; but ye know him; for he dwelleth
with you, and shall be in you (John 14:16-17).

And, behold, I send the promise of my Father upon you: but
tarry ye in the city of Jerusalem, until ye be endued with power
from on high (Luke 24:49).

For John truly baptized with water; but ye shall be baptized with
the Holy Ghost not many days hence. . . . But ye shall receive
power, after that the Holy Ghost is come upon you. . . (Acts
1:5, 8).

This Jesus hath God raised up, whereof we all are witnesses.
Therefore being by the right hand of God exalted, and having

received of the Father the promise of the Holy Ghost, he hath shed forth this, which ye now see and hear (Acts 2:31-32).

Then Peter said unto them, Repent, and be baptized every one of you in the name of Jesus Christ for the remission of sins, and ye shall receive the gift of the Holy Ghost. For the promise is unto you, and to your children, and to all that are afar off, *even* as many as the Lord our God shall call (Acts 2:38-39).

6. *Healing for believers*

Who his own self bare our sins in his own body on the tree, that we, being dead to sins, should live unto righteousness: by whose stripes ye were healed (1 Pet. 2:24).

Is any among you afflicted? Let him pray, Is any merry? Let him sing psalms. Is any sick among you? Let him call for the elders of the church; and let them pray over him, anointing him with oil in the name of the Lord: And the prayer of faith shall save the sick, and the Lord shall raise him up; and if he have committed sins, they shall be forgiven him. Confess *your* faults one to another, and pray for one another, that ye may be healed. The effectual fervent prayer of a righteous man availeth much (James 5:13-16).

7. *The ability of believers to ask in the name of Jesus Christ*

And whatsoever ye shall ask in my name, that will I do, that the Father may be glorified in the Son. If ye shall ask anything in my name, I will do *it* (John 14:13-14).

And Peter, fastening his eyes upon him [the man lame from his mother's womb] with John, said, Look on us. And he gave heed unto them, expecting to receive something of them. Then Peter said, Silver and gold have I none; but such as I have give I thee: In the name of Jesus Christ of Nazareth, rise up and walk. And he took him by the right hand and lifted him up; and immediately his feet and ankle bones received strength. And he leaping up stood, and walked, and entered with them into the temple, walking, and leaping, and praising God (Acts 3:4-8).

8. *The gathering together of believers on his return*

For this we say unto you by the word of the Lord, that we which are alive *and* remain unto the coming of the Lord shall not prevent [precede] them which are asleep. For the Lord himself shall descend from heaven with a shout, with the voice of the archangel, and with the trump of God: and the dead in Christ shall rise first: Then we which are alive and remain shall be caught up together with them in the clouds to meet the Lord in the air; and so shall we ever be with the Lord (1 Thess. 4:15-17).

And to you who are troubled rest with us, when the Lord Jesus shall be revealed from heaven with his mighty angels, In flaming fire taking vengeance on them that know not God, and that obey not the gospel of our Lord Jesus Christ. Who shall be punished with everlasting destruction from the presence of the Lord, and from the glory of his power; When he shall come to be glorified in his saints, and to be admired in all them that believe (because our testimony among you was believed) in that day (2 Thess. 1:7-10).

Now this I say, brethren, that flesh and blood cannot inherit the kingdom of God; neither doth corruption inherit incorruption. Behold, I shew you a mystery; We shall not all sleep, but we shall all be changed. In a moment, in the twinkling of an eye, at the last trump: for the trumpet shall sound, and the dead shall be raised incorruptible, and we shall be changed. For this corruptible must put on incorruption, and this mortal *must* put on immortality (1 Cor. 15:50-53).

For as in Adam all die, even so in Christ shall all be made alive. But every man in his own order: Christ the firstfruits; afterward they that are Christ's at his coming (1 Cor. 15:22-23).

9.   *Deliverance of believers from the wrath to come*

> But God commendeth his love toward us, in that, while we were
> yet sinners, Christ died for us.
> Much more then, being now justified by his blood, we shall be
> saved from wrath through him.
> For if, when we were enemies, we were reconciled to God by
> the death of his Son, much more, being reconciled, we shall be
> saved by his life (Rom. 5:8-10)

> For they themselves shew of us what manner of entering in we
> had unto you, and how ye turned to God from idols to serve the
> living and true God;
> And to wait for his Son from heaven, whom he raised from the
> dead, *even* Jesus, which delivered us from the wrath to come (1
> Thess. 1:9-10)

> For God hath not appointed us to wrath, but to obtain salvation
> by our Lord Jesus Christ, Who died for us, that, whether we
> wake or sleep, we should live together with him (1 Thess. 5:9-
> 10).

7

Sin, Love, Choice, and Obedience

For all have sinned, and come short of the glory of God (Rom. 3:22)

He that loveth not knoweth not God; for God is love. In this was manifested the love of God toward us, because that God sent his only begotten Son into the world, that we might live through him. Herein is love, not that we loved God, but that he loved us, and sent his Son *to be* the propitiation for our sins. Beloved, if God so loved us, we ought also to love one another (1 John 4:8-10)

And this is love, that we walk after his commandments (2 John 6)

Whosoever transgresseth, and abideth not in the doctrine of Christ, hath not God. He that abideth in the doctrine of Christ, he hath both the Father and the Son (2 John 9)

God's Ways, and God's Mercy and Grace

There's a story about "silent Cal" Coolidge, former U.S. President, and his remarks about the sermon Coolidge had heard in church. When asked what the sermon was about, Cal simply said, "Sin."

When asked what the minister had said, Cal replied, "He's against it."

And so is God! The Word of God minces no words when it declares what God wants and what He doesn't want. Our Creator makes clear that man's ways are not God's ways:

> Know therefore that the Lord thy God, he *is* God, the faithful God, which keepeth covenant and mercy with them that love him and keep his commandments to a thousand generations; And repayeth them that hate him to their face, to destroy them: he will not be slack to him that hateth him, he will repay him to his face. Thou shalt therefore keep the commandments, and the statutes, and the judgments, which I command thee this day, to do them (Deut. 7:9-11).

> As for God, his way *is* perfect; the word of the Lord *is* tried: he *is* a buckler to all them that trust in him. For who *is* God, save the Lord? And who *is* a rock, save our God? (2 Sam. 22:31-32).

> There is a way which seemeth right unto a man, but the end thereof *are* the ways of death (Prov. 14:12).

> For my thoughts are not your thoughts, neither are your ways my ways, saith the Lord, For as the heavens are higher than the earth, so are my ways higher than your ways, and my thoughts than your thoughts (Isa. 55:8-9).

But there is more to the story. It has to do with God's grace and mercy. "Grace" is considered to be "unmerited favour"– something we receive as a gift even though we didn't earn it and don't necessarily deserve it. "Mercy" is considered to be "deserved punishment withheld"–something for which we should have been judged, condemned, and punished, but were not because of the "mercy" of the adjudicator.

And of his fulness have all we received, and grace for grace. For the law was given by Moses, *but* grace and truth came by Jesus Christ (John 1:16-17).

But now the righteousness of God without the law is manifested, being witnessed by the law and the prophets; Even the righteousness of God *which is* by faith of Jesus Christ unto all and upon all them that believe: for there is no difference. For all have sinned and come short of the glory of God; Being justified freely by his grace through the redemption that is in Christ Jesus: Whom God hath set forth to be a propitiation through faith in his blood, to declare his righteousness for the remission of sins that are past, through the forbearance of God (Rom. 3:21-25).

There is therefore now no condemnation to them which are in Christ Jesus. . . (Rom. 8:1).

For the law of the Spirit of life in Christ Jesus hath made me free from the law of sin and death. For what the law could not do, in that it was weak through the flesh, God sending his own Son in the likeness of sinful flesh, for sin, condemned sin in the flesh: That the righteousness of the law might be fulfilled in us, who walk not after the flesh, but after the Spirit (Rom. 8:4-5).

But God, who is rich in mercy, for his great love wherewith he hath loved us, Even when we were dead in sins, hath quickened us together with Christ (by grace ye are saved) (Eph. 2:4-5).

Paul, an apostle of Jesus Christ by the will of God, according to the promise of life which is in Christ Jesus, To Timothy, *my* dearly beloved son: Grace, mercy, *and* peace, from God the Father and Christ Jesus our Lord (2 Tim. 1:1-2).

Paul, a servant of God, and an apostle of Jesus Christ, according to the faith of God's elect, and the acknowledging of the truth which is after godliness;

To Titus, *mine* own son after the common faith: Grace, mercy, *and* peace, from God the Father and the Lord Jesus Christ our Saviour (Titus 1:1, 4).

Grace and peace be multiplied unto you through the knowledge of God, and of Jesus our Lord (2 Pet. 1:2).

Sin

There has been plenty of "sin" in the lives of most alcoholics. And the Bible tells us what sin is. Literally, it is "missing the mark." God establishes the mark and provides the way and path to it. Man is to hit the mark. When he scores, he receives the blessing of God for doing just that. When he fails to aim for the mark, shoots in the other direction, falls short of the mark, or misses the whole target completely, there are consequences for his actions.

There is a great deal of theology involved in the concept of "sin;" and the author does not propose to set out expert opinion or present extended theology on the subject. There is a book by Charles C. Ryrie, *Basic Theology: A Popular Systematic Guide to Understanding Biblical Truth*. And we will quote some portions of it–verbatim or nearly so–immediately below. This is not to prove that Ryrie's statements are correct, non-controversial, or comprehensive. But rather, they can provide a starting point for those who wish to explore the subject in much more depth. Here, then, are some excerpts:

> The biblical concept of sin comes from a study of words used in both Testaments for sin. . . . there are at least eight basic words for sin in the Old Testament and a dozen in the New. Together they furnish the basic concepts involved in the doctrine. (Ryrie, p. 239).

The present author's guidebook will not quote all the words or review all the concepts discussed by Ryrie, but will attempt to show the material that can be studied.

"Sin" in the Old Testament

> In all of its forms, the basic Hebrew word for
> "sin"–*chata*–occurs about 522 times in the Hebrew Old
> Testament. Its basic meaning is "to miss the mark." It is
> equivalent to the basic Greek word for "sin"–*hamartanō*. But
> missing the mark also involves hitting some other mark. [Ryrie
> includes at this point a study of other words for sin.]. From the
> word study we may draw certain conclusions about the Old
> Testament teaching on sin. (1) Sin may take many forms, and
> because of the variety of words used, an Israelite could be aware
> of the particular form his sin took. (2) Sin is that which is
> contrary to a norm, and ultimately it is disobedience to God. (3)
> Although disobedience involved both positive and negative ideas,
> the emphasis is on the positive commission of wrong. . . . Sin
> was not only missing the mark, but hitting the wrong mark.
> [Ryrie, pp. 239-41, nearly word-for-word.]

"Sin" in the New Testament

The Greek New Testament employs at least a dozen words to
describe sin. [Here, too, Ryrie includes a study of these words.]

> The Greek word *hamartia* is the most frequently used word for
> sin, occurring in its various forms about 227 times. . . . The
> metaphor behind the word is "missing the mark," but, as in the
> Old Testament, this is not only a negative idea but includes the
> positive idea of hitting some wrong mark. Several conclusions
> may be drawn from the New Testament word study. (1) There
> is always a clear standard against which sin is committed. (2)
> Ultimately all sin is a positive rebellion against God and a
> transgression of His standards. (3) Evil may assume a variety of
> forms. (4) Man's responsibility is definite and clearly
> understood. [Ryrie, pp. 241, 43, nearly word-for-word.]

> . . . [I]t might be a good idea to define it thus: sin is missing the
> mark, badness, rebellion, iniquity, going astray, wickedness,

wandering, ungodliness, crime, lawlessness, transgression, ignorance, and a falling away. . . . Certainly the chief characteristic of sin is that it is directed against God. . . . Any definition that fails to reflect this is not a biblical one. . . . And sin is so damaging that only the death of God's Son can take it away (John 1:29) [Ryrie, pp. 243-44].

Some Sources of Sin

- Satan
- The World
- The Heart (Ryrie, p. 249)

Some Consequences of Sin

Sin causes people to be lost. . . . If unforgiven it causes them to perish. . . . It brings people into judgment. . . . The Lord made it clear that the Pharisees were slaves to the desires of the devil. . . . Of course not all sickness is the result of sin (John 9:3), but some evidently is. . . . Additionally, the sins warned against in the Sermon on the Mount all have their effect on others. No one can sin in total isolation (Ryrie, pp. 249-50).

The Forgiveness of Sin

John the Baptist announced the purpose of it when he pointed to Jesus as the Lamb of God who takes away the sin of the world (John 1:29). . . . Forgiven people should forgive others. This is a recurring theme in the Lord's teaching. . . . (Ryrie, p. 250).

The Inheritance of Sin

The Bible clearly states that all aspects of man's being are corrupt. . . . Every facet of man's being is affected by this sin nature. (1) His intellect is blinded (2 Cor 4:4). His mind is reprobate or disapproved (Rom.1:28). His understanding is darkened, separated from the life of God (Eph 4:18). (2) His emotions are degraded and defiled (Rom. 1:21, 24, 26; Titus 1:15). (3) His will is enslaved to sin, and therefore stands in opposition to God (Rom. 6:20; 7:20). . . . The penalty that is particularly related to inherited sin is spiritual death. . . . We are separated from the dominion of sin by Christ's death, and we are free from its domination by the power of the Spirit (Ryrie, pp. 252-54).

Personal Sins

In Rom. 3:9-18 Paul demonstrates the condemnation of all people on the basis of their committing sins personally. . . . If we need one idea to describe the result of all personal sins, it would be the loss of fellowship. The unbeliever has no fellowship with God because of his sins, and the believer who has been brought into the fellowship of God's family loses the enjoyment of that fellowship when he sins. He is not expelled from the family, though he may lose some of the privileges of being in the family. When he confesses and is forgiven, he is restored to fellowship. . . . For the unbeliever who receives Christ, that forgiveness covers all the guilt of his sins (Eph.1:7). For the believer, that forgiveness restores the enjoyment of fellowship in the family of God (1 John 1:9) [Ryrie, pp. 261-63]

The Standard for the Believer

The standard is God's holiness. The requirement is to walk in the light. Our experience should always be a growing one, growing to maturity. That is true biblical perfectionism. (Ryrie, pp. 263-64)

The Enemies of the Believer

The believer is continually opposed by the world [with Satan as its head and controlling force], the flesh [The flesh is the

principle of sin within all of us. Some equate the sin nature and
the flesh], the devil [his work in attacking believers] (Ryrie, pp.
264-66).

The Preventives for Sin

The Word of God. God's Word in our hearts will serve to
prevent sin, for it will warn, remind, encourage, strengthen,
and guide us when we are tempted to sin (Ps. 119:11). . . The
Intercession of Christ. Our Lord ever lives to pray for us (Heb.
7:25). . . The Indwelling of the Spirit. . . we need to walk in
the Spirit. . .Teaching us the deep things of the Word helps us
to discern good and evil. . . Leading us in our prayers. . .
(Ryrie, pp. 267-68).

God doesn't cause man to sin. Man does the sinning. When he does,
he brings upon himself the justice meted out by a righteous God:

Whosoever commiteth sin transgresseth also the law; for sin is
the transgression of the law (1 John 3:4).

Now we know that what things soever the law saith, it saith to
them who are under the law: that every mouth may be stopped,
and all the world may become guilty before God. Therefore by
the deeds of the law there shall no flesh be justified in his sight:
for by the law is the knowledge of sin (Rom. 3:19-20).

Sin entered the world, states the Bible, because the first man
(Adam) disobeyed the command of God even when there was no
law. Adam's transgression was disobeying God:

Wherefore, as by one man sin entered into the world, and death
by sin; and so death passed upon all men, for that all have
sinned; (For until the law sin was not in the world: but sin is not
imputed when there is no law. Nevertheless death reigned from
Adam to Moses, even over them that had not sinned after the
similitude of Adam's transgression, who is the figure of things

to come. But not as the offence, so also *is* the free gift. For if through the offence of one many be dead, much more the grace of God, and the gift by grace, *which is* by one man, Jesus Christ, hath abounded unto many (Rom. 5:12-15).

Today, far too many in and out of Twelve Step Fellowships (Christian or otherwise) and in and out of church-sponsored groups, dwell on sin, instead of victory. Meetings often reek of self-condemnation, guilt, shame, fear, sin-consciousness, justifications, and rationalizations.

Such behavior and topics need to be examined in light of what early AAs borrowed from the Bible. Yet it is very important to talk about the alcoholism/sin issue for a moment. First, because there are Christian critics of A.A. who point to excessive and nonmedicinal drug use and even occasional intoxication as "sin," note the following:

> While the terms "alcoholic" and "drug addict" do not appear in Scripture, God's Word does speak clearly to the issue of alcohol abuse. It calls those addicted to alcohol drunkards (Deut. 21:20; Prov. 23:21; 26 :9; Isa. 24: 20; 1 Cor. 5:11). Certainly, the alcoholic or drug addict is a person *controlled* by his or her habit. . . . To be "under the power" includes not only excessive drinking or nonmedicinal drug use as a way of life, but also occasional intoxication. If one is not guilty of the former, he will not succumb to the latter. Such dissipation is strictly forbidden by God and hence is sin (Eph. 5:18). The unrighteous person is listed right along with other sinners–"fornicators," "idolaters," "adulterers," "homosexuals," "drunkards: (1 Cor. 6:9-10). . . . Such uncontrolled lifestyle is called unrighteousness (sin). (Playfair, *The Useful Lie*, p. 29).

Whereas admission of being a sinner, who is totally depraved and under the domination of sin, is involved in conversion to Christianity, the Step One of AA is the admission that the problem is **not** sin, but rather disease–that one is not under the domination of sin, as clearly stated in the Bible, but under the domination of a destructive disease (The Bobgans, *12 Steps to Destruction,* p. 73).

And, even though the Bible clearly refers to drunkenness as sin, most Christians have hopped onto the AA bandwagon of faith and believe that habitual drunkenness is due to a disease called "alcoholism" or "addiction" rather than to sin. In fact AA's influence has been so pervasive and widespread that Christians and non Christians alike believe that addictions of all sorts are serious diseases to be treated rather than sinful habits to be changed (The Bobgans, *12 Steps to Destruction,* p. 74).

By God's law, all are guilty. Before a person is converted to Jesus Christ, he is under the domination of sin, whether he acts it out in sinful habits of substance abuse or in other sinful ways. Nevertheless, such a pronouncement of guilt does not lead to hopelessness or helplessness. Instead, it should lead to Christ. . . . Jesus Christ is the answer and faith in Him is the way out of hopelessness, helplessness, powerlessness, and sinfulness. Jesus empowers believers to overcome sin and to please God (The Bobgans, *12 Steps to Destruction*, pp. 92-93).

Whether "alcoholism" and "addiction" are diseases or illnesses or not, when a person is drunk (or abusing drugs), that person misses the mark. That person disobeys God. That person receives no blessing from God for that conduct, but instead brings upon himself or herself some very dire consequences. Today's A.A. literature, however, will have nothing to do with that idea.

In the past and in the present A.A. has spoken of many *other* "sins" which need to be "removed." Such sin or sins are, in the lingo of the Oxford Group and of Sam Shoemaker, "blocks" to a relationship with God. And A.A. has treated them as such, often speaking of the "blocks" to God (Big Book, 3rd ed., pp. 54, 64, 71, 72, 76).

Initially, A.A. took its cue as to what was or was not "sin" from Dr. Robert Speer's "Four Standards"(or "Four Absolutes," as they were later called). The four standards were: Absolute Honesty,

Absolute Purity, Absolute Unselfishness, and Absolute Love. Those were the "marks" that Jesus laid down for conduct, said Dr. Speer. Man was to shoot for those marks. And it is hardly necessary to cite the Bible verses which were said to support the idea that ignoring these standards constituted sin.

Dr. Speer cited John 8:44 for eliminating lying, and replacing it with honesty. He cited Mark 10:45 for rejecting selfishness, and living unselfish ministry and service. He cited Mark 7:15 for removing the things defiling a man from within and, instead, seeking purity. He cited John 13:34 for turning away from hatred and violation of God's commandments to love, and heeding instead Jesus's commandment: "as I have loved you, that ye also love one another." The Oxford Group and early A.A. followed suit. (See Dick B., *The Good Book and The Big Book*, pp.148-51.)

Soon becoming unhappy with "absolute" moral standards, particularly the Four Absolutes of the Oxford Group, Bill Wilson began listing certain "negatives" as "sins," or shortcomings, or "character defects" to be eliminated. Nonetheless, even Bill's list of negatives was founded on biblical injunctions against them. They included resentments and grudges (James 5:9); fears (Mark 5:36); selfishness (1 Cor. 13:4-5); dishonesty (1 Cor. 13:4, 6); harms done (Num. 4: 6-7).

Possibly under the influence of his later Jesuit editors, Bill Wilson began adding other "sins" which were to be "removed." He mentioned the so-called "seven deadly sins" as a "universally recognized list of major human failings." These seven were pride, greed, lust, anger, gluttony, envy, sloth; and we will leave it to our readers to get out a Bible concordance and trace the verses declaring these seven "failings" were transgressions abhorred in the Bible. But the confusing emphasis was on God's *removing the sins*, rather than upon man's being able to decide for himself to abandon them and then ask for God's help and guidance in eliminating them.

Somewhere along the line, AAs began talking about being "on the beam" and "off the beam." That's not far from the biblical concept of hitting or missing the mark. A laundry list of activities were declared to be "off;" and they often were accompanied by a parallel list of opposites declared to be "on." One example of "off the beam" "characteristics" can be found in Clarence Snyder's Fourth Step "moral inventory checklist":

> Self-pity; self-justification; egotism; self-condemnation; dishonesty; impatience; hate; resentments; false pride; jealousy; envy; laziness; procrastination; insincerity; negative thinking; vulgar-immoral thinking; criticizing; lying; fear; greed (See Dick B., *That Amazing Grace: The Role of Clarence and Grace S. in Alcoholics Anonymous*, pp. 69-71).

Clarence Snyder got sober in February, 1938; was one of the forty "pioneers" who had achieved sobriety when A.A.'s basic text was undertaken; and was sponsored by Dr. Bob. Snyder was an ardent Bible student; and he frequently quoted Mark 7:18-23 and Gal. 5:16-26 for lists of defiling, defeating, evil things man had been nurturing in himself and which needed to be purged. You can see in our list of biblical "sins" below just how much of Clarence's thinking and that of the "beamers" (as summarized above) was influenced by Bible verses describing sinful behavior. The following are some of the "sins" that are mentioned in the Bible:

> Lust (Rom. 1:24); lesbianism (Rom. 1:26); homosexuality (Rom. 1:27); unrighteousness (Rom. 1:29); fornication (Rom. 1:29); wickedness (Rom. 1:29); covetousness (1 Cor. 5 :10); maliciousness (Rom. 1:29); deceitfulness (Rom. 1:29); whispering (Rom. 1:29); back-biting (Rom. 1:30); haters of God (Rom. 1:30); pride (Rom. 1:30); boasting (Rom. 1:30); stealing (Rom. 2:21); adultery (Rom. 2:22); slothfulness (Rom. 12:11); vengeance (Rom. 12:19); killing (Rom. 13:9); bearing false witness (Rom. 13:9); rioting (Rom. 13:13); drunkenness (Rom. 13:13); strife (Rom. 3:13); envy (Rom. 13:13); idolatry (1 Cor. 5:10; 10:7); extortion (1 Cor. 5:10).

There are many more in both the Old Testament and in the New. In
fact, there are enough sins mentioned above to keep the alcoholic
drunk; or in despair; or in fear; or in a guilty frame of mind for
years to come. This is the case whether he or she drinks or not. You
can hear sin-consciousness frequently in today's meetings. Weeping
and penitent souls all too often lay trips on themselves, describing
themselves as "broken," "bruised," "sinners," "failures," "stupid,"
"worthless," "losers," "sick," and on and on.

One Christian lady I knew used to jump up in A.A. meetings
and say: "I'm Sarah. I'm an alcoholic, an Episcopalian, a lesbian,
and a church organist." Someone finally told her to sit down
because she was "confusing the newcomers." The point is that guilt,
guilt, guilt, fear, fear, fear, and self-loathing permeate the
expressions in meetings where sin and sins are the focus. To the
point that many wind up saying: "I'm a grateful alcoholic," or "I'm
grateful that I am an alcoholic." What's more, if you have been a
sponsor (and the author has sponsored more than 80 men in their
A.A. program), you will have heard many of these "sins." They are
frequently listed by the newcomer as his moral shortcomings in his
Fourth Step inventory, and then confesses them in his Fifth Step
revelations to the sponsor. The author often heard the joking
statement, "There is no *original* sin in A.A." AAs have done it all!

And that's enough for sin. It exists. God defines what it is. God
didn't cause it. God's against it. He provided a solution through
Jesus Christ. He expects us to steer clear of it, whether it's
drunkenness or idolatry. But *our* focus here–for the alcoholic who
is working on his or her way out–is on redemption, remission,
forgiveness, power, love, grace, and mercy. On what Jesus Christ
accomplished for those who accept him as their savior, and what
they can do with the power thus received..

Early AAs were looking to better lives through Christ, not lives
of self-pity, self-condemnation, and self-centeredness. Their Big
Book still retains emphasis on eliminating the defeating
manifestations of "self," *sans mention of Jesus Christ*:

Selfishness–self-centeredness! That, we think, is the root of our troubles. Driven by a hundred forms of fear, self-delusion, self-seeking, and self-pity, we step on the toes of our fellows and they retaliate. . . . Above everything, we alcoholics must be rid of this selfishness (Big Book, 3rd ed., p. 62).

But what a guilt trip such language lays on us as we haltingly creep into meetings seeking relief! How much better it would be to hear this verse which Clarence Snyder taught his sponsees over a period of many years:

Therefore if any man *be* in Christ, *he is* a new creature: old things are passed away; behold, all things are become new (2 Cor. 5:17).

And these verses:

That ye put off concerning the former conversation the old man, which is corrupt according to the deceitful lusts; And be renewed in the spirit of your mind; And that ye put on the new man, which after God is created in righteousness and true holiness (Eph. 4:22-24).

Let this mind be in you, which was also in Christ Jesus (Phil. 2:5).

Love

Alcoholics and addicts crave love. Loneliness, a sense of separation, a feeling of abandonment and worthlessness, a fear of rejection, an overwhelming guilt and shame are common ingredients in the mind of the newcomer. Bill Wilson stated these points very well in the Big Book. So did many of the personal stories that accompanied Bill's basic text.

Love, for most of the pioneers, offered the answer. Dr. Bob said all the Steps could be simmered down to "love and service." Those who get the most out of A.A. are very likely to be those who give the most. Dr. Bob was well-known for speaking about our "God of love" (See also 2 Cor. 13:11). A.A. literature abounds with mention of a loving God. Anne Smith (Dr. Bob's wife) very often comforted hurting newcomers with the simple quote, "God is love" (See 1 John 4:8, 16).

Both the Old and the New Testaments commanded that we love God with our heart, soul, mind, and strength, and our neighbor as ourselves. These themes were repeated over and over in the Church Epistles, particularly the injunction to "love thy neighbor as thyself" (Rom. 13:9; Gal. 5:13; James 2:8; 1 John 3:23; 5:1-2).

There are many definitions of love in the Bible. John 3 shows the love of God in giving His only begotten son Jesus in order that the world might, through him, be saved. Jesus certainly spelled out the required loving conduct that was considered to be in accord with God's will. 1 Corinthians 13 detailed the "ingredients" of the love of God. 1 Cor. 13:8 states plainly "Charity never faileth." 1 Cor. 13:13 states "And now abideth faith, hope, charity, these three; but the greatest of these *is* charity [love]."

Galatians specifies the relationship of faith and love:

For in Jesus Christ neither circumcision availeth anything, nor uncircumcision; but faith which worketh by love (Gal. 5:6).

Ephesians states what God's kids are to do in their walk:

Be ye therefore followers of God, as dear children; And walk in love, as Christ also hath loved us, and hath given himself for us an offering and a sacrifice to God for a sweetsmelling savour (Eph. 5:1-2).

1 Peter provides an interesting contrast between love and sin:

> And above all things have fervent charity among yourselves: for
> charity shall cover the multitude of sins (1 Pet. 4:8).

Romans quotes several of the "shalt nots" of the commandments;
and says if there be any other commandment, it is briefly
comprehended in this saying, namely, "Thou shalt love thy
neighbor as thyself." It continues:

> Love worketh no ill to his neighbor: therefore love *is* the
> fulfilling of the law (Rom. 13:10).

Choosing

A.A.'s thesis of "powerlessness" urges that *will-power is of no
avail* when it comes to quitting drinking (Big Book, 3rd ed., p. 5).
It emphasizes that *self-knowledge* (education as to alcohol's danger
and consequences of drunkenness) *assures no protection* (p. 7). It
stresses that *"fear" will not keep one sober* (p. 8). It culminates its
powerless presentation by declaring *"probably no human power"*
can relieve the alcoholic of his or her alcoholism (p. 60).

All those points are made in Bill's Story at the beginning of the
Big Book. They are clear from other parts of the basic text. They
are clear from the so-called a,b,c's (p. 60). They are summed up in
two further statements: (1) "As to two of you men, whose stories I
have heard [said a renowned doctor], there is no doubt in my mind
that you were 100% hopeless apart from divine help" (p. 43). (2)
"Lack of power, that was our dilemma. We had to find a power by
which we could live. . . . And it means, of course, that we are
going to talk about God" (p. 45).

That's where today's "powerless" controversies begin to foam.
If alcoholism is a "disease" which the human is "powerless" to
overcome, some say alcoholism cannot be "cured." The alcoholic

can only receive a "daily reprieve," which could perhaps be seen as walking in fellowship with God, *if* we were talking about believers. However, God's availability to help His kids is *unconditional*. Man makes the choice–to walk in harmony with God's will, or to walk toward drunkenness at the bar. God can help and guide. But God doesn't take away either the choice or the help; man's actions, however, can abandon both. Does that mean he is "powerless" or simply that he has turned away from the "power?"

Early AAs felt very clearly that alcoholism can be *cured* (p. 191). By the power of God. So did Bill Wilson's medical mentor, Dr. William D. Silkworth, who wrote the "Doctor's Opinion" for A.A.'s Big Book. (See Norman Vincent Peale, *The Positive Power of Jesus Christ: Life-changing Adventures in Faith,* 1980, pp. 59-62). See also:

[Wilson to Silkworth:] "Well, doc," he said, "my troubles are all over. I've got religion." "Why you're the last man" [said Dr. Silkworth]. Sure, I know all that. But I've got it. And I know I'm cured of this drinking business for good" [said Wilson] (quotes from *Liberty Magazine*, September, 1939).

Here is how it works: Every member of the group–which is to say every person who has been saved–is under obligation to carry on the work, to save other men. That, indeed, is a fundamental part of his own mental cure (quote from *Liberty Magazine, supra*).

Is there hope for habitual drunkards? A cure that borders on the miraculous–and it works! (Headline of *Liberty Magazine* article, *supra*).

If, as some of A.A.'s Christian critics assert, alcoholism is a "sin," then *overcoming it begins with choices*. Man may be "powerless" by himself (by his own fleshly walk) to avoid drunkenness; but many of A.A.'s Christian detractors would say he first has the choice to accept Christ (Rom. 10:9-10)–the Christ who became sin for us. Then man has the choice of standing fast in the liberty wherewith Christ has made him free--free to choose, free so that he is appropriately commanded: "Let not sin therefore reign in your mortal body, that ye should obey it in the lusts thereof" (Rom. 6:12). Note, that in almost every biblical reference to *a* sin, believers are urged to "put off" the sin, to cease the sinning, to "do God's will," and to be delivered from the consequences of disobeying God (Compare Gal. 5:1; John 8:30-36; Rom. 6:1-11, 8:2-4). Therefore, if God commands a believer to do something–to walk in love, to put off sinful behavior, to do God's will–the believer must have a choice. It must be possible to do that which God commands.

The interesting question, then, is whether there is that much difference between early A.A., *properly understood*, and one Christian view of "sin" that is propounded by many Christian writers today. Early A.A. was, despite today's protests to the contrary, grounded in the idea that there *was* a sin problem with alcoholism. You won't find it stated in A.A. literature. In fact, it is hard to find the sin problem in the remarks of the founders. Yet Dr. Bob, Anne, Bill, and Lois all spoke of sin in connection with the program. Note the following remarks they made:

> List of sins: Feeling of being special, self-conscious, feeling of inferiority, self-indulgence in small things, dependency on human law (remarks of **Lois Wilson** in her Oxford Group notebook at Stepping Stones. See Dick B., *The Akron Genesis of Alcoholics Anonymous*, 3rd ed., p. 150-52).

> Sin blinds, binds, multiplies, deadens (**Lois Wilson**, *supra*).

> There ain't no white lies. All sins have blue eyes & dimples when they are young (**Lois Wilson**, *supra*).

Confess your sins to God and another human being (**Lois Wilson** in *Lois Remembers*, p. 92).

Christ can only remove them [sins such as possessiveness, temper, selfishness, dishonesty, and pride] and replace them with a new quality of life. Read Rom. 12 (remarks by **Anne Smith**. See Dick B., *Anne Smith's Journal*, 3rd ed., p. 47).

A small sense of sin means a small sense of Christ. The closer you get to Christ, the more sensitive you become to sin.. The whiter the cloth, the more easily it is stained (**Anne Smith**, *Anne Smith's Journal*, *supra*, p. 44).

It is because we have ignored sin in our presentation of the Gospel that the message of the Gospel has lost its sting and blasting power. Our first need is an emetic, not a narcotic (**Anne Smith**, *Anne Smith's Journal*, *supra*, p. 44).

Be willing to ask God where I am failing and to admit sin (**Anne Smith**, *Anne Smith's Journal*, *supra*, p. 43).

We made a moral inventory of our defects or sins (wrote **Bill Wilson**. See Dick B., *The Akron Genesis of Alcoholics Anonymous*, 3rd ed., p. 256).

He must remove from his life other sins such as hatred, adultery, and others which frequently accompany alcoholism (report of **A.A.'s Trustee-to-be Frank Amos** in his report to Rockefeller on the early A.A. "Program" requirements See Dick B., *The Akron Genesis of Alcoholics Anonymous*, 3rd ed., p. 258).

They spoke of the need for the power of God. They spoke of the need for the guidance of God. Dr. Bob, Anne, and Bill all recognized the need for Christ–Bill, from the moment Bill made his decision for Christ at Calvary Rescue Mission. And the simplest understanding of real A.A. history provides the backdrop.

Oxford Group founder Dr. Frank Buchman was fond of making this statement: "Sin is the problem. Jesus Christ is the cure. The result is a miracle." Sam Shoemaker never demurred to Buchman's view in Sam's teachings which Bill Wilson heard so often. And all these "founders" spoke of receiving "power" through conversion (the acceptance of Jesus Christ as Lord and Saviour)–a fact that many Christian A.A. critics seem to ignore

There is no claim here that this discussion will resolve anyone's muddy thinking. Today's AAs could be dead wrong about "disease." They could be dead wrong about their lack of "willpower." They could be dead wrong about lacking "power." They could even have some weird ideas about "a god." And they *sometimes do today*. But their forbears *did* recognize sin. They *did* speak of cure. Most pioneers became Christians, belonged to a Christian Fellowship, surrendered to Jesus Christ, and (in Akron) called themselves a Christian Fellowship.

And that is probably as far as this historical guide should go on the matter of early A.A. and sin. To be sure, no one in Twelve Step groups today can fairly be labeled as an advocate of "sin." For example, no one in Twelve Step groups could be expected to claim a recovery that still involved drunkenness, smoking, gambling, and so on. And it seems appropriate to suggest that Christian detractors who talk of sin, as well as AAs who talk of disease, all need to examine very carefully the *original* emphasis in A.A. on many aspects of *willpower*.

Willpower was required to *seek God*: "God, I offer myself to Thee. . ." (Big Book, 3rd ed, p. 63). Willpower was required to *"find" God*: "We asked His protection and care with complete abandon" (Big Book, 3rd ed., p. 59–setting forth the starting point for the Steps that purported to do just that). Willpower was required to *live in harmony with God's will*: "all of us. . . are the children of a living Creator with whom we may form a relationship upon simple and understandable terms as soon as we are willing and honest enough to try" (Big Book, 3rd ed., p. 28). It was required to *improve one's relationship with his Creator*: "See that your relationship with Him is right, and great events will come to pass for you and countless others" (Big Book, 3rd ed., p. 164). Wilson wrote this:

> Every day is a day when we must carry the vision of God's will into all of our activities. "How can I best serve Thee–Thy will (not mine) be done." These are thoughts which must go with us constantly. We can exercise our will power along this line all we wish. It is the proper use of the will (Big Book, 3rd ed., p. 85).

The Bible is emphatic that believers are to *change their minds*–to renew their minds to what God says and put that Word in their minds and act upon it. They are to put their wills to choosing God's way, and to "doing" God's will. This, whether the Bible is speaking of choosing to become children of God, choosing to abstain from sin, or choosing to walk in love. Let's look at a few of the "musts" that make it clear that people have a choice, are to make the choice, and that their choice–the choice to serve God or mammon--will have consequences.

> And the LORD [Yahweh] God commanded the man [Adam], saying, Of every tree of the garden thou mayest freely eat: But of the tree of the knowledge of good and evil, thou shalt not eat of it: for in the day that thou eatest thereof thou shalt surely die (Gen. 2:16-17).

In Exodus, Yahweh spoke to Moses on mount Sinai and gave Moses choices:

> Now therefore, if ye will obey my voice indeed, and keep my
> covenant, then ye shall be a peculiar treasure unto me above all
> people: for all the earth is mine (Exod. 19:5).

> And the LORD [Yahweh] said unto Moses, Lo, I come unto
> thee in a thick cloud, that the people may hear when I speak
> with thee, and believe thee forever (Exod. 19:9a)

> And the LORD [Yahweh] came down upon mount Sinai, on the
> top of the mount; and the LORD [Yahweh] called Moses *up* to
> the top of the mount; and Moses went up (Exod. 19:20).

Then God spoke the "ten commandments," and other "laws,"
beginning with: "Thou shalt have no other gods before me. . . ."
(Exod. 20:3-18). The people said, ". . . All the words which the
LORD [Yahweh] hath said will we do" (Exod. 24:3). But before
long, the people made choices–choosing to disobey. God then said
to Moses:

> Go, get thee down; for thy people, which thou broughtest out of
> the land of Egypt, have corrupted *themselves*. They have turned
> aside quickly out of the way which I commanded them. . . .
> Now therefore let me alone, that my wrath may wax hot against
> them, and that I may consume them; and I will make of thee a
> great nation (Exod. 32:7-10).

Then, in spite of the pleas from Moses, came the *consequences of
disobedience*:

> And the LORD [Yahweh] said unto Moses, Whosoever hath
> sinned against me, him will I blot out of my book (Exod. 32:33)

God offers many other choices to man. All require the exercise
of willpower which acts in compliance with the will of God. Here
are just a few examples of God's commands to choose:

But I say unto you, Love your enemies, bless them that curse you, do good to them that hate you, and pray for them which despitefully use you, and persecute you (Matt. 5:44).

Not everyone that saith unto me, Lord, Lord, shall enter the kingdom of heaven; but he that doeth the will of my Father which is in heaven (Matt. 7:22).

Jesus answered, Verily, verily, I say unto thee, Except a man be born of water and of the Spirit, he cannot enter into the kingdom of God. . . . Marvel not that I said unto thee, Ye must be born again (John 3:5, 7).

Then Peter said unto them, Repent, and be baptized every one of you in the name of Jesus Christ for the remission of sins, and ye shall receive the gift of the Holy Ghost (Acts 2:38).

That ye put off concerning the former conversation the old man, which is corrupt according to the deceitful lusts. . . . And that ye put on the new man, which after God is created in righteousness and true holiness (Eph. 4:22, 24).

Charge them that are rich in this world that they be not highminded, nor trust in uncertain riches, but in the living God, who giveth us richly all things to enjoy (1 Tim. 6:17).

But be ye doers of the word, and not hearers only, deceiving your own selves (James 1:22).

Humble yourselves therefore under the mighty hand of God, that he may exalt you in due time; Casting all your care upon him, for he careth for you (1 Pet. 5 :6-7).

Love not the world, neither the things *that are* in the world. . . . (1 John 2:15).

Note the imperative language in most of the foregoing verses: *Humble yourselves*; *love not* the world; *charge them* that are rich; *put off*; *put on*; and so on. All imply that there is a choice; and all enjoin action that God wants. In other words, through exercise of the free will that God Almighty has given us, we *can* choose. Our Creator Yahweh has offered us choices: The choice of accepting Jesus as Saviour; the choice of putting off the old man and putting on the new man; the choice of doing the word and will of God; and the choice of loving and obeying God or of loving the world:

> Love not the world, neither the things that are in the world. If any man love the world, the love of the Father is not in him. For all that is in the world, the lust of the flesh, and the lust of the eyes, and the pride of life, is not of the Father, but is of the world. And the world passeth away, and the lust thereof: but he that doeth the will of God abideth for ever (1 John 2:15-17).

> From whence *come* wars and fightings among you? *come they* not hence, even of your lusts that war in your members. Ye lust, and have not; ye kill, and desire to have, and cannot obtain; ye fight and war, yet ye have not, because ye ask not. Ye ask, and receive not, because ye ask amiss, that ye may consume *it* upon your lusts. Ye adulterers and adulteresses, know ye not that the friendship of the world is enmity with God? whosoever therefore will be a friend of the world is the enemy of God (James 4:1-4).

> Dearly beloved, I beseech *you* as strangers and pilgrims, abstain from fleshly lusts, which war against the soul (1 Pet. 2:11).

The Need to Obey

By now, it should not be necessary to assert that God's Word proclaims God's will that the whole world, particularly His children, shall obey His commands. God makes that very plain:

> And hereby do we know that we know him, if we keep his commandments. He that saith, I know him, and keepeth not his commandments, is a liar, and the truth is not in him. But whoso keepeth his word in him verily is the love of God perfected; hereby know we that we are in him. He that saith he abideth in him ought himself so to walk, even as he walked (1 John 2:3-6).

> But be ye doers of the word, and not hearers only, deceiving your own selves (James 1:22).

Receive the power. Choose to utilize the power. Walk according to God's will. And thus be in obedience to God. The old saws that have become so prevalent in meeting chatter today just don't conform to what the Bible said and early AAs believed. You don't become fatalistic and "accept" the misery that "must have been meant to be" and play the "cards that were dealt you." There is an old hymn, Lutheran, I believe. It begins: RISE UP O MEN OF GOD!

Some Questions for the Critics

Lots today, including most AAs, are still contending that alcoholism *is* a disease. If that conclusion is sound, can God Almighty cure it? If not, why not?

Many today are now saying that alcoholism is *not* a disease. If that be so, can the power of God Almighty still lead a believer to sanity, wholeness, and deliverance? If not, why not?

Still others (usually Christians) claim that alcoholism is a *sin*. If that be so, is there any doubt in their minds that if one accepts Christ, utilizes the power of God thus received, and resists the devil, that such a person cannot stay sober? If not, why not?

Is not the answer in each case at least this: There should not be a repudiation of early A.A. history which shows–by results–exactly how the pioneers were cured; or, if not cured, then given sanity and deliverance from self-destruction; or, if engaged in sinning, overcame that sin by accepting Christ, submitting themselves to God, and resisting the devil (cp. James 4:7).

Is the not the following a fruitful approach for the believer's study? (and note the choices involved):

> He that covereth his sins shall not prosper: but whoso confesseth and forsaketh *them* shall have mercy (Prov. 28:13).

> But God, who is rich in mercy, for his great love wherewith he loved us, Even when we were dead in sins, hath quickened us together with Christ, (by grace ye are saved). . . . For we are his workmanship, created in Christ Jesus unto good works, which God hath before ordained that we should walk in them (Eph. 2:4-5, 10).

> Wherefore putting away lying, speak every man truth with his neighbor. . . . Be ye angry, and sin not: let not the sun go down on your wrath: Neither give place to the devil. Let him that stole steal no more: but rather let him labour, working with *his* hands the thing which is good, that he may have to give to him that needeth. Let no corrupt communication proceed out of your mouth, but that which is good to the use of edifying, that it may minister grace unto the hearers (Eph. 4:25-29).

> And be not drunk with wine, wherein is excess; but be filled with the Spirit (Eph. 5:18).

> That ye might walk worthy of the Lord unto all pleasing, being fruitful in every good work, and increasing in the knowledge of God; Strengthened with all might, according to his glorious power, unto all patience and longsuffering with joyfulness; Giving thanks unto the Father, which hath made us meet to be partakers of the inheritance of the saints in light: Who hath

delivered us from the power of darkness, and hath translated us into the kingdom of his dear Son (Col. 1:11-13).

I can do all things through Christ which strengtheneth me (Phil. 4:13).

Nevertheless, whereto we have already attained, let us walk by the same rule, let us mind the same thing. Brethren, be followers together of me, and mark them which walk so as ye have us for an ensample (Phil. 3:16-17).

As ye have therefore received Christ Jesus the Lord, so walk ye in him: . . . . For in him dwelleth all the fulness of the Godhead bodily. And ye are complete in him, which is the head of all principality and power (Col. 2:10).

Be not unequally yoked together with unbelievers: for what fellowship hath righteousness with unrighteousness? And what communion hath light with darkness (2 Cor. 6:14)?

Be sober, be vigilant; because your adversary the devil, as a roaring lion, walketh about, seeking whom he may devour. Whom resist stedfast in the faith, knowing that the same afflictions are accomplished in your brethren that are in the world. But the God of all grace, who hath called us into his eternal glory by Christ Jesus, after that you have suffered a while, make you perfect, stablish, strengthen, settle you (2 Pet. 5:8-10).

Pray without ceasing. In every thing give thanks; for this is the will of God in Christ Jesus concerning you. . . . Prove all things; hold fast that which is good. Abstain from all appearance of evil. And the very God of peace sanctify you wholly; and I pray God your whole spirit and soul and body be preserved blameless unto the coming of our Lord Jesus Christ (1 Thess. 5:17-18, 21-23).

We will close with some words about Dr. Bob–and then a question:

> Prayer, of course, was an important part of Dr. Bob's faith.
> According to Paul S., "Dr. Bob's morning devotion consisted
> of a short prayer, a 20 minutes study of a familiar verse from
> the Bible, and a quiet period of waiting for directions as to
> where he, that day, should find use for his talent. Having heard,
> he would religiously go about his Father's business, as he put
> it." (*DR. BOB and the Good Oldtimers*, p. 314).

[The following is from an interview of Dorothy S.M. by Bill Wilson
on August 30, 1954]

> DOROTHY: Did you know that he [Dr. Bob] prayed three
> times a day regularly?
> BILL WILSON: He [Dr. Bob] went up to his room three times
> a day on the hour. I think it was about 9, 11, and 4, as I recall,
> that he prayed not only for his own understanding but for
> different groups of people who requested him to pray for them.
> I was always glad that I was included in those prayers (Dick B.,
> *The Akron Genesis of Alcoholics Anonymous*, p. 204).

Was Dr. Bob wrong in any of these situations when he said: "Your
Heavenly Father will never let you down!" The Good Book offers
these confirmations:

> I sought the LORD [Yahweh], and he heard me, and delivered
> me from all my fears (Ps. 34:4).

> This poor man cried, and the LORD [Yahweh] heard him, and
> saved *him* out of all his troubles (Ps. 34:6)

> The angel of the LORD [Yahweh] encampeth round about them
> that fear him, and delivereth them (Ps. 34:7).

O taste and see that the LORD [Yahweh] *is* good: blessed *is* the man *that* trusteth in him (Ps. 34:8).

The righteous cry, and the LORD [Yahweh] heareth, and delivereth them out of all their troubles (Ps. 34:17).

Many *are* the afflictions of the righteous: but the LORD [Yahweh] delivereth him out of them all.
He keepeth all his bones: not one of them is broken (Ps. 34:19-20).

The LORD [Yahweh] redeemeth the soul of his servants: and none of them that trust in him shall be desolate (Ps. 34:22),

. . . for he hath said, I will never leave thee, nor forsake thee. So that we may boldly say, The Lord *is* my helper, and I will not fear what man shall do unto me (Heb. 13:5-6).

Sound like what Dr. Bob had to say? Well he read and believed the Good Book; and why not you!

8

Release from Your Prisons

Verily, verily, I say unto you, He that believeth on me, the
works that I do shall he do also; and greater works than these
shall he do; because I go unto my Father.
And whatsoever ye shall ask in my name, that will I do, that the
Father may be glorified in the Son (John 14:12-13).

Then Jesus said to those Jews which believed on him, If ye
continue in my word, *then* are ye my disciples indeed;
and ye shall know the truth, and the truth shall make you free.
If the Son therefore shall make you free, ye shall be free indeed
(John 8:31-32, 36).

Giving thanks unto the Father, which hath made us meet to be
partakers of the inheritance of the saints in light:
Who hath delivered us from the power of darkness, and hath
translated us into the kingdom of his dear Son (Col. 1:12, 13).

The author is indebted to a wonderful Bible teacher for the
deliverance he received in very early sobriety. He was delivered
from endless and seemingly unbearable fears, anxieties,
hopelessness, despair, and very real problems. The following is a
quote from that teacher's writings–an inspirational passage that
started the author on his way to victory:

153

God's will is for every one of us to be released today from
whatever prison is holding us. Prisons are not only made of bars
of steel. The prisons of our secret sins, things in our lives which
we don't want to share with any other person in the world, are
the most frustrating and defeating. The thoughts of self-
condemnation that have been gnawing in the back of one's
conscious and subconscious mind for years and years–thoughts
of sickness and disease, fear, worry, anxiety, suicide, death–are
the most tormenting and wretched kinds of prisons. It is not
God's will for us to be so mentally bound: God's will is just the
opposite as He has given total release from all negatives. . . . It
is the will of God that all self-condemnation be gone because He
wants to make us free indeed–not just half-free, but a wholly-
free person. Not only does God want us free of all the secret
condemnation but He wants us to be free from all the powers of
darkness in this world.

For personal reasons and reasons of anonymity, the author of the
foregoing passage will not be named. But this author (the author of
this present guide) was liberated by the foregoing truths once he
investigated their veracity in the Bible and discovered the "how."
Since those early days of sobriety, the author has also been able to
help many self-condemning alcoholics and addicts overcome prisons
that have been far more defeating than any of their sojourns in jails,
prisons, and other detention facilities.

First, about God's Will

There is not much point in believing God will do something if God
has not declared it to be available. For some of His general
promises as to what He has made available, we do not have to look
far. The author has believed the following assurances, tried to keep
them solidly in his mind for many years now, and reaped the
benefits of seeing God make good on that which He says He can and
will do.

Power Available to Believers:

And when he had called unto him his twelve disciples, he gave
them power against unclean spirits, to cast them out, and to heal
all manner of sickness and all manner of disease.
Heal the sick, cleanse the lepers, raise the dead, cast out devils:
freely ye have received, freely give (Matt. 10:1, 8).

After these things the Lord appointed other seventy also and
sent them two and two before his face into every city and place,
whither he himself would come.
And heal the sick that are therein, and say unto them, The
kingdom of God is come nigh unto you.
Behold, I give unto you power to tread on serpents and
scorpions, and over all the power of the enemy: and nothing
shall by any means hurt you (Luke 10:1, 9, 19).

And, behold, I send the promise of my Father upon you: but
tarry ye in the city of Jerusalem, until ye be endued with power
from on high (Luke 24:49).

Verily, verily, I say unto you, He that believeth on me, the
works that I do shall he do also; and greater *works* than these
shall he do; because I go unto my Father.
And whatsoever ye shall ask in my name, that will I do, that the
Father may be glorified in the Son (John 14:12-13).

And he [Jesus] said unto them, Go ye into all the world, and
preach the gospel to every Creature.
He that believeth and is baptized shall be saved; but he that
believeth not shall be damned.
And these signs shall follow them that believe; In my name shall
they cast out devils; they shall speak with new tongues.
They shall take up serpents; and if they drink any deadly thing,
it shall not hurt them; they shall lay hands on the sick, and they
shall recover (Mark 16:15-18).

But ye shall receive power after that the Holy Ghost is come
upon you. . . (Acts 1:8).

Above All They Can Ask or Think

And God *is* able to make all grace abound toward you; that *ye,*
always having all sufficiency in all *things*, may abound to every
good work (2 Cor. 9:8).

Now unto him that is able to do exceeding abundantly above all
that we ask or think, according to the power that worketh in us
(Eph. 3:20).

Forgiveness, Healing, Deliverance

Bless the LORD [Yahweh], O my soul, and forget not all his
benefits:
Who forgiveth all thine iniquities; who healeth all thy diseases;
Who redeemeth thy life from destruction: who crowneth thee
with loving kindness and tender mercies (Ps. 103:2-4).

Grace and peace be multiplied unto you through the knowledge
of God, and of Jesus our Lord,
According as his divine power hath given unto us all things that
pertain unto life and godliness, through the knowledge of him
that hath called us to glory and virtue:
Whereby are given unto us exceeding great and previous
promises: that by these ye might be partakers of the divine
nature, having escaped the corruption that is in the world
through lust (2 Pet. 1:2-4).

Who his own self bare our sins in his own body on the tree, that
we, being dead to sins, should live unto righteousness: by
whose stripes ye were healed (1 Pet. 2:24).

For all have sinned, and come short of the glory of God;
Being justified freely by his grace through the redemption that is in Christ Jesus (Rom. 3:23-24).

And hope maketh not ashamed; because the love of God is shed abroad in our hearts by the Holy Ghost which is given unto us.
For when we were yet without strength, in due time Christ died for the ungodly.
But God commendeth his love toward us in that, while we were yet sinners, Christ died for us (Rom. 5:5-6, 8).

There is therefore no condemnation to them which are in Christ Jesus. . . (Rom. 8:1).

Grace *be* to you and peace from God the Father, and *from* our Lord Jesus Christ,
Who gave himself for our sins, that he might deliver us from this present evil world, according to the will of God and our Father (Gal. 1:3-4).

Giving thanks unto the Father, which hath made us meet to be partakers of the inheritance of the saints in light:
Who hath delivered us from the power of darkness, and hath translated *us* into the kingdom of his dear Son (Col. 1:12-13).

But the manifestation of the Spirit is given to every man to profit withal.
For to one is given by the Spirit the word of wisdom; to another the word of knowledge by the same Spirit.
To another faith by the same Spirit; to another the gifts of healing by the same Spirit;
To another, the working of miracles; to another prophecy; to another discerning of spirits; to another *divers* kinds of tongues; to another the interpretation of tongues.
But all these worketh that one and selfsame Spirit, dividing to every man severally as he will (1 Cor. 12:7-11).

Believing in Order to Receive:

> And all things, whatsoever ye shall ask in prayer, believing, ye shall receive (Matt. 21:22).

> For unto us was the gospel preached, as well as unto them; but the word preached did not profit them, not being mixed with faith in them that heard *it* (Heb. 4:2).

> If any of you lack wisdom, let him ask of God, that giveth to all *men* liberally, and upbraideth not; and it shall be given him.
> But let him ask in faith, nothing wavering. For he that wavereth is like a wave of the sea driven with the wind and tossed.
> For let not that man think he shall receive anything of the Lord (James 1:5-7).

> And this is the confidence that we have in him, that, if we ask anything according to his will, he heareth us:
> And if we know that he hear us, whatsoever we ask, we know that we have the petitions that we desired of him (1 John 5:14-15).

> For this cause also thank we God without ceasing, because, when ye received the word of God which ye heard of us, ye received it not *as* the word of men, but as it is in truth, the word of God, which effectually worketh also in you that believe (1 Thess. 2:13).

The Release Available

Release from Fear

> Notice that the word "fear" is bracketed. . . . This short word somehow touches about every   aspect of our lives. It was an evil and corroding thread: the fabric of our existence was shot through with it *(Alcoholics Anonymous*, 3rd ed., p. 67).

The fear of man bringeth a snare: but whoso putteth his trust in the LORD [Yahweh] shall be safe (Prov. 29:25).

For God hath not given us the spirit of fear; but of power, and of love, and of a sound mind (2 Tim. 1:7).

Believers receive the power, need to know God promises safety, and need to know God makes good on His promises when His promises are believed.

He [Abraham] staggered not at the promise of God through unbelief; but was strong in faith, giving glory to God.
And being fully persuaded that, what he [God] had promised, he was able to perform (Rom. 4:20-21).

Release from Guilt

With increasing guilt and never ending depression, I was too weak to continue this day-by-day suicide (*Alcoholics Anonymous*, 3ʳᵈ ed., p. 355).

Incalculable are the intangible initiation fees that A.A. members have paid: the sick, sick hangovers, the remorse, guilt, broken homes, jails, and institutions, and the mental anguish in general that has been generated over the years (*Alcoholics Anonymous*, 3ʳᵈ ed., p. 399).

Who shall lay anything to the charge of God's elect? *It is* God that justifieth (Rom. 8:33).

The same formula applies. Do we believe what our minds, the world, or the devil hand out in accusations and guilt; or do we believe what God says:

There is therefore now no condemnation to them which are in Christ Jesus. . . (Rom. 8:1).

Release from Anxiety

Same formula:

> Be careful for [or "anxious about"] nothing; but in every thing
> by prayer and supplication with thanksgiving let your requests
> be made known unto God.
> And the peace of God, which passeth all understanding, shall
> keep your hearts and minds through Christ Jesus (Phil. 4:6-7).
>
> But seek ye first the kingdom of God, and his righteousness;
> and all these things shall be added unto you (Matt. 6:33).

Do we believe, "But my God shall supply all your need according
to his riches in glory by Christ Jesus" (Phil. 4:19)? Or don't we!

Release from Cares:

> Casting all your care upon him; for he careth for you (1 Pet.
> 5:7).

Will you, or won't you. Does He, or doesn't He!

Release from Shame

> According as he hath chosen us in him before the foundation of
> the world, that we should be holy and without blame before him
> in love (Eph. 1:4).

Did He, or didn't He!

Release from Insecurity

> Fear of people and of economic insecurity will leave us
> (*Alcoholics Anonymous*, 3rd ed., p. 84).

How about the real thing:

> But seek ye first the kingdom of God, and his righteousness; and all these things [food, clothing, shelter] shall be added unto you (Matt. 6:33).

Will they, or won't they!

Release from Poverty

> But thou shalt remember the LORD [Yahweh] thy God: for it is he that giveth thee power to get wealth, . . . (Deut. 8:18a)

> The blessing of the LORD [Yahweh], it maketh rich, and he addeth no sorrow with it (Prov. 10:22)

> But my God shall supply all your need according to his riches in glory by Christ Jesus (Phil. 4:19)

> Beloved, I wish above all things that thou mayest prosper and be in health, even as thy soul prospereth (3 John 2)

Here's how much Anne Smith thought of the last verse above:

> Read further in John III:2 [she meant 3 John 2]–Beloved I wish above all things that thou mayest prosper and be in health even as thy soul prospereth. . . . Imagine the President speaking over a nation-wide hookup saying: My fellow citizens, my best wish for you is that your material prosperity and your physical health may be just in proportion to your spiritual well-being (Dick B., *Anne Smith's Journal*, 3rd ed., p. 71).

Release from Confusion

For God is not the author of confusion, but of peace, as in all churches of the saints (1 Cor. 14:33)

And the very God of peace sanctify you wholly; and I pray God your whole spirit and soul and body be preserved blameless unto the coming of our Lord Jesus Christ (1 Thess. 5:23)

And let the peace of God rule in your hearts, to the which also ye are called in one body; and be ye thankful (Col. 3:15)

Thou wilt keep *him* in perfect peace, *whose* mind is stayed on *thee*: because he trusteth in thee (Isa. 26:3)

Will He, or won't He!

Release from Weakness

Finally, my brethren, be strong in the Lord, and in the power of his might (Eph. 6:10)

I can do all things through Christ which strengtheneth me (Phil. 4:13)

But we had the sentence of death in ourselves, that we should not trust in ourselves, but in God which raiseth the dead:
Who delivered us from so great a death, and doth deliver: in whom we trust that he will yet deliver us (2 Cor. 1:9-10)

And such trust have we through Christ to God-ward:
Not that we are sufficient of ourselves to think any thing as of ourselves; but our sufficiency is of God;
Who also hath made us able ministers of the new testament; not of the letter, but of the spirit: for the letter killeth, but the spirit giveth life (2 Cor. 3:4-6)

For which cause we faint not; but though our outward man perish, yet the inward man is renewed day by day (2 Cor. 4:16)

I can do all things through Christ which strengtheneth me (Phil. 4:13)

Can we, or can't we!

Release from Doubt

In thinking about our day we may face indecision. We may not be able to determine which course to take. Here we ask God for inspiration, an intuitive thought or a decision. We relax and take it easy. We don't struggle. We are often surprised how the right answers come after we have tried this for a while (*Alcoholics Anonymous*, 3rd ed., p. 86).

The following verses of scripture profitably may be compared with the quotation above:

Commit thy works unto the LORD [Yahweh], and thy thoughts shall be established (Proverbs 16:3)

A man's heart deviseth his way: but the LORD [Yahweh] directeth his steps (Proverbs 16:9)

There is a way that seemeth right unto a man, but the end thereof are the ways of death (Proverbs 16:25)

For we walk by faith, not by sight (2 Cor. 5:7)

If any of you lack wisdom, let him ask of God, that giveth to all men liberally, and upbraideth not; and it shall be given him. But let him ask in faith, nothing wavering. For he that wavereth is like a wave of the sea driven with the wind and tossed.

For let not that man think that he shall receive any thing of the Lord.
A double minded man is unstable in all his ways (James 1:5-8)

Trust in the LORD [Yahweh] with all thine heart; and lean not unto thine own understanding.
In all thy ways acknowledge him, and he shall direct thy paths (Prov. 3:5-6)

Which would you prefer: the intuitive thought and surprise, or the absolute promise in Proverbs 3:5-6? Acknowledge God in all your ways, and He SHALL direct thy paths! Not merely surprise you.

Release from Temptation

There hath no temptation taken you but such as is common to man: but God is faithful, who will not suffer you to be tempted above that ye are able; but will with the temptation also make a way to escape, that ye may be able to bear it (1 Cor. 10:13)

Blessed is the man that endureth temptation: for when he is tried, he shall receive the crown of life, which the Lord hath promised to them that love him.
Let no man say when he is tempted, I am tempted of God: for God cannot be tempted with evil, neither tempteth he any man:
But every man is tempted, when he is drawn away of his own lust, and enticed.
Then when lust hath conceived, it bringeth forth sin: and sin, when it is finished, bringeth forth death.
Do not err, my beloved brethren.
Every good gift and every perfect gift is from above, and cometh down from the Father of lights, with whom is no variableness, neither shadow of turning.
Of his own will begat he us with the word of truth, that we should be a kind of firstfruits of his creatures.

Wherefore, my beloved brethren, let every man be swift to hear, slow to speak, slow to wrath:
For the wrath of man worketh not the righteousness of God.
Wherefore lay apart all filthiness and superfluity of naughtiness, and receive with meekness the engrafted word, which is able to save your souls.
But be ye doers of the word, and not hearers only, deceiving your own selves (James 1:12-22)

God will make a way to escape!

Release from Sickness

And said, If thou wilt diligently hearken to the voice of the LORD [Yahweh] thy God, and wilt do that which is right in his sight, and wilt give ear to his commandments, and keep all his statutes, I will put none of these diseases upon thee, which I have brought upon the Egyptians: for I am the LORD [Yahweh] that healeth thee (Exod. 15:26).

How God anointed Jesus of Nazareth with the Holy Ghost and with power: who went about doing good, and healing all that were oppressed of the devil; for God was with him (Acts 10:38).

For he that eateth and drinketh unworthily, eateth and drinketh damnation to himself, not discerning the Lord's body.
For this cause many *are* weak and sickly among you, and many sleep (1 Cor. 11:29-30).

What about the believers who received the gift of Holy Spirit and went about healing and can still go about healing because God is with them!

Release from Evil Spirits

> And these signs shall follow them that believe; In my name shall they cast out devils; they shall speak with new tongues (Mark 16:17)

> There came also a multitude *out of* the cities round about unto Jerusalem, bringing sick folks, and them which were vexed with unclean spirits: and they were healed every one (Acts 5:16).

Were they, or weren't they!

> And the people with one accord gave heed unto those things which Philip spake, hearing and seeing the miracles which he did.
> For unclean spirits, crying with loud voice, came out of many that were possessed with them: and many taken with palsies, and that were lame, were healed (Acts 8:6-7).

> So that from his body were brought unto the sick handkerchiefs or aprons, and the diseases departed from them, and the evil spirits went out of them (Acts 19:12).

Release from the Devil's Fiery Darts

> Finally, my brethren, be strong in the Lord, and in the power of his might.
> Put on the whole armour of God, that ye may be able to stand against the wiles of the devil.
> For we wrestle not against flesh and blood, but against principalities, against powers, against the rulers of the darkness of this world, against spiritual wickedness in high places.
> Wherefore take unto you the whole armour of God, that ye may be able to withstand in the evil day, and having done all, to stand.

Stand therefore, having your loins girt about with truth, and having on the breastplate of righteousness;
And your feet shod with the preparation of the gospel of peace;
Above all, taking the shield of faith, wherewith ye shall be able to quench all the fiery darts of the wicked.
And take the helmet of salvation, and the sword of the Spirit, which is the word of God:
Praying always with all prayer and supplication in the Spirit, and watching thereunto with all perseverance and supplication for all saints; (Eph. 6:10-18)

Submit yourselves therefore to God. Resist the devil, and he will flee from you (James 4:7)

Be sober, be vigilant; because your adversary the devil, as a roaring lion, walketh about, seeking whom he may devour:
Whom resist stedfast in the faith, knowing that the same afflictions are accomplished in your brethren that are in the world.
But the God of all grace, who hath called us unto his eternal glory by Christ Jesus, after that ye have suffered a while, make you perfect, stablish, strengthen, settle you (1 Pet. 5:8-10)

We know that whosoever is born of God sinneth not; but he that is begotten of God keepeth himself, and that wicked one toucheth him not (1 John 5:18).

Can we "Put on the whole armour of God, that ye [we] may be able to stand against the wiles of the devil" (Eph. 6:11)? Or are we helpless and without strength, power, and armour? Try believing Eph. 6:10-11! Ask the question Dr. Bob asked, "What does the Good Book say?"

Release from Oppression by the Devil

> How God anointed Jesus of Nazareth with the Holy Ghost and
> with power: who went about doing good, and healing all that
> were oppressed of the devil: for God was with him (Acts
> 10:38).

Believers are "anointed" with the same gift of Holy Spirit and with
power when they confess Jesus as their Lord and believe that God
raised Jesus from the dead.

> That if thou shalt confess with thy mouth the Lord Jesus, and
> shalt believe in thine heart that God hath raised him from the
> dead, thou shalt be saved.
> For with the heart man believeth unto righteousness; and with
> the mouth confession is made unto salvation (Rom. 10:9, 10)

> In whom [Christ-verse 12] ye also trusted, after that ye heard
> the word of truth, the gospel of your salvation: in whom also
> after that ye believed, ye were sealed with that holy Spirit of
> promise (Eph. 1:13)

> Now he which stablisheth us with you in Christ, and hath
> anointed us, is God (2 Cor. 1:21)

> But the anointing which ye have received of him abideth in you,
> . . . (1 John 2:27a)

And they can be healed if they are oppressed, for God is with them.

Everlasting Release

> For God so loved the world, that he gave his only begotten Son,
> that whosoever believeth in him should not perish, but have
> everlasting life (John 3:16)

Jesus said unto her, I am the resurrection, and the life: he that
believeth in me, though he were dead, yet shall he live:
And whosoever liveth and believeth in me shall never die.
Believest thou this? (John 11:25-26)

But I would not have you to be ignorant, brethren, concerning
them which are asleep, that ye sorrow not, even as others which
have no hope.
For if we believe that Jesus died and rose again, even so them
also which sleep in Jesus will God bring with him.
For this we say unto you by the word of the Lord, that we
which are alive and remain unto the coming of the Lord shall
not prevent them which are asleep.
For the Lord himself shall descend from heaven with a shout,
with the voice of the archangel, and with the trump of God: and
the dead in Christ shall rise first:
Then we which are alive and remain shall be caught up together
with them in the clouds, to meet the Lord in the air: and so shall
we ever be with the Lord.
Wherefore comfort one another with these words (1 Thess.
4:13-18)

Now our Lord Jesus Christ himself, and God, even our Father,
which hath loved us, and hath given us everlasting consolation
and good hope through grace,
Comfort your hearts, and stablish you in every good word and
work (2 Thess. 2:16-17)

Free indeed!

Then said Jesus to those Jews which believed on him, If ye
continue in my word, then are ye my disciples indeed;
And ye shall know the truth, and the truth shall make you free
If the Son therefore shall make you free, ye shall be free indeed
(John 8:31, 32, 36)

The author of this guidebook has applied, watched his family apply, and watched his sponsees in A.A. apply, the foregoing principles: Look for the promise. Believe God can perform that which He has promised. Walk according to His Word. See God make good. These applications have not been matters of speculation. They have rested on an assured belief. Action is required: Finding the promises, making the choice, believing what God says, having fellowship with Him, and then receiving the benefits require effort. You can *rely* on God! The Good Book says so:

> Bless the LORD [Yahweh], O my soul: and all that is within me, bless his holy name.
> Bless the LORD [Yahweh], O my soul, and forget not all his benefits:
> Who forgiveth all thine iniquities; who healeth all thy diseases;
> Who redeemeth thy life from destruction; who crowneth thee with lovingkindness and tender mercies;
> Who satisfieth thy mouth with good things; so that thy youth is renewed like the eagle's.
> The LORD [Yahweh] executeth righteousness and judgment for all that are oppressed (Ps. 103:1-6)

Yes, He does! And those who wish to study, believe, and obey God's Word have an opportunity to receive the results. The author believes firmly that this is the reason A.A.'s Big Book reassures alcoholics that "God could and would if He were sought."

9

More to Learn

And the brethren immediately sent away Paul and Silas by night
into Berea: who coming thither went into the synagogue of the
Jews.
These were more noble than those in Thessalonica, in that they
received the word with all readiness of mind, and searched the
scriptures daily, whether those things were so.
Therefore many of them believed; also of honorable women
which were Greeks, and of men, not a few (Acts 17:10-12).

There is no thought here of trying to cover all the important topics
in the Bible, either in terms of what A.A. pioneers read, or in terms
of what can be of value today. Dr. Bob read on Bible topics for an
hour every day; and that was after intense training in the Bible as a
youngster and also after having read the Bible in its entirety three
different times in his early Oxford Group days. Anne Smith
recommended reading the Bible every day, and she did so with early
AAs at the Smith home.

Anne in her journal and the later Big Book both spoke
approvingly of further reading which could be as recommended by
clergy or church. Today, the information age has made much much
more available. It has also made information and instruction much
easier to reach.

Many churches have Bible study. There are many Bible study groups. There are many Bible study fellowships, and the author belongs to one. There are a good many books on how to study the Bible. There are still the daily Bible devotionals which offer a verse and further reading for every day of the year. There are wonderful Bible audio-cassette tapes where the entire Bible can be heard. The Bible, in varied versions, can now be seen on the internet. The author's website is linked to several of these for the convenience of surfers. And there are some new video-tape Bible presentations available. Of course, there are endless books of yesteryear and today that cover every facet of the Bible, from Old to New Testament, and on topics such as the prophets, Psalms, Proverbs, the Pentateuch, the Gospels, the church epistles, and Revelation.

Teachers and tools are available: a good Concordance to locate verses and subjects; a good Concordance and lexicon and interlinear to enable study of the underlying Greek and Hebrew words in the earlier texts.

But we have listed here some topics, with a verse or two, that are critical in using the Bible for the purposes it was used in early A.A. and can be used today. Here are a few:

Praying and Prayers

Alcoholics Anonymous, 3rd ed., says the following at pp. 85-86:

> We shouldn't be shy on this matter of prayer. Better men than we are using it constantly. It works, if we have the proper attitude and work at it.

The Good Book offers very specific information on the matter of prayer.

Confess Your Sins to God to Receive His Forgiveness

If we confess our sins, he is faithful and just to forgive us our sins, and to cleanse us from all unrighteousness (1 John 1:9)

He that covereth his sins shall not prosper: but whoso confesseth and forsaketh them shall have mercy (Prov. 28:13)

Ask God for Things in the Name of Jesus Christ

. . . Verily, verily, I say unto you, Whatsoever ye shall ask the Father in my name, he will give it you.
Hitherto have ye asked nothing in my name: ask, and ye shall receive, that your joy may be full (John 16:23b, 24)

Ask God to Supply Your Need

Be careful for [anxious about] nothing; but in every thing by prayer and supplication with thanksgiving let your requests be made known unto God.
And the peace of God, which passeth all understanding, shall keep your hearts and minds through Christ Jesus (Phil. 4:6-7)

And this is the confidence that we have in him, that, if we ask any thing according to his will, he heareth us:
And if we know that he hear us, whatsoever we ask, we know that we have the petitions that we desired of him (1 John 5:14-15)

Thank God for What He Has Done for You

Giving thanks always for all things unto God and the Father in the name of our Lord Jesus Christ (Eph. 5:20)

Continue in prayer, and watch in the same with thanksgiving (Col. 4:2)

In every thing give thanks: for this is the will of God in Christ Jesus concerning you (1 Thess. 5:18)

Praise God for What He Has Done

Praise ye the LORD [*YH,* Yah]. O give thanks unto the LORD [*YHWH,* Yahweh]; for he is good: for his mercy endureth for ever (Ps. 106:1)

"Praise ye the LORD" in the Hebrew text of Ps. 106:1 is *Hallelu Yah.*

Oh that men would praise the LORD [Yahweh] for his goodness, and for his wonderful works to the children of men! (Ps. 107:15)

I will worship toward thy holy temple, and praise thy name for thy lovingkindness and for thy truth: for thou hast magnified thy word above all thy name (Ps. 138:2)

Pray in the Spirit

Likewise the Spirit also helpeth our infirmities: for we know not what we should pray for as we ought: but the Spirit itself maketh intercession for us with groanings which cannot be uttered (Romans 8:26)

For if I pray in an unknown tongue, my spirit prayeth, but my understanding is unfruitful.
What is it then? I will pray with the spirit, and I will pray with the understanding also: I will sing with the spirit, and I will sing with the understanding also (1 Corinthians 14:14, 15)

Praying always with all prayer and supplication in the Spirit, and watching thereunto with all perseverance and supplication for all saints (Ephesians 6:18)

Seek God When You Need Healing

[You, Isaiah,] Turn again, and tell Hezekiah the captain of my people, Thus saith the LORD [Yahweh], the God of David thy father, I have heard thy prayer, I have seen thy tears: behold, I will heal thee: on the third day thou shalt go up unto the house of the LORD [Yahweh] (2 Kings 20:5)

Have mercy upon me, O LORD [Yahweh]; for I am weak: O LORD [Yahweh], heal me; for my bones are vexed (Ps. 6:2)

O LORD [Yahweh] my God, I cried unto thee, and thou hast healed me (Ps. 30:2)

Bless the LORD [Yahweh], O my soul, and forget not all his benefits:
Who forgiveth all thine iniquities; who healeth all thy diseases (Ps. 103:2,3)

Seek God for Deliverance

I sought the LORD [Yahweh], and he heard me, and delivered me from all my fears (Ps. 34:4)

God is our refuge and strength, a very present help in trouble (Ps. 46:1)

In God is my salvation and my glory: the rock of my strength, and my refuge, is in God.
Trust in him at all times; ye people, pour out your heart before him: God is a refuge for us. Selah (Ps. 62:7-8)

In thee, O LORD [Yahweh], do I put my trust: let me never be put to confusion.
Deliver me in thy righteousness, and cause me to escape: incline thine ear unto me, and save me (Ps. 71:1-2)

Who redeemeth thy life from destruction; who crowneth thee
with lovingkindness and tender mercies (Ps. 103:4)

Then they cry unto the LORD [Yahweh] in their trouble, and he
saveth them out of their distresses.
He sent his word, and healed them, and delivered them from
their destructions (Ps. 107:19-20)

Deliver me, O LORD [Yahweh], from the evil man: preserve
me from the violent man (Ps. 140:1)

Seek God for Guidance

Trust in the LORD [Yahweh] with all thine heart; and lean not
unto thine own understanding.
In all thy ways acknowledge him, and he shall direct thy paths
(Prov. 3:5-6)

If any of you lack wisdom, let him ask of God, that giveth to all
men liberally, and upbraideth not; and it shall be given him
(James 1:5)

Pray to God for Others As God Directs

So Abraham prayed unto God: and God healed Abimelech, and
his wife, and his maidservants; and they bare children (Gen.
20:17)

For a multitude of the people, even many of Ephraim, and
Manasseh, Issachar, and Zebulun, had not cleansed themselves,
yet did they eat the passover otherwise than it was written. But
Hezekiah prayed for them, saying, The good LORD [Yahweh]
pardon every one
That prepareth his heart to seek God, the LORD [Yahweh] God
of his fathers, though he be not cleansed according to the
purification of the sanctuary.

And the LORD [Yahweh] hearkened to Hezekiah, and healed the people (2 Chron. 30:18-20)

And these signs shall follow them that believe; In my name shall they cast out devils; they shall speak with new tongues; They shall take up serpents; and if they drink any deadly thing, it shall not hurt them; they shall lay hands on the sick, and they shall recover (Mark 16:17-18)

Is any sick among you? let him call for the elders of the church; and let them pray over him, anointing him with oil in the name of the Lord:
And the prayer of faith shall save the sick, and the Lord shall raise him up; and if he have committed sins, they shall be forgiven him.
Confess your faults one to another, and pray one for another, that ye may be healed. The effectual fervent prayer of a righteous man availeth much (James 5:14-16)

Cast out Evil Spirits in the Name of Jesus Christ As God Directs

When the even was come, they brought unto him [Jesus] many that were possessed with devils: and he cast out the spirits with his word, and healed all that were sick (Matt. 8:16)

And when he [Jesus] had called unto him his twelve disciples, he gave them power against unclean spirits, to cast them out, and to heal all manner of sickness and all manner of disease (Matt. 10:1)

And the seventy returned again with joy, saying, Lord, even the devils are subject unto us through thy name.
And he [Jesus] said unto them, I beheld Satan as lightning fall from heaven.

Behold, I give ["have given"–NASV] unto you power to tread on serpents and scorpions, and over all the power of the enemy: and nothing shall by any means hurt you
Notwithstanding in this rejoice not, that the spirits are subject unto you; but rather rejoice, because your names are written in heaven (Luke 10:17-20)

And these signs shall follow them that believe; In my name shall they cast out devils; they shall speak with new tongues (Mark 16:17)

And it came to pass, as we went to prayer, a certain damsel possessed with a spirit of divination met us, which brought her masters much gain by soothsaying:
The same followed Paul and us, and cried, saying, These men are the servants of the most high God, which shew unto us the way of salvation.
And this did she many days. But Paul, being grieved, turned and said to the spirit, I command thee in the name of Jesus Christ to come out of her. And he came out the same hour (Acts 16:16-18)

Renewing Your Mind to God's Word

What you put in your mind; what you believe in your heart; and what you confess with your mouth are vital matters in establishing fellowship and victory with God.

Finally, brethren, whatsoever things are true, whatsoever things are honest, whatsoever things are just, whatsoever things are pure, whatsoever things are lovely, whatsoever things are of good report; if there be any virtue, and if there be any praise, think on these things (Phil. 4:8)

Keep thy heart with all diligence; for out of it are the issues of life (Prov. 4:23)

Not that which goeth into the mouth defileth a man; but that which cometh out of the mouth, this defileth a man (Matt. 15:11)

Much of the fatalism today comes from a lack of understanding of the Bible's statements about the renewed mind. Man needs to have the power of God that comes with the gift of the Holy Spirit. God says something. Man needs to learn it. Man needs to put God's words in his mind. Man needs to believe those words, hold them in his mind, and act accordingly. God makes good on what He says. Many of the following verses were known, mentioned, and studied in early A.A. They have to do with renewing the mind:

And be not conformed to this world: but be ye transformed by the renewing of your mind, that ye may prove what *is* that good, and acceptable, and perfect, will of God (Rom. 12:2).

For who hath known the mind of the Lord, that he may instruct him? But we have the mind of Christ (1 Cor. 2:16).

For which cause we faint not; but though our outward man perish, yet the inward *man* is renewed day by day.
While we look not at the things which are seen, but at the things which are not seen: for the things which *are* seen are temporal, but the things which are not seen *are* eternal (2 Cor. 4:16, 18).

Casting down imaginations, and every high thing that exalteth itself against the knowledge of God, and bringing into captivity every thought to the obedience of Christ (2 Cor. 10:5).

If so be that ye have heard him, and have been taught by him, as the truth is in Jesus
That ye put off concerning the former conversation the old man, which is corrupt according to the deceitful lusts;
And be renewed in the spirit of your mind;

And that ye put on the new man, which after God is created in righteousness and true holiness (Eph. 4:21-24).

Let this mind be in you, which also was in Christ Jesus (Phil. 2:5).

If ye then be risen with Christ, seek those things which are above, where Christ sitteth on the right hand of God. Set your affections on things above, not on things on the earth.
Lie not one to another, seeing that ye have put off the old man with his deeds; And have put on the new *man*, which is renewed in knowledge after the image of him that created him (Col. 3:1-2, 9-10).

Manifesting the Gift of the Holy Spirit

Much of importance to Christians occurred and began on the day of Pentecost described in Acts chapter 2. That event is often called the birth of the Christian Church. For it was then that the accomplishments of Jesus Christ were made available to all who believed on him. Jesus had promised that believers could do the things he had done, and more, because he was going to his Father. He promised the baptism of the Holy Spirit which would make the power available. And on the day of Pentecost, the power became available to both Jew and Gentile–though the proof of the latter was to await some of the other happenings described in the Book of Acts.

Take 1 Corinthians chapters 12-14 as your starting point and as an interrelated group of chapters. Then begin your study of the important topic of the manifestations of the gift of Holy Spirit:

- Speaking with (or "in") tongues
- Interpretation of tongues
- Prophecy
- Word of knowledge

- Word of wisdom
- Discerning of spirits
- Faith
- Workings of Miracles
- Gifts of Healings

No believer should be without knowledge of these nine manifestations of the gift of the Holy Spirit and of their purposes.

Some believe that these manifestations of the gift of the Holy Spirit are not available at all today. Others believe that only some are available to only some. The author believes that a prayerful, careful, and ongoing study of the Word of God will make plain that all Christian believers can manifest the gift of the Holy Spirit in all nine of the ways listed in 1 Corinthians 12:8-12 if they know that it is available for them to do so and if they really want to; and that has been his experience.

Resisting the Devil

Bill Wilson made an observation which, whether seriously believed or not, provides important insight into his spiritual plight:

> If there was a Devil, he seemed the Boss Universal, and he certainly had me (*Alcoholics Anonymous*, 3rd ed., p. 11).

It is very clear from the writings of Rev. Sam Shoemaker that Sam believed in, wrote about, and explained the spiritual battle and how to win it. Sam's book *God Control* is particularly eloquent on the subject. Anne Smith recognized the Devil as her Adversary. And the important point here is that the Bible sets forth the armor needed to win the fight.

> Finally, my brethren, be strong in the Lord, and in the power of his might.

Put on the whole armour of God, that ye may be able to stand against the wiles of the devil.

For we wrestle not against flesh and blood, but against principalities, against powers, against the rulers of the darkness of this world, against spiritual wickedness in high places.

Wherefore take unto you the whole armour of God, that ye may be able to withstand in the evil day, and having done all, to stand.

Stand therefore, having your loins girt about with truth, and having on the breastplate of righteousness;

And your feet shod with the preparation of the gospel of peace;

Above all, taking the shield of faith, wherewith ye shall be able to quench all the fiery darts of the wicked.

And take the helmet of salvation, and the sword of the Spirit, which is the word of God:

Praying always with all prayer and supplication in the Spirit, and watching thereunto with all perseverance and supplication for all saints (Ephesians 6:10-18)

Who [the Father] hath delivered us from the power of darkness, and hath translated *us* into the kingdom of his dear Son (Col. 1:13).

Submit yourselves therefore to God. Resist the devil, and he will flee from you (James 4:7).

Be sober, be vigilant: because your adversary the devil, as a roaring lion, walketh about, seeking whom he may devour. Whom resist stedfast in the faith, knowing that the same afflictions are accomplished in your brethren that are in the world.

But the God of all grace, who hath called us to eternal glory by Christ Jesus, after that ye have suffered a while, make you perfect, stablish, strengthen, settle *you* (1 Pet. 5:8-10).

And these signs shall follow them that believe; In my name shall they cast out devils. . . . (Mark 16:17)

Believing

It is not clear that Bill Wilson fully understood the importance of what the Bible calls "believing." For Wilson seemed much more concerned about "coming to believe" in what he called a "Power greater than" yourself, than with believing itself. However, he did write the following:

> Here are thousands of men and women, worldly indeed. They flatly declare that since they have come to believe in a Power greater than themselves, to take a certain attitude toward that Power, and to do certain simple things, there has been a revolutionary change in their way of living and thinking. In the face of collapse and despair, in the face of total failure of their human resources, they found that a new power, peace, happiness, and sense of direction flowed into them. . . . When many hundreds of people are able to say that consciousness of the Presence of God is today the most important fact of their lives, they present a powerful reason why one should have faith (*Alcoholics Anonymous*, 3rd ed., pp. 50-51).

The Bible speaks about believing the Word of God, not just "consciousness" or "attitude" or "faith," as Wilson seems to talk of it:

> And Jesus said unto the centurion, Go thy way; and as thou hast believed, so be it done unto thee. And his servant was healed in the selfsame hour (Matt. 8:13).

> And all things, whatsoever ye shall ask in prayer, believing, ye shall receive (Matt. 21:22).

Jesus said unto him, If thou canst believe, all things *are* possible
to him that believeth (Mark 9:23).

And what *is* the exceeding greatness of his power to usward
who believe, according to the working of his mighty power
(Eph. 1:19).

Now faith is the substance of things hoped for, the evidence of
things not seen (Heb. 11:1).

But without faith, *it is* impossible to please *him*: for he that
cometh to God must believe that he is and *that* he is a rewarder
of them that diligently seek him (Heb. 11:6).

Understanding the Bible As an Eastern Book

When you read about camels, candles, bushels, wells, and the many
other items involved in life during Bible times, it is very important
to remember that the Bible is not a Western book. The Bible is an
Eastern Book, and needs to be read and interpreted with that
backdrop in mind. Take a look at Freeman's *Manners and Customs
of the Bible*, 1972.

Understanding Figures of Speech in the Bible

Just as you wouldn't expect someone to strip off his clothing when
he said he would "give you the shirt off his back," you will need to
be aware that figures of speech occur in the Bible. We begin by
taking every word in the Word of God literally. And when we come
upon words or phrases that seem as though they couldn't be literally
true, that is the time to consider whether a figure of speech is being
employed. An excellent resource for your study in the area of how
figures of speech are used in the Bible that have been of help to this
author is E. W. Bullinger's, *Figures of Speech Used in the Bible*,
1968.

Learning about the Early Manuscripts of the Bible

For a start, see Sharpe and Van Kampen, *The Bible As Book: The Manuscript Tradition*, 1998; Samuel C. Gipp, *An Understandable History of the Bible* (1987); and Josh McDowell, *Evidence That Demands a Verdict* (1972).

Reading for Scope

Whether studying individual verses, chapters, or books in the Bible, reading the context is very important. The idea of "reading for scope" involves reading the context around the verse, chapter, or book you are studying specifically. It involves getting background knowledge that you can then bring to bear on the specific verse, chapter, or book you are studying. That is, to understand Ephesians 6:12 better, one would read all of Ephesians chapter 6, and so forth. See *Anne Smith's Journal,* 3rd ed., pp. 82-83.

Word Studies

The author and his son have often used two of the many possible tools that assist in studying words in the Bible by going to their Hebrew and Greek sources. One is *Young's Analytical Concordance to the Bible* by Robert Young, newly revised and corrected, Nashville, TN: Thomas Nelson, 1982. The other is the two-volume set: *The Word Study New Testament* and *The Word Study Concordance* both published by Tyndale House, 1978.

10

It's Not So Tough

Blessed is the man that endureth temptation: for when he is tried, he shall receive the crown of life, which the Lord hath promised to them that love him.

Let no man say when he is tempted, I am tempted of God: for God cannot be tempted with evil, neither tempteth he any man: But every man is tempted, when he is drawn away of his own lust, and enticed.

Then when lust hath conceived, it bringeth forth sin: and sin, when it is finished, bringeth forth death.

Do not err, my beloved brethren.

Every good and perfect gift is from above, and cometh down from the Father of lights, with whom is no variableness, neither shadow of turning (James 1:12-17).

I have never found it difficult to get people onto the early A.A. path. You meet them in an A.A. meeting and pick out a sick one. You let that person know you care. You let him get comfortable through offering coffee or goodies or introductions. You ask him about himself. (Alcoholics, even sick ones, would rather talk about themselves than just about anything. So would most people). Lots of this can be found in the Big Book. Lots can be found in *DR. BOB and the Good Oldtimers*. And *Anne Smith's Journal* contains an abundance of hints on how to deal with the new person. That's one reason for getting her journal out of the shadows and into the light again. Anne was legendary in her wonderful handling of new people.

If the newcomer is in detox state, you get him to the doctor or the hospital. No kidding. You stay with him and help him during and after the visit or stay. My first grandsponsor just suggested that I use orange juice and honey. I was so sick that I bought the oranges and put them in the micro-wave. I'm still looking for the honey. In no time at all–sans doctor, oranges, and honey– I had three grand mal seizures and almost died! You don't fool around with sick ones!

You help them through their fog about what to do, where to go, how to eat, where to sleep, how to get financial sustenance, and how to handle the myriad legal problems that confront them. You don't solve these problems. You help!

Back of it all is God, the Creator of the heavens and the earth. That's where the simplicity comes in. As Dr. Bob did, you ask if they believe in God. You ask them about their alcoholism and desire to stop drinking. You ask them if they are willing to do *anything–go to any lengths*–to get well. You can remind them of the statement they hear from the Big Book at almost any meeting: *Remember that we deal with alcohol–cunning, baffling, powerful! Without help it is too much for us. But there is One who has all power–that One is God. May you find Him now*! Does that "One" suggest that you "find" Santa Claus, a lightbulb, a group, or "not-god?" Of course, not. The confusion begins when someone in A.A. tells you it does.

This guidebook and this approach is not about returning A.A. to the status of a Protestant Christian fellowship. It ain't gonna happen. But it is about working within the Traditions and rooms of A.A. with someone who is a Christian, wants to be a Christian, wonders what a Christian is, and wants to "find" God but gets trounced if he brings up the subject.

You don't talk about higher powers or lightbulbs or chairs. You talk about Almighty God, the Creator. The new guys know who the

Creator is. God is mentioned on the dollar bill. In fact, the dollar bill says we trust in Him. He is mentioned, or was mentioned, in the Pledge of Allegiance. So the new guys have heard of Him. They just never needed Him as much as they do now. If they don't need or want Him, you can decline to serve. The author has, on the very few occasions when someone told him that didn't believe in God, wouldn't believe in God, and didn't want to hear about God. If they want Him, there is a simple path and simple beginning.

They come to God, the Creator, through His Son, Jesus Christ. Note Jesus' statement in John 14:6:

> Jesus saith unto him, I am the way, the truth, and the life: no man cometh unto the Father, but by me.

John 3:16 gives the background of God's love:

> For God so loved the world, that he gave his only begotten Son, that whosoever believeth in him should not perish, but have everlasting life.

And Rom. 10:9, 10 state and explain the requirement:

> That if thou shalt confess with thy mouth the Lord Jesus, and shalt believe in thine heart that God hath raised him from the dead, thou shalt be saved.
> For with the heart man believeth unto righteousness; and with the mouth confession is made unto salvation.

Can they buy that? If you explain to the person what "Lord" means in Rom. 10:9 [i.e., "the Lord Jesus" or "Jesus is Lord" (NIV)] and what Jesus did to buy us back, redeem us, and save us, you won't have much of a problem. They've been told about the birth of the Saviour, regrettably with too many jingle bells. They know about crosses and the crucifixion. They've seen crosses on church buildings for years. They may even know why our calendars talk about A.D. and B.C. If they don't, tell them. They also probably understand what "Easter"–the pagan name–is really about. Not about bunnies, or bonnets, or chocolate eggs. But about the great truth that God, the Creator of the heavens and the earth, raised His Son, Jesus Christ, from the dead. They know that. They'll even laugh if you make the point. Many have laughed over that one in my discussions with them.

Then you can tell them what early AAs really did and believed. How simple it was: Come to God through Jesus Christ; and have meetings and hang out with fellow believers. Pray, read the Bible, ask God for help and guidance at every turn. Tell them to join a newcomer patrol. To get a newcomer net. To start working with someone else, even if it's just saying hello and welcome to the meeting. Is that so tough?.

The rest of it has to do with what we've been talking about–learning *more*! The customary A.A. lingo about avoiding slippery places, slippery people, and "HALT" (not getting too hungry, angry, lonely, or tired); going to lots of meetings, getting phone numbers, getting commitments, sticking with the winners, using the phone, and so on, are not cures. They are supports–A.A. variety supports. These are time-honored supports along the early A.A. path to receiving God's help and deliverance. I have used them all. And I still suggest them: Don't get too hungry, angry, lonely, or tired. Stay away from the old haunts and habits. Communicate! Participate! Stay in the center of the herd!

Go for it. "Pass It On." Why dilute the original message and facts. Why compromise on the power of God. Dr. Bob ended his story in the Big Book with: "Your Heavenly Father will never let you down!" There is no evidence that He will let you down. He won't. It just takes information about Him. It takes your believing; and it takes your steadfastness.

Now about this "God" business. There was an old gal named Maxine (about my age) who had twenty years of sobriety when I came in. They tell me she's still going strong in A.A. She's a staunch Roman Catholic. She literally saved my life by calling an ambulance when I had grand mal seizures at one of my first A.A. meetings. Everyone thought she was a character because of her make-up and dress. But she had been around the Horn and wasn't afraid to talk about God, prayer, and Christianity. And how many times I heard her say: "If the word 'God' scares you out of these rooms, a bottle of booze will scare you back–if you live"! I never saw one person walk out of the room when Maxine said that, and I heard lots of people quote that statement from time to time in other meetings. Yet the idea persists among many in our fellowship that mention of God, Jesus Christ, or the Bible might "scare away the newcomer."

Despite what Bill Wilson actually asserted in earlier A.A. years about people's fear of being "God-bitten," I have never, ever seen one newcomer leave A.A. because of the mention of God or Jesus Christ or the Bible. Not one! I've seen people criticized for mentioning those things. And I've seen many leave to "have fun," and to drink, and then get drunk and stay drunk for several years. I've personally known two young women who believed in God, who left A.A. for heroin, and who died of overdoses. But I've never seen anyone drop dead, go to jail, or leave A.A. because "God" was mentioned. Never!

In fact, my group of sponsees used to say, when a newcomer would come in and mention a "higher power," that the words "higher power" were "forbidden" in our gang of winners. There was usually a peaceful acquiescence, and the newcomer took the point well. Sometimes not!

A reference to the Conference Approved book *DR. BOB and the Good Oldtimers* is appropriate here. According to Clarence Snyder, here is how Dr. Bob–whom Bill W. called the "prince of twelfth-steppers" and who personally helped more than 5,000 alcoholics–approached new comers–in this case, Clarence:

"Then he [Dr. Bob] asked, 'Do you believe in God, young
fella?' (He always called me 'young fella.' When he called me
Clarence, I knew I was in trouble.)
"'What does that have to do with it?'
"'Everything,' he said.
"'I guess I do.'
"'Guess, nothing! Either you do or you don't'
"'Yes, I do.'
"'That's fine,' Dr. Bob replied. 'Now we're getting someplace.
All right, get out of bed and on your knees. We're going to
pray.'
"'I don't know how to pray.'
"'I guess you don't, but that's all right. Just follow what I say,
and that will do for now.'
"I did what I was ordered to do," Clarence said. "There was no
suggestion."

Clearly, Dr. Bob was not concerned about "scaring away the
newcomers" by talking about God. Remember, this was the same
Dr. Bob Smith, co-founder of A.A., who began the work in Akron
where they had a 75% success rate with "medically incurable"
alcoholics who "really tried." And this was the Clarence Snyder
who started A.A. in Cleveland where they had a 93% success rate!

So, back to simplicity and easy does it. It's not hard to find and
work with a newcomer these days because there are so few who still
do it. It's not hard to draw the newcomer out concerning his
alcoholism and problems, and then to draw him into the A.A. scene
if you simply show that you care. And do! Finally, the real message
for the new person, other than the caveats, is itself quite simple:
First, "Put the plug in the jug–forever!" Not one-day-at-a-time.
Forever! Second, ask God for help from the first moment. Third,
decide that you have to change your life completely and work at it.
But only to the best of your ability. The Steps provide a way, if they
are practiced. The Bible provides a way if it is believed and acted
upon.

The mess you found yourself in by following the old way of life does not hold much appeal if you work with someone who shows by example and by teaching what you can do if you quit for good, trust God, and "clean house."

"Clean house" means "clean house." By asking God's help in the process; seeing where you've failed; confessing your actions to another to bring them to the light of day; becoming convinced this all has to change with God's help; accepting the gift of the Holy Spirit with open arms and deciding to put on the new man in Christ; then clearing up the wreckage of the past with amends and restitution. The final step is the hardest. It is resolving to walk with, and for, and in obedience to, Almighty God, our Creator. That means a daily walk, a daily effort to improve, a daily and intense fellowship with God, and–in A.A.–a real effort to help newcomers in every way possible and at every stage.

Put this in the framework of a fellowship of friends, believers, and winners; and you've got it. If that's not A.A., then the forty pioneers who founded A.A. were on the wrong path.

Again, the message: Quit–you are licked! Trust God! Change! Have fellowship with our Heavenly Father by doing what He asks. Willingly receive what He offers; believe what He says; love Him and His kids; and serve Him heartily. That's what Dr. Bob meant by "love" and "service." He preached it. He lived it. He passed it on. You can too.

11
What's on the Platter Today

This *is* the day *which* the LORD [Yahweh] hath made; we will rejoice and be glad in it (Ps. 118:24)

But seek ye first the kingdom of God, and his righteousness; and all these things shall be added unto you (Matt. 6:33)

And whatsoever *ye* do, do *it* heartily, as to the Lord, and not unto men (Col. 3:23)

The Bible was the standard for truth in early Alcoholics Anonymous. Even though many pioneers actually studied the Good Book assiduously, all were *taught* far more than they themselves unearthed in that Good Book itself. There are no persuasive records that large groups of A.A. pioneers took Bible classes, enrolled in seminaries, were ordained ministers, or were hired as Bible teachers. Or were called a sect, denomination, or religion! In fact, when speaking of Anne Smith, one pioneer said that Anne never sought to rewrite the Bible; she just accepted it.

Early A.A., from the beginning, was peopled by alcoholics with various beliefs. Primarily Protestant and male. The primarily Protestant program in Akron was developed, practiced, and proven to be effective. Then came diversity–with the strong new pocket of

Roman Catholics in early Cleveland A.A. The Bible was still frequently quoted and studied there, but some of the Protestant trappings in Akron that had brought on Roman Catholic hostility and condemnation were dropped. Then came lots of diversity–Jews, women, some blacks, some Hispanics, some Native Americans, some atheists, some gays and lesbians, and perhaps a few members who believed in Eastern Religions.

Unfortunately, that growing diversity was accompanied by growing dilution, revision, compromise, universalization, misunderstanding, criticism, and downright invention–seeming to amount to a new religion. And it appeared to be accompanied by a real fear–in the sense of being afraid–of God, Jesus Christ, and the Bible. Ideas about "spirituality," about "new thought," about special "gods and goddesses," became common fare despite the fact that the language of, and ideas in, A.A.'s basic text remained basically the same (though altered to suit some of the new themes). It still is basically the same and still is basically filled with biblical ideas, no matter how badly mangled..

Then came the government agencies, the insurance companies, the treatment centers, the therapists and counselors, and bundles of new books and literature. "Higher Power" with a capital "H" and a capital "P" was heard far more often, and seen more often, than "God Almighty, Creator, Bible, and Christ." "God as we understood Him" became more one's own conception of some "power" than one's understanding of, and progress in understanding, Yahweh, the Creator.

Then followed "chairs," "bulldozers," "groups," "lightbulbs," "somethings," and "not-god" in the vestige of a "god." Such absurdities were heard often, in fact, more often than mention of Jesus Christ, of the Good Book, of the Holy Spirit, or even of Almighty God. This despite the fact that Dr. Bob never minced words when it came to God or the Bible. But he died. Bill Wilson occasionally talked about Jesus Christ, the Bible, and God, but he died too. And the door was flung open to a host of devilish ideas, thoughts, and nomenclature that would, if resurrection of the dead had been available, have probably brought both Bob and Bill back to the scene in horror. Then came the curious idea: "Fake it till you make it."

After Dr. Bob's death, A.A. was also using, emphasizing, and encouraging reliance upon such words, ideas, and practices as "unity" and "service." These to the point that, at times, they have seemed more hallowed than the act of grabbing a newcomer and helping him. And the success rate went down and down and down. Finally, Christian groups and secular groups began to form outside of A.A. Then came lawsuits successfully prosecuted to insure that there is no more *compulsory* A.A. – despite the fact that most of its newcomers were probably coming from probation and court referrals or "compulsory" bussing from treatment centers.

Despite the easily observable new factors, to this very day, the person most likely to be trounced verbally in any meeting is the one who has settled down in A.A. with a substantial period of sobriety, but mentions his Bible, his Saviour Jesus Christ, or his Almighty God, Yahweh, the Creator of the heavens and the earth.

It Is What God Says That Counts

Notice how Jesus handled statements thrown at him that were completely out of line with what God says:

> Then was Jesus led up of the spirit into the wilderness to be tempted of the devil.
> And when he had fasted forty days and forty nights, he was afterward an hungred.
> And when the tempter came to him, he said, If thou be the Son of God, command that these stones be made bread.
> But he answered and said, It is written, Man shall not live by bread alone, but by every word that proceedeth out of the mouth of God.

Then the devil taketh him up into the holy city, and setteth him
on a pinnacle of the temple,
And saith unto him, If thou be the Son of God, cast thyself
down: for it is written, He shall give his angels charge
concerning thee: and in their hands they shall bear thee up, lest
at any time thou dash thy foot against a stone.
Jesus said unto him, It is written again, Thou shalt not tempt the
Lord thy God.
Again, the devil taketh him up into an exceeding high mountain,
and sheweth him all the kingdoms of the world, and the glory
of them;
And saith unto him, All these things will I give thee, if thou wilt
fall down and worship me.
Then saith Jesus unto him, Get thee hence, Satan: for it is
written, Thou shalt worship the Lord thy God, and him only
shalt thou serve.
Then the devil leaveth him, and, behold, angels came and
ministered unto him (Matt. 4:1-11)

You can't effectively evaluate or answer or deal with the untruths
the Devil and those he influences throw at you unless you have the
spirit of God in you and measure statements directed toward you by
what God has to say on the topic. "It is written" is the response that
brings the truth to light and sends the Devil and his forces packing!
For those who believe, it is still the proper response–whether mental
or vocal.

I have seen Christian AAs shrink from intimidation within
meetings. It happened only two days ago at an Alkathon in Maui
this January–two days in a row! One of A.A.'s female "bleeding
deacons" fussed and fumed at each of the meetings because there
was a box of books about A.A. history outside the Alkathon room.
Needless to say, there was mention of Christianity in the books.
Prodded by the "deaconess," the owner of the books moved the box
to an area sufficiently distant from the A.A. meeting room to silence
the old girl. I have seen Christian AAs leave A.A., not necessarily

to drink, but to find Christian fellowships outside of A.A. But I have never seen the hosts of people who share about their "relationships," their atheist leanings, their sexual preference, or their psychological problems in any way intimidated from vocalizing them.

Now, these things are not going to change! You can go to the bank with that statement. But the *attitude* about them among those who have really learned how sick they are, how dangerous their illness is, how great are the number of their problems, and how much they are in need of God's help, *can* change. In fact, modern, fast, complete communication outside of A.A. meetings and literature is already changing it.

No matter what anyone tells you, you *can* mention and believe in God in today's A.A. No matter what anyone tells you, you can mention and study and try to live by the Good Book in today's A.A. No matter what anyone tells you, a group of alcoholics can be formed in Alcoholics Anonymous and listed as a Bible study group, a Christian Fellowship, or a fellowship of believers. Even today, the only requirement for "membership" is a desire to stop drinking. Each group is declared to be autonomous except in matters affecting other groups or A.A. as a whole. And A.A. can neither endorse nor oppose any sect, denomination, religion or cause.

And how could it. Or why should it. For that is where it all started. Religion–through Rev. Samuel M. Shoemaker, Jr., Father Ed Dowling (the Jesuit priest), and Father John C. Ford (the Jesuit moral theologian)–has had a far greater influence on A.A. and its ideas (past and present) than most could ever imagine.

AAs today need freedom to believe, to speak, to heal, to be cured, to be given a way out of their bondage, and to receive the power and love of our Creator if they *choose* to seek these things. If Hindus, atheists, Christians, Moslems and others want to just "not drink and go to meetings" or just be "Big Book thumpers" or adapt the Twelve Steps to their particular religious beliefs, or even believe in "nothing at all," they are as free to do this as they want.

There is no need to create a new, universal, diluted A.A. program for any or all of them. But all could use some good solid information about what A.A. *was*. All in A.A. today should feel under no compulsion, obligation, or tradition to shun or ignore or hide from A.A. exactly as it *was*. They should feel completely free to meet and practice old-time A.A.–in their homes, their churches, their fellowships, their meetings, and their groups.

And here we make some suggestions more applicable to the individual alcoholic.

Become Knowledgeable about the Bible's Place in A.A.

Every A.A., every Christian in A.A., and everyone connected with A.A. needs to feel free to learn as much as possible about the Good Book and early A.A. This particular guidebook will help to that end. So will our titles, *The Good Book and The Big Book: A.A.'s Roots in the Bible; Good Morning!: Quiet Time, Morning Watch, and Meditation in Early A.A.; The Books Early AAs Read for Spiritual Growth*; and *By the Power of God*.

Get Acquainted with the Bible's Contents

My first sponsor and his sponsor were both fond of saying that AAs should not read the Bible and that people who did read the Bible in A.A. got drunk. I happen to know my first sponsor had read the Bible. But I also know that his sponsor flatly stated he had *never* read the Bible. This man went to great lengths to prevent my sponsees from participating in a Bible fellowship. And I venture to say that many of today's "bleeding deacons," who object to mention of the Bible in A.A., are unaware of, or unfamiliar with, its contents and are lacking in knowledge about the Bible's relationship to the language and principles of the Big Book

Boldly Mention God, His Son, and His Word

I've been through the fear route in today's A.A. scene. Fear of speaking up. Fear of losing friends. Fear of being criticized. But no more! If Dr. Bob could do it, why should I fear doing it. If A.A. Number Three [Bill Dotson] taught the Bible at A.A. meetings, what would I need to fear. In fact, the Bible tells me that God has not given us the spirit of fear, but of power and of love and of a sound mind (2 Tim. 1:7). I use it. I don't have to trumpet my convictions to an unbelieving assemblage, but I have no hesitancy now in sharing in my own language and from my own point of view how I established my relationship with God (*Alcoholics Anonymous*, 3rd ed., p. 29)–particularly to a newcomer I'm trying to help.

So today, I study the Bible daily just as most of the pioneers did. I have taught my sponsees about the Bible's role for a long time. I am swamped with messages by phone, fax, email, and letters from people who are delighted to know our history, who are forming Bible study groups, and who are finally sharing *their experiences* with individuals, in meetings and in other groups.

My own view, however, is that there is little value in casting pearls before swine, to use the biblical expression. If it will not serve, glorify, and be to the praise of God Almighty, there is no point in arguing with someone whose prejudices against religion, the Bible, the Creator, or Christianity will really not make much difference in the long run.

The Bible is filled with references to the importance of speaking the word of God boldly. It also has some important references to shaking the dust off your feet and moving on when someone really turns a deaf ear. In fact, if you learn discerning of spirits and also that the natural man does not receive the things of the spirit of God, you will not want to spend much time on some people. The Parable of the Sower (Matt. 13, Mark 4, Luke 8) provides an excellent guide to what God really expects when His Word is mentioned: Not everyone is going to get blessed or even listen.

Grow

Joe and Charlie are fond of saying in their Big Book Seminars that you are either growing or dying. I won't place my imprimatur on the statement, but I will say that the Big Book repeatedly speaks of growing in spiritual understanding and effectiveness.

To sit in A.A. and fondle possibilities of God, of His actually caring and loving, or of His grace and mercy, and yet to learn nothing about any of these things is not for me. I want to know more. So did Bill Wilson and said so at a later point in his A.A. writing about the clergy. I consider it no badge of brilliance or accomplishment to say: "I don't and can't understand God. I don't know how it works. I just don't drink and go to meetings." That's not what the Bible talks about. Nor is it what our founders talked about or did. For Dr. Bob always tried to grow through Bible study. Why not follow his example!

Learn Your Resources

You cannot learn much without a textbook. Those in A.A. who don't study the Big Book make absurd statements about the program all the time. Those who spout off about the Bible and don't know much or anything about it neither glorify God nor help their fellow AAs.

We've mentioned the resources for Bible study. And early A.A. used many of them. But today you have churches, study groups, Bible fellowships, books, articles, pamphlets, classes, audio-cassette tapes, videos, movies, radio and television programs, and internet resources that give you all the tools you need to make knowledge of God, His Son, and His word your own–in depth! Remember this great section from page 89 of the Big Book:

> There are many helpful books also. Suggestions about these
> may be obtained from one's priest, minister, or rabbi. Be quick

to see where religious people are right. Make use of what they offer.

Pass It On!

Never be in doubt about witnessing. As Sam Shoemaker pointed out many times, the "gospel" meant the "good news." And when people preached the gospel, they were preaching the good news about God, the resurrection and return of Jesus Christ, salvation, the new birth, and many other great things. Jesus Christ preached. He told others to preach. They preached. The Book of Acts shows exactly how the message was carried, to the point that thousands were converted at a single event. Paul's letters and Paul's travels involved message-carrying. Secret agent Christianity was not part of the New Testament picture. They didn't just keep their mouths shut, smile, and hope that somehow, someday, someone might accidentally discover that they were Christian believers. A.A. built on that very foundation with its Twelfth Step work.

Now the original message in the Oxford Group was: Tell them what God has done for you. Ebby Thacher's initial message that impacted on Bill Wilson was "God has done for me what I could not do for myself." You'll find that message more than once in the Big Book.

Anne Smith, and the Big Book, point out that you can't talk about an experience you haven't had. So don't try! The best ambassador for Christ is the one who speaks only about what he or she *knows* from the Bible or what God has done for them. Not some dingbat opinion or theory–but what he or she knows from his or her own victorious experience or *exact* knowledge of the Bible.

There Is a Process, Then

Here is a process I suggest. It is in the Bible. These terms summarize it: birth, growth, maturity. Here are some helpful verses:

Birth:

Jesus answered, Verily, verily, I say unto thee, Except a man
be born of water and *of* the Spirit, he cannot enter into the
kingdom of God.
That which is born of the flesh is flesh; and that which is born
of the Spirit is spirit (John 3:5-6).

Being born again, not of corruptible seed, but of incorruptible,
by the word of God, which liveth and abideth forever (1 Pet.
1:23).

Now to Abraham and his seed were the promises made. He
saith not, And to seeds, as of many; but as of one, And to thy
seed, which is Christ (Gal. 3:16).

Growth:

As newborn babes, desire the sincere milk of the word, that ye
may grow thereby (1 Pet. 2:4).

And I, brethren, could not speak unto as unto spiritual, but as
unto carnal, *even* as unto babes in Christ.
I have fed you with milk, and not with meat: for hitherto ye
were not able to *bear it*, neither yet now are ye able.
For ye are yet carnal: for whereas *there is* among you envying,
and strife, and divisions, are ye not carnal, and walk as men (1
Cor. 3:1-3).

Maturity:

For when for the time ye ought to be teachers, ye have need that
one teach you again which *be* the first principles of the oracles
of God; and are become such as have need of milk, and not of
strong meat.

For every one that useth milk is unskilful in the word of righteousness: for he is a babe.

But strong meat belongeth to them that are of full age, even those who by reason of use have their senses exercised to discern both good and evil (Heb. 5:12-14).

Brethren, I count not myself to have apprehended: but *this* one thing I *do,* forgetting those things which are behind, and reaching forth unto those things which are before.

I press toward the mark for the prize of the high calling of God in Christ Jesus.

Let us therefore, as many as be perfect [mature], be thus minded: and if in any thing ye be otherwise minded, God shall reveal even this unto you (Phil. 3:13-15)

Trust God with All Your Heart

Don't you get tired of hearing people talk about "accepting" adversity–becoming proverbial door mats. Don't you get tired of hearing them whining about their "problems" instead of asking how to solve them. Don't you get tired of hearing that "bad things just happen"–instead of looking to their source and the protection and victory that God provides. Don't you get tired of hearing that bad things happen to good people, that prayers don't get answered, and that there must be a "purpose" for everything–like AIDS, hurricanes, auto accidents, disability, bankruptcy, even death.

The people who have and live the love of God usually attract attention, but not necessarily gratitude, from those around them. But love, joy, peace, and all the rest of the fruit of the spirit are theirs for the taking and using. It used to really annoy me that, when I lost something or was waiting for something or was moaning about something, my ever-present sponsee Shane would say: "Victory is just a thought away." Or, Shane would comment: "Have you asked the Father?"

Shane was just a kid–Only 21! But he knew what God's Word said. How simple those solutions are. How much God cares! How great is His performance!

Why not do what Dr. Bob did (and strongly suggested in his 1943 talk in Los Angeles) when he urged cultivating the habit of praying and studying the Bible regularly. Use the Word of God in your searching, believing, and renewing of your mind. Use it in praying, overcoming sicknesses, seeking healing, asking guidance, forgiveness issues, your daily walk, defeating oppressions and depressions, fears, and anxieties. Use it in your planning and requests for help. Above all, believe it (John 3:16 and Rom. 10:9) for salvation.

There is an important approach that is easy to ignore. It means putting on the whole armor of God because the battle is not against flesh and blood. Jesus Christ came to defeat the works of the Devil. He won! So the battle can be won by believers today as well. Ephesians chapter 6 discusses the "how" of it.

Just to conclude with an A.A. topic: I wonder how many people who have seen the "miracles" in A.A. realize that God can assure victory over alcoholism, addiction, and the other problems encountered, in and out of A.A., every single day. A reading of Dr. Bob's personal story should convince you of the scope of God's power that Dr. Bob felt was available.

> For with God nothing shall be impossible,
> And Mary said, Behold the handmaid of the Lord; be it unto me
> according to thy word (Luke 1:37-38).

The angel of God told Mary that she would conceive in her womb, and bring forth a son, and was to call his name JESUS. Mary wondered how this could happen–since she "knew not" a man. The angel re-assured Mary that God was in the impossible business. Mary believed the angel's message. The "babe leaped in" her womb. And there was a "performance of those things which were told her from the Lord." God wanted or willed, that a Saviour should be born into the world. When God says it, that settles it. If we believe it, there will be a performance of those things which God says He will do and cause to happen. In the same context–the presumed impossibility of being delivered from alcoholism–Dr. Bob concluded: "Your Heavenly Father will never let you down!" And He won't.

Why did early A.A. succeed? There are many opinions on this topic floating around. But succeed it did–with "medically incurable" alcoholics. We do know for sure today that the pioneers *knew they could be cured.* We do know for sure that they believed the Creator of the heavens and the earth would not let them down. We do know that they looked to the Good Book for the answers–something the Twelve Step Fellowships no longer do, even though their basic ideas were taken from the Good Book. We do know that the pioneers believed in God Almighty, established a relationship with Him through His only begotten Son, and tried to walk in the light and shun the darkness. And we know that God helped His children as they sought Him in accordance with His Word. How do we know? They said so, and lived to prove it. This author suggests you follow the path of the early AAs who learned about the Creator of the heavens and the earth, sought His help, and received from Him deliverance from "medically incurable" alcoholism.

The End

Appendix 1
The Creator's Name is Yahweh!

We will now go into considerable detail about the name of the Creator of the heavens and the earth, **Yahweh**. Please review this material carefully, as it will answer many questions you may have had about the God, the Creator.

The Creator's Name Is Yahweh

In the main body of this work, we presented statements by scholars indicating that the name of the Creator of the heavens and the earth is *YHWH*, Yahweh. Here are several more:

> Yahweh, the proper name of the God of Israel [Francis Brown, with the Cooperation of S. R. Driver and Charles A. Briggs, *The New Brown-Driver-Briggs-Gesenius Hebrew and English Lexicon* (n.p.: Christian Copyrights, 1983), "YHWH" (spelled in Hebrew letters), p. 217 ("BDB")]

> The Reader will immediately notice that the personal name of the biblical God appears in this volume as "YHWH" [Everett Fox, The Five Books of Moses (New York: Schocken Books, 1995), p. xxix]

The personal name of God is Yahweh. It is a foreign name, quite un-English, and so unlike the good Anglo-Saxon word 'God'. For that reason, if perhaps for no other, the name Yahweh must be preserved. . . . [David J. A. Clines, "Yahweh and the God of Christian Theology," *Theology* 83 (1980), pp. 323-30)]

The Creator's Name Is Not "God"

Perhaps you are like many people who have been taught or believe that "God" is God's name, so to speak. The word "God"—as used in the KJV (and in the NIV) in reference to the Creator of the heavens and the earth—is really a title. This can be seen clearly from verses such as the following:

> And I will make thee swear by the LORD [Yahweh], the God **of heaven**, and the God **of the earth**, that thou shalt not take a wife unto my son of the daughters of the Canaanites, among whom I dwell: (Gen 24:3; emphasis added)

> And the LORD [Yahweh] appeared unto him the same night, and said, I *am* the God **of Abraham thy father**: fear not, for I *am* with thee, and will bless thee, and multiply thy seed for my servant Abraham's sake. (Gen 26:24; emphasis added)

> And I will take you to me for **a people**, and I will be to you **a God**: and ye shall know that *I am* the LORD [Yahweh] **your God**, which bringeth you out from under the burdens of the Egyptians. (Exod 6:7; emphasis added)

> And I will dwell among the children of Israel, and will be **their God**.
> And they shall know that I am the LORD [Yahweh] **their God**, that brought them forth out of the land of Egypt, that I may dwell among them: I am the LORD [Yahweh] **their God**. (Exod 29:45, 46; emphasis added)

The Hebrew word translated "God" in Genesis 1:1 and in the verses immediately above is *elohim*, Strong's number 430 (pronounced "el-o-heem' "). This plural Hebrew noun occurs a total of 2,606 times in the Hebrew Old Testament text from which the KJV was translated [BLB, (www.blueletterbible.org)], and 2,600 times in that from which the NIV was translated (HECOT, p. 98). *Elohim* is translated as the singular English word "God"—as a plural of majesty or a plural intensive with a singular meaning—more than 2,300 times in both the KJV and the NIV, beginning with Genesis 1:1. And it is by far the word most commonly translated "God" in the Old Testament.

The *New Bible Dictionary* explains the Hebrew word *elohim* as follows:

> Though a plural form (*elohim*), Elohim can be treated as a singular, in which case it means the one supreme deity, and in [English versions] is rendered "God." Like its English equivalent, it is, grammatically considered, a common noun, and conveys the notion of all that belongs to the concept of deity, in contrast with man (Nu. 23:19) and other created beings. It is appropriate to cosmic and world-wide relationships (Gn. 1:1), because there is only one supreme and true God, . . . [I]t approaches the character of a proper noun, while not losing its abstract and conceptual quality. . . .
>
> Strictly speaking, Yahweh is the only "name" of God (*New Bible Dictionary*, 2d ed., organizing ed., J. D. Douglas., under "God, Names of," pp. 429-30.)

And Barker states in *The NIV: The Making of a Contemporary Translation*:

> God himself identifies his name as Yahweh in Exodus 3:15; 6:3. Strictly speaking, all other "names" are either generic

terms (e.g., *Elohim*, "God") or apellative [sic] titles or epithets
(e.g., *Adonai*, "Lord") [Barker, "YHWH Sabaoth: 'The Lord
Almighty'" (http://www.gospelcom.net/ibs/niv/mct/9.php)]

(For more information on the occurrences and meaning of the
Hebrew word *elohim*, see *BDB*, p. 43.)

The Creator's Name Is Not "the LORD"

Since the Creator's name is actually Yahweh, why did the KJV and
many modern versions (such as the NIV and the NASV) translate
YHWH as "(the) LORD" in Isa. 42:8 and nearly all other places?

> I am **the LORD** [Yahweh]: that is my name: and my glory will
> I not give to another, neither my praise to graven images (Isa.
> 42:8 KJV).

> I am **the LORD** [Yahweh]; that is my name! I will not give my
> glory to another or my praise to idols (Isa. 42:8 NIV).

To understand how the more familiar terms "[the] LORD" and
"Jehovah" came to be substituted for the Creator's name, Yahweh,
we begin with the discussion of "Yahweh" in the Preface to the
NIV:

> In regard to the divine name *YHWH*, commonly referred to as
> the *Tetragrammaton*, the translators adopted the device used in
> most English versions of rendering that name as "LORD" in
> capital letters to distinguish it from *Adonai*, another Hebrew
> word rendered "Lord," for which small letters are used.
> Whenever the two names stand together in the Old Testament as
> a compound name of God, they are rendered "Sovereign
> LORD." (quoted in the *Interlinear NIV Hebrew-English Old
> Testament*, p. xxxv).

The Hebrew word *adonai*—Strong's number 136 (pronounced "ad-o-noy'")—means "lord" (BDB, pp. 10, 11). It occurs 442 times in the Hebrew Old Testament underlying the NIV (HECOT, p. 29); and the NIV always translates it as some form of "lord" (i.e., "the Lord," "Lord," and "the Lord's"), except where it is translated "Sovereign," as explained in the NIV Preface quoted above. *Adonai* is translated as some form of "lord" in 433 of the 434 places where it occurs in the Hebrew Old Testament underlying the KJV. (It is translated "God" once in the KJV.)

You may have already anticipated the problem which the NIV, and other modern translations—including the NASV and the Revised Standard Version (RSV)—caused for themselves by choosing not to translate *YHWH* as the proper name "Yahweh." When *YHWH* is used with *adonai*, the NIV (and other translations which took its tack) had to change the translation (and meaning) of *adonai* to "Sovereign" (or something else) in order to avoid an awkward translation like "Lord LORD." We can see this clearly in the first two occurrences of *adonai* in the Hebrew Old Testament (where, in both cases, it is used together with *YHWH*).

> But Abram said, "O Sovereign LORD [*adonai YHWH*], what can you give me since I remain childless and the one who will inherit my estate is Eliezer of Damascus?"
> But Abram said, "O Sovereign LORD [*adonai YHWH*], how can I know that I will gain possession of it?" (Gen. 15:2, 8 NIV)

To see the appropriate solution to this "dilemma" (which the NIV and other translations caused for themselves), we now turn to the Introduction of the *Interlinear NIV Hebrew-English Old Testament* [previously published as *The NIV Interlinear Hebrew-English Old Testament* (NIVIHEOT)]:

> The proper name of God . . . [*YHWH*] is translated "LORD" in the NIV and most other English versions. The NIVIHEOT consistently renders this name as "Yahweh." This is the spelling

and pronunciation generally acknowledged by Bible scholars. Further, according to Scripture, this is God's special name, and it has no direct connection with the idea of lordship. Thus the use of the name Yahweh is a major—and, I think, meaningful—exception to the NIV. (pp. xx, xxi).

The JB translation illustrates how the use of God's name, Yahweh, in the English translation accurately and clearly sets forth the truth.

'My Lord Yahweh,' Abram replied 'what do you intend to give me? I go childless...'
'My Lord Yahweh,' Abram replied 'how am I to know that I shall inherit it?' (Gen. 15:2, 8 JB)

Here is how the KJV translates *adonai* in these two verses:

And Abram said, Lord GOD [*adonai YHWH*] , what wilt thou give me, seeing I go childless, and the steward of my house [is] this Eliezer of Damascus?
And he said, Lord GOD [*adonai YHWH*], whereby shall I know that I shall inherit it? (Gen. 15:2, 8 KJV)

The KJV uses the "device" here of translating *YHWH* as "GOD" in small capitals when it follows *adonai* ("lord") in the Hebrew Old Testament. This is certainly no better than the NIV's "device," as *YHWH* also does not mean "God," the English word normally used to translate the Hebrew word *elohim* in the Old Testament.

God's name is not "the LORD." It is Yahweh!

The Creator's Name Is Not "Jehovah"

Before "Yahweh" became commonly accepted among modern biblical scholars as the best representation in English of the Hebrew word *YHWH*, several older translations and versions chose to translate it as "Jehovah." Included in this group were the Darby

Translation (DT, 1890), the Young's Literal Translation of the Bible (YLT, 1898), and the American Standard Version (ASV, 1901). These versions have recently become readily accessible through the Internet at sites such as "The Bible Gateway" (http://bible.gospelcom.net/) and the "Blue Letter Bible" (BLB), (http://www.blueletterbible.org/)]. We again look at Isa. 42:8:

> I am Jehovah, that is my name; and my glory will I not give to another, neither my praise to graven images (DT).

> I [am] Jehovah, this [is] My name, And Mine honour to another I give not, Nor My praise to graven images (YLT).

> I am Jehovah, that is my name; and my glory will I not give to another, neither my praise unto graven images (ASV).

The Internet version of the *Encyclopaedia Britannica* (http://www.britannica.com/), in its article on "Yahweh," explains how the word "Jehovah" came into being as a translation of *YHWH*:

> Yahweh

> the God of the Israelites, his name being revealed to Moses as four Hebrew consonants (YHWH) called the tetragrammaton. After the Exile (6th century BC), and especially from the 3rd century BC on, Jews ceased to use the name Yahweh for two reasons. As Judaism became a universal religion through its proselytizing in the Greco-Roman world, the more common noun Elohim, meaning "god," tended to replace Yahweh to demonstrate the universal sovereignty of Israel's God over all others. At the same time, the divine name was increasingly regarded as too sacred to be uttered; it was thus replaced vocally in the synagogue ritual by the Hebrew word Adonai ("My Lord"), which was translated as Kyrios ("Lord") in the Septuagint, the Greek version of the Old Testament.

The Masoretes, who from about the 6th to the 10th century worked to reproduce the original text of the Hebrew Bible, replaced the vowels of the name YHWH with the vowel signs of the Hebrew words Adonai or Elohim. Thus, the artificial name Jehovah (YeHoWaH) came into being. Although Christian scholars after the Renaissance and Reformation periods used the term Jehovah for YHWH, in the 19th and 20th centuries biblical scholars again began to use the form Yahweh.

The KJV translated *YHWH* as "LORD" with small capitals in more than 6,500 of its 6,519 occurrences in the Hebrew Old Testament [BLB (http://www.blueletterbible.org/)]. In four of the remaining occurrences, *YHWH* was translated "GOD." However, in four other instances— Exod. 6:3; Ps. 83:18; Isa. 12:2; and Isa. 26:4—the KJV translated *YHWH*, Yahweh, as "Jehovah." And *YHWH*, used in conjunction with another Hebrew word, is translated as a compound name including "Jehovah" three times in the KJV: Gen. 22:14; Exod. 17:15; and Jud. 6:24. We will now briefly examine each of the seven places where *YHWH*, Yahweh, is translated as a form of "Jehovah" in the KJV.

The first of the four places where "Jehovah" stands by itself in the KJV is in Book of Exodus.

And God [*elohim*] spake unto Moses, and said unto him, I am the LORD [*YHWH*, Yahweh]:
And I appeared unto Abraham, unto Isaac, and unto Jacob, by *the name of* God Almighty [*el shaddai*], but by my name JEHOVAH [*YHWH*, Yahweh] was I not known to them (Exod. 6:2, 3; English words italicized in the original)

In verse two, the KJV translated *YHWH* as "the LORD" according to its normal pattern. However, in verse three, where God (*elohim*) specifically speaks of "my name," *YHWH* is translated as "Jehovah." The words "the name of" in the first part of verse three are in italics in the KJV to indicate that there were no corresponding Hebrew words in the Hebrew Old Testament text underlying the KJV. Thus Exod. 6:3 is not saying that "God Almighty"—*el shaddai* in Hebrew—is a name of God. It is saying that God's name is *YHWH*, Yahweh.

The second occurrence of "Jehovah" standing by itself in the KJV occurs in the Book of Psalms.

> That *men* may know that thou, whose name alone *is* JEHOVAH [*YHWH*, Yahweh], *art* the most high over all the earth (Ps. 83:18)

Here again we see that God's name is *YHWH*, Yahweh.

The last two places where "Jehovah" stands by itself in the KJV are both in the Book of Isaiah.

> Behold, God *is* my salvation; I will trust, and not be afraid: for the LORD JEHOVAH [*YH YHWH*] is my strength and *my* song; he also is become my salvation (Isa. 12:2)

> Trust ye in the LORD [*YHWH*, Yahweh] for ever: for in the LORD JEHOVAH [*YH YHWH*] *is* everlasting strength (Isa. 26:4)

Strangely, in Isa. 26:4 above, *YHWH* is translated as "the LORD" in the first part of the verse and as "Jehovah" in the second part of the verse. *YH* (Yah)—Strong's number 3050—is translated as "the LORD" in Isa. 12:2 and in Isa. 26:4 (the second "the LORD"). It is a shortened form of Yahweh (BDB, p. 219). The two separate words—Yah and Yahweh—are distinguished in the DT as follows:

. . . for Jah [*YH*, Yah], Jehovah [*YHWH*, Yahweh], is my strength and song, and he is become my salvation (Isa. 12:2b DT)

. . . for in Jah [*YH*, Yah], Jehovah [*YHWH*, Yahweh], is the rock of ages (Isa. 26:4b DT)

In each of the four verses above, the KJV broke with its normal pattern of translating *YHWH* as "the LORD," but without real justification or explanation.

Genesis chapter 22 contains one of the three places where the KJV translates *YHWH* as "Jehovah," when it occurs in conjunction with another Hebrew word, to form a compound name. (These compound names are sometimes known as the "Jehovah titles." See, for example, The Companion Bible, Appendix 4: "The Divine Names and Titles.")

And Abraham called the name of that place Jehovahjireh [*YHWH* + *ra'ah*]: as it is said to this day, In the mount of the LORD [*YHWH*, Yahweh] it shall be seen [*ra'ah*] (Gen. 22:14)

The Hebrew verb *ra'ah*, "to see" [Strong's number 7200 (pronounced "raw-ah'")], is simply transliterated in English as "jireh" in the first part of the verse above, and tacked onto the end of "Jehovah" to form "Jehovahjireh." In the second part of the verse, *ra'ah* is translated "it shall be seen." Earlier in the same chapter, *ra'ah* is translated "will provide" in verse 8: ". . . God [*elohim*] will provide [*ra'ah*] himself a lamb for a burnt offering: . . ." The JB reflects this sense of *ra'ah* as "to provide" in its translation of verse 14:

Abraham called this place 'Yahweh provides', and hence the saying today: On the mountain Yahweh provides.

Once the verb *ra'ah* is translated as a form of "provide" in its three occurrences in verses 8 and 14, one can begin to see the exciting parallel between this record and God's later providing of His Son, Jesus Christ, as a sacrificial offering:

> For God so loved the world, that he gave his only begotten Son, that whosoever believeth in him should not perish, but have everlasting life (John 3:16).

Exodus chapter 17 contains the second place where the KJV translates *YHWH* as "Jehovah," when it occurs in conjunction with another Hebrew word, to form a compound name.

> And Moses built an altar, and called the name of it Jehovahnissi [*YHWH* + *nes*] (Exod. 17:15)

Here, the Hebrew noun *nes* [Strong's number 5251 (pronounced "nace")] is transliterated in English as "nissi" and added onto the end of "Jehovah" to form "Jehovahnissi." Meanings of *nes* include "something lifted up, standard, signal, signal pole, ensign, banner, sign, sail" (Blue Letter Bible). The *Brown-Driver-Briggs Hebrew Lexicon* (BDB) states that *nes* in this verse has the meaning of a "*standard*, as rallying-point, . . . [i.e.,] *my standard*" (emphasis in the original). Thus, the meaning of *YHWH* combined with *nes* in verse 17 above is "Yahweh my banner" or "Yahweh my standard." The Schocken Bible, Volume 1, The Five Books of Moses (SB)—which uses "YHWH" in place of "Yahweh"—translates verse 17 as follows:

> Moshe built a slaughter-site [i.e., altar] and called its name: YHWH My Banner.

Judges chapter 6 contains the final place where the KJV translates *YHWH* as "Jehovah," when it occurs in conjunction with another Hebrew word, to form a compound name.

> And the LORD [*YHWH*, Yahweh] said unto him, Peace [*shalom*] be unto thee; fear not: thou shalt not die.
> Then Gideon built an altar there unto the LORD [*YHWH*, Yahweh], and called it Jehovahshalom [*YHWH* + *shalom*]: unto this day it is yet in Ophrah of the Abiezrites (Judges 6:23, 24)

The Hebrew noun *shalom* [Strong's number 7965 (pronounced "shaw-lome'")] is transliterated in English as "shalom" and added onto the end of "Jehovah" to form "Jehovahshalom." Meanings of the *shalom* include "completeness, soundness, welfare, peace" (BDB). *Shalom* is usually translated "peace" in the KJV, and BDB indicates that it has that meaning in verse 24 (pp. 1022-23). Thus, the meaning of *YHWH* combined with *shalom* in verse 24 above is "Yahweh is (or perhaps "gives" or "sends") peace." The JB translates the verse as follows:

> Gideon built an altar there to Yahweh and called it Yahweh-Peace. This altar still stands at Ophrah of Abiezer (Judges 6:24 JB)

Thus we can see that the Creator's name, Yahweh, could easily have been used in the seven unusual places where the KJV translated *YHWH* as "Jehovah."

What about the So-called "Names of God?"

After this extended discussion of the Creator's name, Yahweh, you may be wondering: "But I thought God had many names in the Bible." Indeed, such books as *The Names of GOD in Holy Scripture* by Andrew Jukes (Grand Rapids, MI: Kregel, 1967) and *Names of*

God by Nathan Stone (Chicago: Moody Press, 1944) would certainly lead one to believe that the Creator of the heavens and the earth had many names. Books with titles such as those just mentioned notwithstanding, scholars almost universally acknowledge that the Creator has only one proper name in Old Testament—*YHWH*, Yahweh:

> Strictly speaking, Yahweh is the only "name" of God. In Genesis wherever the word *sem* ("name") is associated with the divine being that name is Yahweh. When Abraham or Isaac built an altar "he called on the name of Yahweh" (Gn. 12:8; 13:4; 26:25) [*New Bible Dictionary*, under "God, Names of," pp. 429ff.]

> God himself identifies his name as Yahweh in Exodus 3:15; 6:3. Strictly speaking, all other "names" are either generic terms (e.g., *Elohim*, "God") or apellative [sic] titles or epithets (e.g., *Adonai*, "Lord") [Barker, *The NIV*, chapter on "YHWH Sabaoth" (http://www.gospelcom.net/ibs/niv/mct/9.php)]

> Yahweh, the proper name of the God of Israel [Under "YHWH" (spelled in Hebrew letters), BDB, p. 217]

Yahweh is **the** personal, proper name of the Creator of the heavens and the earth!

The Creator's Name in the New Testament

We have seen that the Creator's name, Yahweh, occurs more than 6,500 times in the Hebrew Old Testament. But what about in the New Testament? There are four verses in the Book of Revelation that contain a form of the name of Yahweh in the KJV:

And after these things I heard a great voice of much people in heaven, saying, **Alleluia**; Salvation, and glory, and honour, and power, unto the Lord our God:
And again they said, **Alleluia** And her smoke rose up for ever and ever.
And the four and twenty elders and the four beasts fell down and worshipped God that sat on the throne, saying, Amen; **Alleluia**.
And I heard as it were the voice of a great multitude, and as the voice of many waters, and as the voice of mighty thunderings, saying, **Alleluia**: for the Lord God omnipotent reigneth.(Rev. 19:1, 3, 4, 6; emphasis added)

The English word "Alleluia" in the four verses above [Greek *allelouia* (Strong's number 239)] is translated "Hallelujah" in the NIV, the NASV, and the RSV. Strong's Concordance states that *allelouia* is of Hebrew origin and etymologically derives from the Hebrew verb *halal*, "to praise" [pronounced "haw-lal'" (Strong's number 1984)], and from *Yah* (Strong's number 3050), the shortened form or contraction for Yahweh. In other words, the Greek word *allelouia* means "Praise Yah(weh)." For example, look at the following verse from Ps. 104:

Let the sinners be consumed out of the earth, and let the wicked be no more. Bless thou the LORD, O my soul. Praise ye [*halal*] the LORD [*YH*, Yah] (Ps. 104:35)

The Interlinear NIV Hebrew-English Old Testament translates the clause "Praise ye the LORD" in verse 35 as "Praise Yahweh."
Another aspect of studying the use of the Creator's name in the New Testament is to look at verses from the Old Testament that are quoted in the New Testament.

> The LORD [*YHWH*, Yahweh] said unto my Lord [*adon*], "Sit thou at my right hand, until I make thine enemies thy footstool." (Ps. 110:1)

The second "Lord" in the verse above is the translation of the Hebrew word *adon*—Strong's number 113 (pronounced "aw-done'")—and means "lord" or "master," and is usually so translated in the KJV and other English versions such as the NIV.

> And David himself saith in the book of Psalms, The LORD [*kurios*] said unto my Lord [*kurios*], Sit thou on my right hand, Till I make thine enemies thy footstool. (Lu. 20:42, 43)

Even though the KJV put the first "LORD" in small capitals (which in the Old Testament would indicate that it was the Hebrew word *YHWH*, Yahweh), both occurrences of "Lord" in the verse 42 above are translations of the Greek word *kurios*—Strong's number 2962 (pronounced "koo'-ree-os"). According to *Young's Analytical Concordance to the Bible*, *kurios* means "lord, sir, master," and it is usually translated as "lord" in the KJV.

You can probably already see the problem that arises in trying to track the Creator's name through the New Testament. The Hebrew Old Testament consistently uses *YHWH*, Yahweh, for the Creator's name and etymologically unrelated words for "lord" [including *adon* and *adonai* (which comes from *adon*)]. The Greek New Testament, however, uses *kurios*—the Greek equivalent of the Hebrew *adon* and *adonai*—to represent both the Creator's name Yahweh and the Hebrew word for "lord," *adon(ai)*.

The historical and other reasons why the Creator's name, Yahweh, does not occur in any publicly known manuscripts of the Greek New Testament are beyond the scope of this present discussion. However, learning as much as you can about the use of the Creator's name throughout the Bible will make for a very rewarding study.

Appendix 2
The Materials Dr. Bob Considered "Absolutely Essential"

(Jesus's Sermon on the Mount, James, 1 Corinthians 13)

"Dr. Bob, another founder of A.A., also addressed the Shrine assembly [along with Bill W.] As he was introduced, the audience rose to its feet in tribute. The fame of Dr. Bob is great in A.A. In soft, confident and unhurried words he too [along with Bill W.] reiterated the principles of Alcoholics Anonymous. . . He particularly recommended reading the Bible" (*The Tidings*, Friday, March 26, 1943, p. 47).

Many of the Bible's Books, Parts, and Verses Were Important, of Course!

A.A.'s Bible roots are as numerous and varied as the A.A. sources that used them. If you start with the Bible *devotionals* in wide use by A.A.'s old-timers, you'll see lots of mention of *all* the Bible verses, chapters, and books we'll discuss. Key among those devotionals were *The Upper Room, The Runner 's Bible, Daily Strength for Daily Needs,* and *My Utmost For His Highest.* These covered many verses and segments of the Bible other than the

Sermon on the Mount, the Book of James, and 1 Corinthians 13. Many of these other verses and segments were studied by, and important to, A.A.'s pioneers.

If you start with the books Dr. Bob's wife Anne recommended and shared from her journal with early AAs and their families, you will find Anne recommending the Book of Acts, Psalms, Proverbs, and other specific sections. She also recommended Fosdick's book on *The Meaning of Prayer,* which is filled with Bible references pertaining to prayer. She recommended several books on the life of Jesus Christ which also are filled with Bible references. She recommended life-changing books by Sam Shoemaker and others. These titles spell out appropriate Bible sources for the very spiritual ideas Rev. Shoemaker was teaching early AAs. So too with the Glenn Clark books and E. Stanley Jones books.

If you start with some of the books Dr. Bob recommended, you'll be looking at *The Greatest Thing in the World* by Drummond, which discusses 1 Corinthians 13. You'll look at several commentaries about Matthew chapters 5-7 (the sermon on the mount delivered by Jesus). These include books by Oswald Chambers, Glenn Clark, E. Stanley Jones, Emmet Fox, and others. Most of those authors discuss almost every single verse in the sermon. Though there is no commentary on the Book of James, *The Runner's Bible* (which Dr. Bob widely recommended) discusses many parts of James--the book Anne frequently read to Bob and Bill at the Smith home in the summer of 1935. The many books by Rev. Sam Shoemaker, Oxford Group writers, new thought writers, and others such as Toyohiko Kagawa and Glenn Clark all became rich sources for the simple ideas AAs extracted from the Good Book and incorporated into their spiritual program of recovery. That program, of course, involved intensive work with newcomers, prayer, Bible study, and daily fellowship with like-minded believers.

The Special Role of the Books of
Matthew, James, and 1 Corinthians

The focus here will be on the three portions of the Bible which Dr. Bob said he and the early A.A. pioneers considered "absolutely essential." Pointing directly to the roles of the three segments are the following pioneer comments about Matthew chapters 5-7, the Book of James, and 1 Corinthians 13:

> When we started in on Bill D. [who was A.A. Number Three], we had no Twelve Steps [said Dr. Bob]. But we were convinced that the answer to our problems was in the Good Book. To some of us older ones, the parts that we found absolutely essential were the Sermon on the Mount, the thirteenth chapter of First Corinthians, and the Book of James (*The Co-founders of Alcoholics Anonymous: Biographical sketches Their last major talks*, 1972, 1975, pp. 9-10).

> [Dr. Bob said, in Youngstown, Ohio:] Members of Alcoholics Anonymous begin the day with a prayer for strength and a short period of Bible reading. They find the basic messages they need in the Sermon on the Mount, in Corinthians and the Book of James (Wally P., *But for the Grace of God,* p. 45).

> [Dr. Bob's son "Smitty" recently recalled:] Before there was a Big Book—in the period of "flying blind," God's Big Book was the reference used in our home. The summer of 1935, when Bill lived with us, Dr. Bob had read the Bible completely three times. And the references that seemed consistent with the program goals were the Sermon on the Mount, I Corinthians 13, and the Book of James (Dick B., *The Good Book and The Big Book,* p. ix).

> [An early pamphlet commissioned by Dr. Bob stated:] There is the Bible that you haven't opened for years. Get acquainted with it. Read it with an open mind. You will find things that will

amaze you. You will be convinced that certain passages were written with you in mind. Read the Sermon on the Mount (Matthew V, VI, and VII). Read St. Paul's inspired essay on love (I Corinthians XIII). Read the Book of James. Read the Twenty-third and Ninety-first Psalms. These readings are brief but so important (*A Manual for Alcoholics Anonymous*, rev ed., AA of Akron, 1989, p. 8).

[Bill Wilson said of his stay with Dr. Bob and Anne for three months in 1935:] Each morning there was devotion. After the long silence Anne [Dr. Bob's wife] would read out of the Good Book. James was our favorite (*RHS*. New York: The AA Grapevine, Inc., 1951, p. 5).

The definition of love in Corinthians also played a great part in our discussions (Kurtz, *Not-God*. Hazelden, 1991, p. 320, n. 11).

The Sermon on the Mount [Matthew chapters 5-7] contains the underlying spiritual philosophy of A.A. [said both Bill Wilson and Dr. Bob] (Dick B., *The Good Book and The Big Book: A.A.'s Roots in the Bible,* p. 4).

The key Bible segments, then--considered absolutely essential in putting together A.A.'s spiritual program of recovery--were the Sermon, James, and 1 Corinthians 13.

And there seems little doubt that any study of A.A. history, A.A. principles, A.A. literature, and the A.A. fellowship requires a knowledge of what the early AAs took from the three key Bible sources. Those three segments of Biblical materials clearly influenced or found their way into the Big Book and the Twelve Steps. And those Bible segments are of such historical significance that they justify the following, separate, item-by-item review.

The Sermon on the Mount

This discussion will not deal with a particular book or commentary on Matthew chapters 5-7. It will focus on the Sermon on the Mount itself; for this Sermon, which Jesus delivered, was not the property of some present-day commentator or writer. The fact that Dr. Bob read the Matthew chapters *themselves,* as well as many interpretations of them, verifies the A.A. belief that the Sermon was one of the principles comprising "the common property of mankind," which Bill Wilson said the AAs had borrowed. And here are some major points that appear to have found their way from the Sermon into the basic ideas of the Big Book. The points were, of course, in the sermon itself. In addition, the pioneers read many books and articles on and about the sermon which are thoroughly documented in the author's title, *The Good Book and The Big Book: A.A.'s Roots in the Bible.* Those items further illustrate some of the points made in the sermon that might have found their way into A.A.

The Lord's Prayer—Matthew 6:9-13

Oxford Group meetings closed with the Lord's Prayer in New York and in Akron. Moreover, the author has attended at least two thousand A.A. meetings, and almost every one has closed with the Lord's Prayer. At the 1990 International A.A. Conference in Seattle, which was a first for this author, some 50,000 members of Alcoholics Anonymous joined in closing their meetings with the Lord's Prayer. The question here concerns what parts, if any, of the Lord's Prayer found their way into the Big Book, Twelve Steps, A.A. Slogans, and the A.A. fellowship; and we hasten to remind the reader that the prayer is *part of the Sermon on the Mount.* Here are the verses of the Lord's Prayer (*King James Version*) as found in Matt. 6:9-13. Jesus instructed the Judaeans, "After this manner therefore pray ye":

Our Father which art in heaven, Hallowed be thy name.
Thy kingdom come. Thy will be done in earth, as *it is* in
heaven. Give us this day our daily bread.
And forgive us our debts, as we forgive our debtors.
And lead us not into temptation, but deliver us from evil: For
thine is the kingdom, and the power, and the glory, for ever.
Amen.

Dr. Bob studied commentaries on the Sermon by Oswald Chambers,
Glenn Clark, Emmet Fox, and E. Stanley Jones. And these writers
extracted a good many teachings, prayer guides, and theological
ideas from Lord's Prayer verses in the Sermon. But there are a few
concepts and phrases in the Lord's Prayer itself which either
epitomize A.A. thinking or can be found in its language—whether
the A.A. traces came from the Lord's Prayer or from other portions
of the Bible. For example, the Big Book uses the word "Father"
when referring to God; and the context shows that this usage and
name came from the Bible. The Oxford Group also used the term
"Father," among other names, when referring to God. The concept
and expression of God as "Father" is not confined to the Sermon on
the Mount. It can be found in many other parts of the New
Testament. But AAs have given the "Our Father" prayer a special
place in their meetings. Thus the Lord's Prayer seems the likely
source of their use of the word "Father."

The phrase "Thy will be done" is directly quoted in the Big
Book several times. It underlies A.A.'s contrast between "self-will"
and "God's will." The Oxford Group stressed, as do A.A.'s Third
and Seventh Step prayers, that there must be a *decision to do God's
will and surrender to His will*. These ideas were also symbolized in
the A.A. prayer's "Thy will be done."

Finally, "Forgive us our debts" or "trespasses" certainly states
that God can and will "forgive"; and these concepts can be found in
the Big Book, whether they came from the Lord's Prayer or from
other important Biblical sources such as the Book of James.

The Full "Sermon on the Mount": Matthew Chapters 5-7

Dr. Bob studied, and circulated among early AAs, an E. Stanley
Jones book, *The Christ of the Mount* (Nashville: Abingdon, 1931;
Festival ed., 1985, pp. 36-37) which outlined the Sermon's contents
in this fashion:

1. The goal of life: To be perfect or complete as the Father in
    heaven is perfect or complete (5:48); with twenty-seven
    marks of this perfect life (5:1-47).

    [Jones wrote of these verses:] The perfect life consists in
    being poor in spirit, in mourning, in being meek, in
    hungering and thirsting after righteousness, in being
    merciful, pure in heart, in being a peacemaker, persecuted
    for righteousness sake and yet rejoicing and being
    exceeding glad, in being the salt of the earth, the light of
    the world, having a righteousness that exceeds, in being
    devoid of anger with the brother, using no contemptuous
    words, allowing no one to hold anything against one,
    having the spirit of quick agreement, no inward lustful
    thinking, relentless against anything that offends against the
    highest, right relations in the home life, truth in speech and
    attitude, turning the other cheek, giving the cloak also,
    going the second mile, giving to those who ask and from
    those who would borrow turning not away, loving even
    one's enemies, praying for those that persecute (pp. 50-
    51).

2. A diagnosis of the reason why men do not reach or move
    on to that goal: Divided personality (6:1-6; 7:1-6).

3. The Divine offer of an adequate moral and spiritual re-
    enforcement so that men can move on to that goal: The
    Holy Spirit to them that ask him (7:7-11).

4.   After making the Divine offer he gathers up and
      emphasizes in two sentences our part in reaching that goal.
      Toward others we are to do unto others as we would that
      they should do unto us (7:12); toward ourselves—we are to
      lose ourselves by entering the straight gate (7:13).

5.   The test of whether we are moving on to that goal, or
      whether this Divine Life is operative within us: By their
      fruits (7:15-23).

6.   The survival value of this new life and the lack of survival
      value of life lived in any other way: The house founded on
      rock and the house founded on sand (7:24-27).

Our own discussion will review Jesus's Sermon, chapter by chapter,
to locate some principal thoughts that Dr. Bob and Bill may have
had in mind when they each said A.A. embodied the philosophy of
the Sermon.

Matthew Chapter 5

1. **The Beatitudes**. The Beatitudes are found in Matt. 5:3-11.
The word "beatitudes" refers to the first word "Blessed" in each of
these verses. Merriam Webster's says "blessed" means "enjoying
the bliss of heaven." The word in the Greek New Testament from
which "blessed" was translated means, "happy," according Biblical
scholar Ethelbert Bullinger. *Vine's Expository Dictionary of Old
and New Testament Words* explains the word "Blessed" as follows:
"In the beatitudes the Lord indicates not only the characters that are
blessed, but the nature of that which is the highest good." Dr. Bob's
wife Anne Smith described the Beatitudes in the Sermon on the
Mount as "the Christ-like virtues to be cultivated" (Dick B., *Anne
Smith's Journal,* p. 135).
The beatitude verses can be found at the very beginning of
Jesus's sermon and read as follows:

And seeing the multitudes, he went up into a mountain: and
when he was set, his disciples came unto him:
And he opened his mouth, and taught them, saying,
Blessed are the poor in spirit: for theirs is the kingdom of
heaven.
Blessed are they that mourn: for they shall be comforted.
Blessed are the meek: for they shall inherit the earth.
Blessed are they which do hunger and thirst after righteousness:
for they shall be filled.
Blessed are the merciful: for they shall obtain mercy.
Blessed are the pure in heart: for they shall see God.
Blessed are the peacemakers: for they shall be called the
children of God.
Blessed are they which are persecuted for righteousness' sake:
for theirs is the kingdom of heaven.
Blessed are ye, when men shall revile you, and persecute you,
and shall say all manner of evil against you falsely, for my
sake.
Rejoice, and be exceeding glad: for great is your reward in
heaven: for so persecuted they the prophets which were before
you (Matt. 5:1-12)

Italicized below are Webster's definitions for the key words in each
"beatitude" verse, with quotes also from the *King James Version*,
which was the version Dr. Bob and early AAs most used. As the
verses appear in the King James, they state: "Blessed" are:

- the poor *(humble)* in spirit [renouncing themselves, wrote
  Jones]: for theirs is the kingdom of heaven (v. 3) ;
- they that mourn *(feel or express grief or sorrow):* for they
  shall be comforted (v. 4);
- the meek *(enduring injury with patience and without
  resentment);* for they shall inherit the earth (v. 5);
- they which do hunger and thirst after righteousness *(acting
  in accord with divine or moral law):* for they shall be filled
  (v. 6);

- the merciful *(compassionate):* for they shall obtain mercy (v. 7);
- the pure *(spotless, stainless)* in heart [has a passion for righteousness and a compassion for men–seeks law and shows love, wrote Jones]: for they shall see God (v. 8);
- the peacemakers: for they shall be called the children of God (v. 9);
- they which are persecuted for righteousness sake: for theirs is the kingdom of heaven (v. 10);
- ye when men shall revile you, and persecute you, and shall say all manner of evil against you falsely, for my sake *(end or purpose):* for great is your reward in heaven: for so persecuted they the prophets which were before you (v. 11).

Did Dr. Bob, Anne, Bill, or Henrietta Seiberling study and draw specifically on these beatitude verses as they put together A.A.'s recovery program? The author can neither provide nor document an answer. But there are some ideas common to A.A.'s spiritual principles in the beatitudes. These are: (1) Humility–overcoming self; (2) Comfort for the suffering; (3) Patience and tolerance to the end of eliminating resentment; (4) Harmonizing one's actions with God's will; (5) Compassion, which Webster defines as "sympathetic consciousness of others distress together with a desire to alleviate;" (6) "Cleaning house"–which means seeking obedience to God and straightening out harms based on the principle of love; (7) Making peace; (8) Standing for and acting upon spiritual principles because they are God's principles, whatever the cost. The foregoing are Twelve Step ideas that can be found in the Beatitudes; and A.A. founders probably saw them there as well.

2. **Letting your light shine**. Matt. 5:13-16 suggest glorifying your Heavenly Father by letting others *see* your good works. That is, "Letting your light shine" does not mean glorifying yourself, but

rather glorifying God by letting others see the spiritual walk *in action*—see the immediate results of surrender to the Master. These ideas may be reflected in the Big Book's statement: "Our real purpose is to fit ourselves to be of maximum service to God. . . ." (p. 77).

3. **Obeying the Ten Commandments**. In Matt. 5:17-21, Jesus reiterates the importance of obeying the law and the prophets, specifically referring to Exod. 20:13 (Thou shalt not kill), but obviously referring to the other important commandments such as having no other god but Jehovah (Exod. 20:2-3), worshiping no other god (Exod. 20:4-5), eschewing adultery (Exod. 20:14), not stealing (Exod. 20:15), and so on. And even though some of these commandments may have fallen between the cracks in today's A.A., they very clearly governed the moral standards of early A.A. that Dr. Bob and the Akron AAs embraced. The Ten Commandments were part of early A.A. pamphlets and literature, and (for example) Dr. Bob and the Akron AAs would have nothing to do with a man who was committing adultery.

4. **The Law of Love in action**. In Matt. 5:17-47, Jesus confirms that the Law of Love fulfills the Old Testament Law. He rejects anger without cause, unresolved wrongs to a brother, quibbling with an adversary, lust and impurity, adultery, retaliation, and hatred of an enemy. The author's title *The Oxford Group & Alcoholics Anonymous* covers many of these ideas as roots of A.A. principles. And the foregoing verses in Matthew may very well have influenced A.A. language about: (1) Overcoming resentments [". . .I say unto you, That whosoever is angry with his brother without a cause shall be in danger of the judgment. . .]; (2) Making restitution ["Therefore if thou bring thy gift before the altar, and there rememberest that thy brother hath ought against thee; Leave there thy gift before the altar, and go thy way; first be reconciled to thy brother, and then come and offer thy gift"]; (3) Avoidance of

retaliation for wrongdoing by others ["Ye have heard that it hath been said, An eye for an eye, and a tooth for a tooth: But I say unto you, That ye resist not evil: but whosoever shall smite thee on thy right cheek, turn to him the other also"]; and (4) Making peace with our enemies ["Ye have heard that it hath been said, Thou shalt love thy neighbor, and hate thine enemy. But I say unto you. Love your enemies, bless them that curse you, do good to them that hate you, and pray for them which despitefully use you, and persecute you"]

Matthew Chapter 6

1. **Anonymity**. Matt. 6:1-8, 16-18 (urging almsgiving "in secret," praying "in secret," fasting "in secret," and avoiding "vain repetitions," and hypocrisy) very possibly played a role in the development of A.A.'s spiritual principle of anonymity. Jesus said, "your Father knoweth what things ye have need of, before ye ask him" and "thy Father, which seeth in secret. shall reward thee openly." The vain practices which Jesus condemned were focused on inflation of the ego and the importance of self--something A.A. disdains. We have located no direct tie between the teachings of Jesus on anonymity and A.A.'s traditions on this "spiritual" principle. But the concepts are parallel; and *The Runner's Bible* and other A.A. biblical sources discuss their significance at some length.

2. **Forgiveness**. Matt. 6:14-15 refer to forgiving men their trespasses; and Emmet Fox's forceful writing about these verses may well have influenced the A.A. amends process. Fox said:

> The forgiveness of sins is the central problem of life. . . . It is, of course, rooted in selfishness. . . . We must positively and definitely extend forgiveness to everyone to whom it is possible that we can owe forgiveness, namely, to anyone who we think can have injured us in any way. . . When you hold resentment

against anyone, you are bound to that person by a cosmic link, a real, tough metal chain. You are tied by a cosmic tie to the thing that you hate. The one person perhaps in the whole world whom you most dislike is the very one to whom you are attaching yourself by a hook that is stronger than steel (Fox, *The Sermon on the Mount,* pp. 183-88).

There is no assurance that Fox's writing on this forgiveness point specifically influenced the Big Book's emphasis on forgiveness. At least two A.A. history writers have claimed that Fox's writings did influence Bill Wilson. However, other books that were read by early AAs used language similar to that used by Fox in his discussion of forgiveness of enemies. And the Sermon on the Mount is not the only place in the New Testament where forgiveness is stressed. Thus, after, and even though, Christ had accomplished remission of past sins of believers, Paul wrote:

Forbearing one another, and forgiving one another, if any man have a quarrel against any: even as Christ forgave you, so also *do ye* (Col. 3:13)

See also the following verse, a favorite used by Henrietta Seiberling:

If a man say I love God, and hateth his brother. he is a liar: for he that loveth not his brother whom he hath seen, how can he love God whom he hath not seen? (1 John 4:20)

In any event, the Big Book, Third Edition, states at page 77:

The question of how to approach the man we hated will arise. It may be he has done us more harm than we have done him and, though we may have acquired a better attitude toward him, we are still not too keen about admitting our faults. Nevertheless, with a person we dislike, we take the bit in our teeth. It is harder to go to an enemy than to a friend, but we find it more beneficial to us. We go to him in a helpful *and forgiving spirit,* confessing our former ill feeling and expressing our regret. Under no condition do we criticize such a person or argue. Simply we tell him that we will never get over drinking until we have done our utmost to straighten out the past (italics added).

3. **"The sunlight of the Spirit?"** Speaking of the futility and unhappiness in a life which includes deep resentment, the Big Book states: "when harboring such feelings we shut ourselves off from the sunlight of the Spirit." One often hears this "sunlight" expression quoted in A.A. meetings. Yet its origins seem unreported and undocumented. Anne Smith referred frequently in her journal to the verses in 1 John which had to do with fellowship with God and walking in the light as God is light. So did A.A.'s Oxford Group sources. And the following are the most frequently quoted verses from 1 John having to do with God as "light" and the importance of walking in the light (rather than walking in darkness) in order to have fellowship with Him:

That which we have seen and heard declare we unto you, that
ye may have fellowship with us: and truly our fellowship *is* with
the Father, and with his Son, Jesus Christ.
And these things write we unto you, that your joy may be full.
This then is the message which we have heard of him, and declare
unto you, that God is light, and in him is no darkness at all.
If we say that we have fellowship with him, and walk in darkness,
we lie, and do not the truth:
But if we walk in the light, as he is in the light, we have fellowship
one with another, and the blood of Jesus Christ his Son cleanseth us
from all sin (1 John 1:3-7).

Though this particular discussion is concerned with the Sermon on the Mount, we have mentioned also the foregoing verses from 1

John 1:3-7 (having to do with walking in God's light as against walking in darkness). For very possibly those ideas in 1 John, together with the following verses in the Sermon, may have given rise to Bill's references to the alcoholic's being blocked from the "sunlight of the Spirit" when he or she dwells in such dark realms as excessive anger. Matt. 6:22-24 (in the Sermon) state:

> The light of the body is the eye: if therefore thine eye be single, thy whole body shall be full of light.
> But if thine eye be evil, thy whole body shall be full of darkness. If therefore the light that is in thee be darkness, how great *is* that darkness!
> No man can serve two masters: for either he will hate the one, and love the other: or else he will hold to the one, and despise the other. Ye cannot serve God and mammon.

4. **Seek ye first the kingdom of God**. Matt. 6:24-34 seem to have had tremendous influence on A.A. The substance of these verses is that man will be taken care of when he seeks *first* the kingdom of God and His righteousness. Verse 33 says:

> But seek ye first the kingdom of God, and his righteousness; and all these things [food. clothing, and shelter] shall be added unto you.

Dr. Bob specifically explained the origin of our A.A. slogans "Easy Does It" and "First Things First." *(DR. BOB and the Good Oldtimers,* pp 135, 144). When he was asked the meaning of "First Things First," Dr. Bob replied. "Seek ye first the kingdom of God and His righteousness, and all these things shall be added unto you." He told his sponsee Clarence S. that "First Things First" came from Matt. 6:33 in the Sermon on the Mount. And this verse was widely quoted in the books that Dr. Bob and the Akron AAs read and recommended (Dick B., *The Good Book and The Big Book,* p. 125, n.119).

On page 60, the Big Book states the A.A. solution for relief from alcoholism: "God could and would if He were sought." This concept of "seeking" results by reliance on God instead of reliance on self is a bedrock idea in the Big Book (see Third Edition, pp. 11, 14, 25, 28, 43, 52-53, 57, 62). In view of Dr. Bob's explanations as to the origin of "First Things First," the Big Book's emphasis on "seeking" very likely came from the "seeking the kingdom of God first" idea in Matt. 6:33.

Matthew Chapter 7

1. **Taking your own inventory**. Much of A.A.'s Fourth, Ninth, Tenth, and Eleventh Step actions involve looking for your own part, for your own fault in troublesome matters. This self-examination process (as part of the house-cleaning and life-changing process in the Steps) was expected to result in that which, in Appendix II of the Third Edition of the Big Book, became described as "the personality change sufficient to bring about recovery from alcoholism" (Big Book, p. 569). Matt. 7:3-5 states:

> And why beholdest thou the mote [speck] that is in thy brother's eye, but considerest not the beam [log] that is in thine own eye? Or how wilt thou say to thy brother, Let me pull the mote [speck] out of thine eye; and, behold, a beam [log] *is* in thine own eye.
> Thou hypocrite, first cast out the beam [log] out of thine own eye; and then shalt thou see clearly to cast out the mote [speck] out of thy brother's eye.

These verses from Matthew were frequently cited by A.A.'s spiritual sources as the Biblical foundation for self-examination and thus finding one's own part, one's own erroneous conduct, in a relationship problem.

2. **Ask, seek, knock**. Matt. 7:7-11 states:

> Ask, and it shall be given you; seek, and ye shall find; knock,
> and it shall be opened unto you;
> For every one that asketh receiveth; and he that seeketh findeth;
> and to him that knocketh it shall be opened.
> Or what man is there of you, whom if his son ask bread, will he
> give him a stone? Or if he ask a fish, will he give him a
> serpent?
> If ye then, being evil, know how to give good gifts unto your
> children, how much more shall your Father which is in heaven
> give good things to them that ask him?

Bill Wilson's spiritual teacher, Rev. Sam Shoemaker, wrote:

> Our part [in the crisis of self-surrender] is to ask, to seek, to
> knock. His [God's] part is to answer, to come, to open
> (Shoemaker, *Realizing Religion,* p. 32).

The Runner's Bible (one of the most important of the early A.A.
Bible devotionals) has an entire chapter titled, "Ask and Ye shall
receive." Another favored devotional among the A.A. pioneers was
My Utmost for His Highest, by Oswald Chambers. Chambers says,
about the foregoing verses beginning with Matt. 7:7:

> The illustration of prayer that Our Lord uses here is that of a
> good child asking for a good thing. . . . It is no use praying
> unless we are living as children of God. Then, Jesus says:
> "Everyone that asketh receiveth."

The foregoing verses, and relevant comments by A.A. sources,
underline the importance of becoming a child of God, establishing
a harmonious relationship with Him, and *then* expecting good
results from God, as our Heavenly Father. Given the emphasis in
early A.A. on the Sermon, those verses from Matt. 7 very probably

influenced the following similar ideas in the Big Book's Third Edition:

> If what we have learned and felt and seen means anything at all, it means that all of us, whatever our race, creed, or color are the children of a living Creator with whom we may form a relationship upon simple and understandable terms as soon as we are willing and honest enough to try (p. 28).

> God will constantly disclose more to you and to us. Ask Him in your morning meditation what you can do each day for the man who is still sick. The answers will come, *if your own house is in order*. But obviously you cannot transmit something you haven't got. See *to it that your relationship with Him is right*, and great events will come to pass for you and countless others. This is the Great Fact for us (p. 164, italics added).

In this same vein. Dr. Bob's wife, Anne, wrote, in the spiritual journal she shared with early AAs and their families:

> We can't give away what we haven't got. We must have a genuine contact with God in our present experience. Not an experience of the past, but an experience in the present—actual, genuine (Dick B., *Anne Smith's Journal*, p. 121).

3. **Do unto others**. The so-called "Golden Rule" cannot, as such, be readily identified in A.A.'s Big Book though it certainly is a much-quoted portion of the Sermon on the Mount which Bill and Dr. Bob said underlies A.A.'s philosophy. The relevant verse is Matt. 7:12:

> Therefore all things whatsoever ye would that men should do to you, do ye even so to them: for this is the law and the prophets.

Perhaps the following two Big Book segments bespeak that philosophy as Bill may have seen it:

> We have begun to learn tolerance, patience and good will toward all men, even our enemies, for we look on them as sick people. We have listed the people we have hurt by our conduct, and are willing to straighten out the past if we can (p. 70).

> Then you will know what it means to give of yourself that others may survive and rediscover life. You will learn the full meaning of "Love thy neighbor as thyself" (p. 153).

4. **He that doeth the will of my Father.** There are *several* key verses in the sermon on the mount which could have caused Bob and Bill to say that it contained A.A.'s underlying philosophy. The verses are those in the Lords Prayer itself (Matt. 6:9-13), the so-called Golden Rule quoted above (Matt. 7:12), and the phrase "Thy will be done" (Matt. 6:10). However, the author believes that perhaps the major spiritual principle that A.A. seems to have borrowed from the Sermon on the Mount—can be found in Matt. 7:21:

> Not every one that saith unto me. Lord, Lord, shall enter into the kingdom of heaven; but he that doeth the will of my Father which is in heaven.

Bill Wilson said clearly in the Big Book and in his other writings that the key to success in A.A. is doing the will of the Father--the Father Who is the subject of the Lord's Prayer, and the Creator upon whom early AAs depended. Wilson wrote:

> I was to sit quietly when in doubt, asking only for direction and strength to meet my problems as He would have me (Bill's Story, Big Book, 3rd ed., p. 13).

He humbly offered himself to his Maker—then he knew (Big Book, 3rd ed., p. 57).

. . . praying only for knowledge of His will for us and the power to carry that out (Step Eleven, Big Book, 3rd ed., p. 59).

May I do Thy will always (portion of "Third Step Prayer," Big Book, 3rd ed., p. 63)!

Thy will be done (Big Book, 3rd ed, pp. 67, 88).

Grant me strength, as I go out from here, to do your bidding. Amen (portion of "Seventh Step Prayer," Big Book, 3rd ed., p. 76).

There is God, our Father, who very simply says, 'I am waiting for you to do my will' *(Alcoholics Anonymous Comes of Age,* p. 105).

The Book of James

Of probably even greater importance (than the Sermon) in the day-by-day thinking of early A.A. was the Book of James. It was much studied by A.A.'s co-founders. Quotes and ideas from the Apostle James can be found throughout the Big Book and in A.A. literature. The Book of James was considered so important that many favored calling the A.A. fellowship the "James Club" *(DR. BOB and the Good Oldtimers,* p. 71; *Pass It On,* p. 147). And even the most fundamental phrases in A.A., such as "It Works" and Bill Wilson's own "Works Publishing Company" (which published the First Edition of the Big Book), probably have their origin in the "Faith without works is dead" phrases in the Book of James (See: Nell Wing, *Grateful to Have Been There,* pp. 70-71).

Let's therefore review the Book of James, chapter by chapter. As we do so, we will point to traces of that book which we believe can be found in, or probably influenced the text of, the Big Book. At the outset, we would report that as our research into the Biblical roots of A.A. has progressed, so has our understanding of some root sources that previously went unnoticed.

For example, some time back, Dr. Bob's son, Robert R. Smith, told the author by phone that his father had placed great stake in *The Runner's Bible*. We had encountered difficulty locating a copy. And we were still looking for some commentary on the Book of James similar to the many on the Sermon on the Mount (by Oswald Chambers, Glenn Clark, Emmet Fox, and E. Stanley Jones) and on 1 Corinthians 13 (by Henry Drummond, for example) which Dr. Bob had studied. We believed such above-mentioned commentaries probably impacted upon the thinking of Dr. Bob, Anne, Henrietta, and the early AAs just as the actual Bible verses in Matthew chapters 5-7 and 1 Corinthians 13 have.

But we could find no similar commentary that the pioneers used with the Book of James, despite A.A.'s specific emphasis on James. Finally, as we studied the spiritual literature early AAs read, we noticed in *The Runner's Bible* the frequency with which all the books and chapters that Dr. Bob called "absolutely essential" (Matthew chapters 5-7, 1 Corinthians 13, and James) were there mentioned. We particularly noticed the frequency with which *The Runner's Bible* mentioned and discussed verses from the Book of James. Hence our reader will find many references to *The Runner's Bible* in the footnotes of our title *The Good Book and The Big Book;* for we believe that the little devotional book may have provided Dr. Bob, Anne Smith, and perhaps even Bill Wilson, with much of the fodder that caused them to focus on James and conclude that James was their "favorite" book of the Bible.

In a phone conversation with the author in 1995, from his home in Texas, Dr. Bob's son stated he felt it would be almost impossible for him, at this late date, to confirm that *The Runner's Bible* was the source of either A.A.'s or its founders' emphasis on James or other parts of the Bible. But he pointed out that the little Biblical devotional book was used by those who wanted a quick and easy source for Biblical ideas in which they were interested. Perhaps, then, that book became a reference source for Dr. Bob, Anne, and even Bill Wilson when they were studying the pertinent Biblical ideas they extracted from 1 Corinthians 13, the Sermon on the Mount, and particularly James. Now let's look at the chapters in James.

James Chapter 1

1. **Patience.** Chapter One is not the only chapter in the Book of James which mentions patience. Nor is it the only portion of the Bible that stresses patience. But we've noted that James was a favored Biblical source in early A.A., and James 1:3-4 do state:

> Knowing *this,* that the trying of your faith worketh patience. But let patience have *her* perfect work, that ye may be perfect and entire, wanting nothing.

Patience certainly wound up as one of the most frequently mentioned spiritual principles in the Big Book (pp. 67, 70, 83, 111, 118, 163).

2. **Asking wisdom of God with unwavering believing**. James 1:5-8 state:

> If any of you lack wisdom, let him ask of God, that giveth to all *men* liberally, and upbraideth not; and it shall be given him.
> But let him ask in faith, nothing wavering. For he that wavereth is like a wave of the sea driven with the wind and tossed.
> For let not that man think that he shall receive anything of the Lord. A double minded man *is* unstable in all his ways.

Asking for God's direction and strength and receiving "Guidance" from Him, are major themes in both the Old and New Testaments.

They were important Oxford Group ideas as well. We therefore discussed them at length in our titles on the Oxford Group and on Anne Smith's spiritual journal. Certainly the Big Book, including the Eleventh Step itself, is filled with such Guidance concepts (3rd ed., pp.13, 46, 49, 62-63, 69-70, 76, 79-80, 83, 84-88, 100, 117, 120, 124, 158, 164).

3. **Resisting temptation.** It should surprise no one that AAs of yesteryear and of today are interested in resisting temptation, and having the power to do that—the power of God. James 1:12-16 state:

> Blessed *is* the man that endureth temptation: for when he is tried, he shall receive the crown of life, which the Lord hath promised to those that love him.
> Let no man say when he is tempted, I am tempted of God: for God cannot be tempted with evil, neither tempteth he any man:
> But every man is tempted when he is drawn away of his own lust and enticed.
> Then when lust bath conceived, it bringeth forth sin: and sin, when it is finished, bringeth forth death.
> Do not err, my beloved brethren.

4. **Every good and perfect gift comes from God, the Father of lights.** James 1:17 states:

> Every good gift and every perfect gift is from above, and cometh down from the Father of lights, with whom is no variableness, neither shadow of turning.

Bill seemed to be referring to this verse when he wrote on page 14 of *Alcoholics Anonymous*, 3rd ed.:

I must turn in all things to the Father of Light [sic] who presides over us all. [Alcoholics Anonymous, 1st ed., has "the Father of Lights," p. 23.]

Bill made the same reference to God, the Father of lights, who presides over us all, in Appendix I of *Alcoholics Anonymous*, 3rd ed.:

This to the end that our great blessings may never spoil us; that we shall forever live in thankful contemplation of Him who presides over us all (p. 568).

The "Him" who presides over us all was, of course, James 1:17's "Father of lights"– Almighty God.

5. **Let every man be slow to speak, slow to wrath**. James 1:19-20 state:

Wherefore, my beloved brethren, let every man be swift to hear, slow to speak, slow to wrath: For the wrath of man worketh not the righteousness of God.

The same verse is quoted in *The Runner's Bible* and seems quite relevant to the Big Book's injunction, "If we were to live, we had to be free of anger. . . . God save me from being angry" (Third Edition, pp. 66-67).

6. **Be ye doers of the word, and not hearers only**. James 1:21-22 state:

Wherefore lay apart all filthiness and superfluity of naughtiness, and receive with meekness the engrafted word, which is able to save your souls.
But be ye doers of the word, and not hearers only, deceiving your own selves.

Reverend Sam Shoemaker made this comment on the foregoing:

> I think St. James' meaning is made much clearer in Dr. Moffatt's translation, "Act on the Word, instead of merely listening to it." Try it out in experiment, and prove it by its results—otherwise you only fool yourself into believing that you have the heart of religion when you haven't (Shoemaker, *The Gospel According to You,* pp. 44-55).

In the same chapter, Shoemaker also pointed out that prayer is often more a struggle to find God than the enjoyment of Him and cooperation with His will. He added that "God is and is a Rewarder of them that seek Him." (See *The Gospel According to You,* p. 47; and Heb. 11:6).

We cannot find a specific reference to James 1:21-22 in the Big Book; but A.A. declares over and over that A.A. is a program of *action,* that probably no human power can relieve a person of his alcoholism, and "That God could and would if He were *sought"* (p. 60). A.A.'s program emphasizes action in the experiment of faith it adopted from John 7:17—*seeking* God by *following* the path that leads to a relationship with God. James 1:22 enjoins *doing* God's will as expressed in His Word—not merely listening to it. James was an Akron favorite. Shoemaker was a Wilson favorite. "Faith without works" was a Big Book favorite; and it therefore seems possible that A.A.'s emphasis on *action* might well have derived in part from James 1:21-22.

7. Pure religion and undefiled before God . . . to visit the fatherless and widows in their affliction. James 1:27 states:

> Pure religion and undefiled before God and the Father is this,
> To visit the fatherless and widows in their affliction, *and* to
> keep oneself unspotted from the world.

At the very least, this verse bespeaks unselfishness and helpfulness to others which were cardinal A.A. principles–particularly the principles embodied in Step Twelve. In fact, that's the point made in one of early A.A.'s pamphlets:

> And all we need to do in the St. James passage is to substitute the word "Alcoholic" for "Fatherless and Widows" and we have Step Twelve (*Spiritual Milestones*, AA of Akron, pp. 12-13).

James Chapter 2

Chapter Two of the Book of James may have made two direct and major contributions to the language of the Big Book and also to A.A.'s philosophy. Those two contributions were "Love thy neighbor as thyself" and "Faith without works is dead."

1. **Love thy neighbor as thyself**. James 2:8 states:

> If ye fulfill the royal law according to the scripture, Thou shalt love thy neighbor as thyself, ye do well.

This commandment to "Love thy neighbor" exists in other parts of both the Old and New Testaments. Thus, when the Big Book incorporated this phrase, there is no assurance that the quote is from James rather than from another Bible verse to the same effect (*e.g.*, Rom. 13:9). But the Big Book certainly does state:

> Then you will know what it means to give of yourself that others may survive and rediscover life. You will learn the full meaning of "Love thy neighbor as thyself" (p. 153).

The Book of James is very probably the specific source of this Biblical quote since Dr. Bob, early AAs, and Bill Wilson himself spoke with such frequency about "love" as the code of A.A. *and* the Book of James as their favorite book.

2. **Faith without works is dead**. Said to be the favorite verse of Anne Smith and perhaps the origin of many expressions in A.A. concerning "works," this sentence, or variations of it, appears several times in Chapter Two of the Book of James. For example, James 2:20 states:

> But wilt thou know, 0 vain man, that faith without works is dead?

"Faith without works" as a phrase, and as an A.A. "action" concept, are quoted or referred to many times in the Big Book (3rd ed., pp. 14-15, 76, 88, 93, 97). A.A.'s original Oxford Group connection also put emphasis on these James verses, using them in connection with the importance of witnessing.

3. **Helping Others**. It hardly requires citation or documentation to state that A.A.'s cardinal objective is to help others. And this service concept is underlined in Chapter 2 of James, beginning with verses 1 to 7. James 2:15-16 state the principle very well:

> If a brother or sister be naked, and destitute of daily food, And one of you say unto them, Depart in peace, be ye warmed and filled; notwithstanding ye give them not those things which are needful to the body; what doth it profit? Even so, faith, if it hath not works, is dead, being alone.

And every alcoholic who has helped one of his miserable, suffering, destitute brothers in need will instantly relate to those verses and hence to the importance of James to the early AAs.

4. **The Ten Commandments. Again!** James 2:10-11 state:

> For whosoever shall keep the whole law, and yet offend in one
> *point,* he is guilty of all. For he that said, Do not commit
> adultery, said also, Do not kill. Now if thou commit no
> adultery, yet if thou kill, thou art become a transgressor of the
> law.

James Chapter 3

1. **Taming the tongue**. In his Farewell Address to A.A., Dr.
Bob said:

> Let us also remember to guard that erring member the tongue,
> and if we must use it, let's use it with kindness and
> consideration and tolerance *(DR. BOB and the Good Oldtimers,*
> p. 338).

A major portion of James chapter 3 is devoted to the trouble that
can be caused by an untamed tongue. Following are a few verses
emphasizing the point:

> Even so the tongue is a little member and boasteth great things.
> Behold, how great a matter a little fire kindleth! And the tongue
> *is* a fire, a world of iniquity; so is the tongue among our
> members that it defileth the whole body, and setteth on fire the
> course of nature; and *it is* set on fire of hell.
> But the tongue can no man tame; it is an unruly evil, full of
> deadly poison.
> Out of the same mouth proceedeth blessing and cursing. My
> brethren, these things ought not to be (James 3:5, 6, 8, 10)

These verses are not quoted in the Big Book. But Anne Smith
referred to them frequently in her journal, as did other A.A. roots
sources (Dick B., *Anne Smith's Journal,* pp. 28, 44, 76, 77; Holm,

The Runner's Bible, p. 68). But, in paraphrasing those verses, Dr. Bob seemed to be speaking of the necessity for tolerance, courtesy, consideration, and kindness in our speech and actions. James makes clear that good *conversation* should be a focus—conversation, we believe, laced with consideration, kindness, and tolerance (See James 3:13). And these latter principles *are* very much in evidence in the Big Book (3ʳᵈ ed., pp. 67, 69-70, 83-84, 97, 118, 125, 135).

2. **Avoidance of envy, strife, and lying**. James 3:14-16 proclaim that a heart filled with envy, strife, and lies has not received that kind of "wisdom" from God, but rather from devilish sources. The verses state:

> But if ye have bitter envying and strife in your hearts; glory not, and lie not against the truth.
> This wisdom descendeth not from above, but is earthly, sensual, devilish.
> For where envying and strife is, there is confusion and every evil work.

"Envy" is not as much decried in the Big Book as jealousy; but a more modern translation of these King James verses equates "envy" *with* "jealousy" (*The Revised English Bible, New Testament*, p, 208). And the Big Book most assuredly condemns jealously (3ʳᵈ ed., pp. 37, 69, 82, 100, 119, 145, 161). In fact, the Big Book states as to jealousy *and* envy:

> Keep it always in sight that we are dealing with that most terrible human emotion—jealousy (p. 82).

> The greatest enemies of us alcoholics are resentment, jealousy, envy, frustration, and fear (p. 145).

And as to strife, the Big Book states:

> After all, our problems were of our own making. Bottles were
> only a symbol. Besides, we have stopped fighting anybody or
> anything. We have to (p. 103)!

James 3:17-18 talk much about making peace and the fruit of
righteousness being sown in peace of them that make peace.

As seen in the quote from James 3:14, lying and dishonesty are
also declared to be devilish; and one should note and compare the
Big Book's frequent emphasis on grasping and developing a manner
of living which "demands rigorous honesty" (p. 58). As to all the
verses in James 3:14-16, however, there is little certainty that these
particular verses were an exclusive or even major source for the Big
Books condemnation of envy, jealousy, strife, and dishonesty
because all these traits are stated to be objectionable by many other
parts of the Bible.

James Chapter 4:

1. **Asking amiss for selfish ends**. A.A.'s writings have much
to say about overcoming selfishness and self-centeredness. But the
following in James 4:3 particularly emphasizes selfishness in
prayer:

> Ye ask, and receive not, because ye ask amiss, that ye may
> consume it upon your lusts.

Several Christian A.A. sources that were favorites of Dr. Bob's
discuss this verse at length. And the Big Book authors may
therefore have borrowed from James 4:3, in this statement:

> We ask especially for freedom from self-will, and are careful to
> make no request for ourselves only. We may ask for ourselves,
> however, if others will be helped. We are careful never to pray

for our own selfish ends. Many of us have wasted a lot of time doing that and it doesn't work (Big Book, 3rd ed., p. 87).

2. **Humility**. The Book of James has no corner on the Biblical injunction to be humble. But the importance of James, and the remarks of Reverend Sam Shoemaker (quoted under Item 3 immediately below) suggest that the following verses from James may have been a source of the Big Book's frequent mention of humility. James 4:7, 10 state:

Submit yourselves therefore to God. Resist the devil, and he will flee from you.
Humble yourselves in the sight of the Lord, and he shall lift you up.

The Big Book's Third Edition is filled with exhortations to be humble, with stress on humbling one's self before God, and with suggestions for humbly asking His help. Examples include:

There I humbly offered myself to God, as I understood Him, to do with me as He would (p. 13).

He humbly offered himself to his Maker—then he knew (p. 57).

Just to the extent that we do as we think He would have us, and humbly rely on Him, does He enable us to match calamity with serenity (p. 68).

We constantly remind ourselves we are no longer running the show, humbly saying to ourselves many times each day "Thy will be done" (pp. 87-88).

3. **Trusting God and cleaning house**. James 4:8 states:

> Draw nigh to God, and he will draw nigh to you. Cleanse your
> hands, ye sinners; and purify your hearts, ye double minded.

The Big Book says on page 98 of the Third Edition:

> Burn the idea into the consciousness of every man that he can
> get well regardless of anyone. The only condition is that he trust
> in God and clean house.

And, in language closely paralleling that in James 4:8, the Big Book
says further that one can establish conscious companionship with
God by simply, honestly, and humbly seeking and drawing near to
Him:

> He has come to all who have honestly sought Him. When we
> drew near to Him He disclosed Himself to us (page 57)!

In Step Seven, the Big Book relates "cleaning house" of one's
character defects to "humbly asking" God to remove them. The
foregoing verses in James, which speak of drawing near to God,
cleansing our hearts, humbling ourselves in His sight, and then
being "lifted" up by God, appear to have been directly involved in
framing the Big Book's Seventh Step language. In fact, many years
after the Big Book was written, Sam Shoemaker thus clarified his
understanding of the Seventh Step, in a 1964 issue of A.A. 's
Grapevine:

> Sins get entangled deep within us, as some roots of a tree, and
> do not easily come loose. We need help, grace, the lift of a kind
> of divine derrick (Shoemaker, "Those Twelve Steps as I
> Understand Them"; *Volume II, Best of the Grapevine*, p. 130).

4. **Taking your own inventory**. James 4:11-12 state:

Speak not evil one of another, brethren. He that speaketh evil
of *his* brother, and judgeth his brother, speaketh evil of the law,
and judgeth the law: but if thou judge the law, thou art not a
doer of the law, but a judge.
There is one lawgiver, who is able to save and to destroy: who
art thou that judgest another?

We discussed the Fourth Step idea of taking your own inventory in
connection with the relevant verses in the Sermon on the
Mount–which were often quoted by Oxford Group people and by
Anne Smith (See Matt. 7:1-5). But the Big Book also speaks of: (1)
looking "for our own mistakes," (2) asking "Where were we to
blame," and (3) realizing, "The inventory was ours, not the other
man's." Considering the importance to AAs of the Book of James
and its insights, the foregoing James verses probably also had an
impact on the A.A. idea of avoiding judgment of another and
focusing on an examination of one's *own* conduct when it comes to
wrongdoing.

James Chapter 5

1. **Patience**. We discussed A.A.'s "patience principle" as
having probably derived from James, Chapter One. As we said,
however, important stress on patience can be found in James 5:7,
8, 10, 11.

2. **Grudges** (covered in A.A.'s 4th Step resentment inventory
process). James 5:9 reads:

Grudge not one against another, brethren, lest ye be
condemned; behold, the judge standeth before the door.

A major portion of the Big Book's Fourth Step discussion is devoted to resentment, about which page 64 says:

> Resentment is the "number one" offender. It destroys more alcoholics than anything else. From it stem all forms of spiritual disease.

The Big Book then suggests putting resentments *on paper*—making a *"grudge list"* (pp. 64-65). Oxford Group spokesman Ebenezer Macmillan wrote at length in his title *Seeking and Finding* about eliminating resentments, hatred, or the *"grudge"* that "blocks God out effectively." Rev. Sam Shoemaker also specified "grudges" as one of the "sins" to be examined in an inventory of self (Shoemaker, *Twice-Born Ministers*, p. 182). Since the Big Book lists resentments or "grudges" as one of the four major "character defects" which block us from God, it quite possible that the "grudge" language in the Big Book was influenced by James, and perhaps specifically by James 5:9.

3. **Asking God's forgiveness for sins**. We repeat James 5:15, which was partially quoted above. The entire verse says:

> And the prayer of faith shall save the sick, and the Lord shall raise him up; and if he have committed sins, they shall be forgiven him.

The Big Book says this about asking God's forgiveness when we fall short:

> If we are sorry for what we have done, and have the honest desire to let God take us to better things, we believe we will be forgiven and will have learned our lesson (3rd ed, p. 70).

When we retire at night, we constructively review our day. . . .
After making our review, we ask God's forgiveness and inquire
what corrective measures should be taken (3rd ed., p. 86).

The foregoing Big Book quotes show that, even after their initial
surrender, wrongdoers may still, in A.A.'s view, seek and receive
God's forgiveness for shortcomings indulged after the initial
surrender. Here again, James has no corner on the statement that
God makes it possible, through forgiveness, for a believer to regain
fellowship with Him. The following in 1 John 1:9 may also have
been a source of such Big Book ideas:

If we confess our sins, he is faithful and just to forgive us *our*
sins, and to cleanse us from all unrighteousness.

See also our discussion of forgiveness in connection with the
Sermon on the Mount. It is fair to say, however, that the Book of
James, 1 John, or Matthew could each, or all, have been the basis
for the Big Book forgiveness concept.

4. **Confess your sins one to another**. It has often been noted
that *both* the Oxford Group concept of sharing by confession *and*
Step Five in the Big Book were derived from James 5:16:

Confess your faults one to another, and pray for one another,
that ye may be healed.

5. **Effectual, fervent prayer works**. James 5:16 states:

The effectual fervent prayer of a righteous man availeth much.

A.A.'s Big Book Third Edition says:

Step Eleven suggests prayer and meditation. We shouldn't be
shy on this matter of prayer. Better men than we are using it

constantly. It works, if we have the proper attitude and work at it.

James 5:16 could well have been a major basis for the Big Book comments on the effectiveness of prayer.

1 Corinthians 13

1 Corinthians 13 is often called the Bible's "love" chapter because it focuses on the importance of love in the Christian's life. In the King James Version, the word "charity" is used in the verses which are speaking of "love;" but the underlying Greek word is *agapē* which is more properly translated "love."

And the most frequently quoted characteristics of love are contained in the following verses from the King James Version of the Bible (which is the version the A.A. pioneers used):

> Charity [love] suffereth long, *and* is kind; charity envieth not; charity vaunteth not itself, is not puffed up,
> Doth not behave itself unseemly, seeketh not her own, is not easily provoked, thinketh no evil;
> Rejoiceth not in iniquity, but rejoiceth in the truth (1 Cor. 13:4-6).

The New International Version, which is much in use today, renders 1 Cor. 13:4-6:

> Love is patient, love is kind. It does not envy, it does not boast, it is not proud.
> It is not rude, it is not self-seeking, it is not easily angered, it keeps no record of wrongs.
> Love does not delight in evil but rejoices with the truth.

One of the most popular books in early A.A. was Professor Henry Drummond's study of 1 Corinthians 13. The title of his book, *The Greatest Thing in the World,* was taken from the last verse of 1 Corinthians chapter 13, which reads:

And now abideth faith, hope, charity, these three; but the greatest of these is charity (1 Cor. 13:13).

Drummond's book was part of Dr. Bob's library, and a copy was still found in, and owned by, Dr. Bob's family when the author interviewed Dr. Bob's son and daughter several years ago. In much earlier years, A.A. Old-timer Bob E. had sent a memo to Bill Wilson's wife, Lois, in which Bob E. listed *The Greatest Thing in the World* as one of three books Dr. Bob regularly provided to alcoholics with whom he worked. In fact, Dr. Bob's enthusiasm for Drummond's book is dramatized by the following remarks by a former wife of A.A. old-timer Clarence S. Clarence's former wife, Dorothy S. M., said:

Once, when I was working on a woman in Cleveland, I called and asked him [Dr. Bob], "What do I do for somebody who is going into D.T.'s?" He told me to give her the medication, and he said, "When she comes out of it and she decides she wants to be a different woman, get her Drummond's 'The Greatest Thing in the World.' Tell her to read it through every day for 30 days, and she'll be a different woman"(See *DR. BOB and the Good Oldtimers,* p. 310).

Henry Drummond himself had made a similar suggestion half a century earlier, at the close of the lecture in which he delivered his 'greatest thing in the world' address–the address which was later published in Drummond's best-seller. Drummond said:

Now I have all but finished. How many of you will join me in reading this chapter [1 Corinthians 13] once a week for the next three months? A man did that once and it changed his whole life. Will you do it? It is for the greatest thing in the world. You might begin by reading it every day, especially the verses which describe the perfect character. "Love suffereth long, and is kind; loveth envieth not; love vaunteth not itself." Get these ingredients into your life (See Drummond, *The Greatest Thing in the World*. p. 53).

The important influence on A.A. that came from 1 Corinthians 13 can be seen in Drummond's own simplified description of love's *ingredients*. Drummond listed nine ingredients of "love" as he saw love specifically defined in that portion of that chapter of the Bible (See Drummond, *The Greatest Thing in the World*, pp. 26-27). And we here set out those nine love ingredients with references to correlative Bible verses and correlative A.A. language:

Drummond's Explanation	Authorized KJV	NIV Version	A.A. Big Book 3rd ed. Examples
1. Patience	"Charity suffereth long."	"Love is patient"	pp. 67, 70, 83 111, 163
2. Kindness	"*and* is kind."	"love is kind"	pp. 67, 82, 83, 86
3. Generosity	"charity envieth not."	"It does not envy"	pp. 145, *cf.* 82
4. Humility	"charity vaunteth not itself "is not puffed up."	"it does not boast, "it is not proud"	pp. 13, 57, 68, 87-88
5. Courtesy	"Doth not behave itself unseemly."	"It is not rude"	p. 69
6. Unselfishness	"seeketh not her own."	"It is not self-seeking"	pp. xxv, 93, 127
7. Good Temper	"is not easily provoked"	"it is not easily angered	pp. 19, 67, 70, 83-84, 125, 118

8. Guilelessness	"thinketh no evil"	"it keeps no record of wrongs	pp. 19, 67, 70, 83-84, 118, 125
9. Sincerity	"Rejoiceth not in iniquity" "but rejoiceth in the truth"	"does not delight in evil" "but rejoices with the truth"	pp. xiv, xxvii, 13 26, 28, 32, 44, 47, 55, 57-58, 63-65, 67, 70, 73, 117,140, 145

Dr. Bob said that A.A.'s Twelve Steps, when simmered down to the last, quite simply resolved themselves into the words "love" and "service" (See *DR. BOB and the Good Oldtimers*, p. 338). He presented God to the old-timers as a God of love who was interested in their individual lives. (*DR. BOB, supra*, p. 110). Dr. Bob's wife, Anne, frequently quoted love verses in 1 John 4:8; 4:16–"God is love" (*DR. BOB supra*, pp. 116-17). Furthermore both Anne and her husband Dr. Bob studied Toyohiko Kagawa's book, *Love: The Law of Life*. In that book, the author Kagawa devoted an entire chapter to 1 Corinthians 13, not only to the Corinthians chapter, but also to Drummond's analysis of that chapter in Drummond's *The Greatest Thing in the World*. Hence there was much emphasis among the A.A. pioneers on the "spiritual" principle of love as it is defined in the Bible. In fact, the Big Book itself talks repeatedly of that principle of love (Big Book, 3rd ed., pp. 83-84, 86, 118, 122, 153).

Love, then--the love of God--was a much cherished principle in early A.A. The AAs needed it, wanted it, studied it, and sought to know it. Despite "higher power" divergences in current A.A. writings and meeting talk, the love of God is still a vital component of A.A. thinking and speech. Even Bill Wilson inserted the phrase "a loving God" in A.A.'s Traditions. And I well remember my good friend Seymour W., a Jew, who tried each morning to comfort his many friends in the fellowship. The telephone on Seymour's "God" line would ring for many about 6:00 A.M. The message to the bedraggled A.A. was "God loves you." And Seymour would hang up. It was a coveted privilege to be on Seymour's "God-loves-you" list. What a way to start the day in early sobriety!

Further illustrating the great store placed on God's love and on the Corinthians love principle by A.A. pioneers is their frequent rendition of Jesus Christ's message in Mark 12:30-31. These Gospel verses deal with what Jesus called the two *great* commandments:

> And thou shalt love the Lord thy God with all thy heart, and with all thy soul, and with all thy mind, and with all thy strength; this is the first commandment. And the second is like, namely this, Thou shalt love thy neighbor as thyself. There is none other commandment greater than these.

The foregoing verses, from the Gospel of Mark in the New Testament, were cited for the standard of "Absolute Love," as it was discussed in AA of Akron's *A Manual for Alcoholics Anonymous* (one of the four pamphlets commissioned by Dr. Bob for use among early AAs). The Old Testament also contained the very same commandments to which Jesus referred, underlining the importance of love of God and of neighbor in all the commandments of the Bible:

> Hear, O Israel: The Lord our God *is* one Lord: And thou shalt love the Lord thy God with all thine heart, and with all thy soul, and with all thy might (Deut. 6:4-5).

> Thou shalt not avenge, nor bear any grudge against the children of thy people, but thou shalt love thy neighbor as thyself: I *am* the Lord (Lev. 19:18).

A.A. literature contains no specifics on, or detailing of, the impact of, 1 Corinthians 13 on A.A. But this cherished "essential," as Dr. Bob put it, deserves to be revived, promulgated, and applied today. The particulars can be seen by reading 1 Corinthians 13 itself; by noting the frequent mention of "Love" in the Big Book; by studying the reading and remarks of Dr. Bob and Anne; by remembering Bill Wilson's specific mention of Corinthians; and by the repeated mention of 1 Corinthians 13 in A.A.'s religious sources. The nine love "ingredients," as they were summarized by Henry Drummond, permeate A.A.'s basic text and can fairly be proclaimed to be among those "principles to be practiced" at the level of A.A.'s Twelfth Step.

The fundamental principle is, of course, love. The component "ingredients" or "virtues" involved in such love are: patience; tolerance; kindness; humility; honesty; unselfishness; consideration for others; and the avoidance of anger, jealousy, envy, pride, and wrongdoing.

As previously covered, almost every one of these virtues can be found as well in Jesus' sermon on the mount and in the Book of James. The principles are defined in the sermon on the mount in specific terms that elaborate upon what constitutes doing the will of God in the love category. And, in James, from the standpoint of action and service to God and service to others through reliance upon God.

These were also the very the principles of love and service of which Dr. Bob spoke in his farewell address and defined as the essence of A.A.'s spiritual program of recovery.

Appendix 3
Yesterday, Today, and Tomorrow

When I studied Economics 40 (Statistics) at the University of California in Berkeley, the professor began the course by presenting the old saw: There are liars, darned liars, and statisticians. However, I also learned from him that statistics is a science; and pollsters have made it a national pastime–whatever its reliability.

Not all the statistics concerning early A.A.'s effectiveness in the 1930's, or its supposed effectiveness in the new millennium, can pass the tests of statistical science. However, if you combine the statistics with what I've seen in the form of evidence, with extant rosters, and present-day revolving door attendance at meetings, I believe you can agree with many of the statements below. Some are from avowed critics of Alcoholics Anonymous–both Christian and atheist. Some are from early A.A. apologists. Some are neither completely adequate nor comprehensive enough.

The Success Factor in Early A.A.

First, let's look at the claims made primarily by Bill Wilson himself. They are varied and tempered by his own desire to "sell" the program. Here's what Wilson said they had to work with as they began to develop a spiritual program of recovery.

The people they helped: Medically incurable; "100% hopeless apart from Divine help"

> The doctor [famed psychiatrist Carl G. Jung] said: "You [Jung's patient, Rowland Hazard] have the mind of a chronic alcoholic. I have never seen one single case recover, where that state of mind existed to the extent that it does in you." Our friend [Rowland Hazard] felt as though the gates of hell had closed on him with a clang (Big Book, 1st ed., 1939, p. 37).

> Many doctors and psychiatrists agree with our conclusions. One of these men, staff member of a world-renowned hospital, recently made this statement to some of us: "What you say about the general hopelessness of the average alcoholic's plight is, in my opinion correct. As to two of you men, whose stories I have heard, there is no doubt in my mind that you were 100% hopeless, apart from Divine help. . . ." (Big Book, 1st ed, 1939, pp. 54-55).

The Success of Akron's Spiritual Program: Several views on what percent recovered:

While the percentage factors re the successes in early A.A. vary, it is difficult to dispute the 75% to 93% claims for Akron and Cleveland if you qualify them with words like "real alcoholics" who "really tried." The reason (even assuming there is no question as to the integrity of those who make the claims) is that the author himself has in his possession, and has studied, the rosters in Akron and Cleveland which show names, sobriety dates, and even addresses and phone numbers of the pioneers. Then there's the fact that the pictures of many early pioneers hang on the walls at Dr. Bob's Home in Akron. The pioneers knew each other, kept track of each other, and–as witnessed by many A.A. old-timers–remained sober for many years. Here are the claims:

Fifty Percent

"In this human laboratory, he [Dr. Bob] has proved that any alcoholic, not too mentally defective, can recover if he so desires. The possible recovery among such cases has suddenly been lifted from almost nil to at least 50 percent, which, quite aside from its social implications, is a medical result of the first magnitude. Though, as a means of our recovery, we all engage in the work, Dr. Smith has had more experience and has obtained better results than anyone else," said Bill Wilson (*DR. BOB and the Good Oldtimers*, p. 174).

Seventy-five Percent

"Of alcoholics who came to A.A. and really tried, 50% got sober at once and remained that way; 25% sobered up after some relapses, and among the remainder, those who stayed on with A.A. showed improvement. Other thousands came to a few A.A. meetings and at first decided they didn't want the program. But great numbers of these–about two out of three–began to return as time passed" (Big Book, 3rd ed., 1976, p. xx. See also Wilson's *Three Talks to Medical Societies*, p. 13; *A Program for You: A Guide to the Big Book's Design for Living*, 1991, p. 15).

Eighty Percent

[Wilson wrote in private correspondence] "We used to pussyfoot on this spiritual business a great deal more out here [in the New York area] and the result was bad, for our record falls a lot short of the performance of Akron and Cleveland, where there are now about 350 alcoholics, many of them sober 2 or 3 years, with less than 20% ever having had any relapse" (Kurtz and Ketcham, *The Spirituality of Imperfection*, 1992, p. 110).

Ninety-three Percent in Early Cleveland A.A.

"Records in Cleveland show that 93% of those who came to us never had a drink again" (*DR. BOB and the Good Oldtimers*, p. 261; Dick B., *That Amazing Grace*, pp. 7, 29, 66; *The Good Book and The Big Book*, p. 8).

"Two years after the publication of the book [in 1939], Clarence [Snyder] made a survey of all of the members in Cleveland. He concluded that, by keeping most of the 'old program,' including the Four Absolutes and the Bible, ninety-three percent of those surveyed had maintained uninterrupted sobriety" (Mitchell K., *How It Worked: The Story of Clarence H. Snyder*, p. 108).

One-hundred-percent with Non-psychotic Drinkers Who Sincerely Wanted to Quit

"One-hundred-percent effectiveness with non-psychotic drinkers who sincerely want to quit is claimed by the workers of Alcoholics Anonymous. . . . As it is impossible to disqualify all borderline applicants, the working percentage of recovery falls below the 100-percent mark" (Reprint of Jack Alexander article in A.A.'s *the Jack Alexander Article about AA*, 1991).

The Wilson factor on the East Coast where the biblical focus was missing

First, Bill Wilson was, by his own characterization, a conservative atheist–and irked at all *organized religions*

"Perhaps I wouldn't need an emotional conversion. After all, a conservative atheist like me ought to be able to get on without anything like that" (Wilson, *W. G. Wilson Reflections*, pp. 123-24. See also, *As Bill Sees It*, p. 276; Dick B., *The Good Book and The Big Book*, p. 68).

[In a 1948 letter to Clem L., Bill wrote:] "The thing that still irks me about all organized religions is their claim how confoundedly right all of them are. Each seems to think it has the right pipeline–no mud in its spiritual water. To secure converts or punish unbelievers, the great religions have violated every known law of man or God. Just now the Hindus and Moslems are at it. Quite obviously, infallibility seems to be much more important than spirituality. The record of the Western world is no better. The Jews crucified Christ; and ever since, Christians have been crucifying Jews–and each other" (*Pass It On*, p. 283).

Second, Bill said he couldn't believe:

"Always, I used to say to myself, 'Yes, this would work if I could only believe it. But I can't believe'" (*Bill W., My First 40 Years*, p. 97).

Third, in attitude, Bill had felt superior to most Christians he knew:

"At any rate I thought I understood as well as anyone what good morals were and with the exceptions of my drinking I felt superior to most Christians I knew. I might be weak in some respects but at least I was not hypocritical. So my interest in Christianity other than its teaching of moral principles and the good I hoped it did on balance was slight" (Wilson, *Bill Wilson's Original Story*, lines 908-15).

Then, there was the attitude of Bill's wife Lois, who felt they should found a universal program, not a Christian one:

"Finally it was agreed that the book should present a universal spiritual program, not a specific religious one, since all drunks were not Christian" (*Lois Remembers*, p. 113).

Next, Lois apparently walked alongside Bill, tuned to spiritualist thinking, rejecting much in Christian belief, and doubting her need for a real conversion. As to her religious views, Lois recounted,

> ". . . [T]he National Board of the YWCA refused because of my religion. Their letter of rejection stated that Swedenborgians (the sect to which I belonged) and Unitarians were not considered Christians! . . . . This seemed to me not only narrow but illogical; a "non-Christian" could instruct children but could not aid wounded soldiers" (*Lois Remembers*, p. 26).

As to her grandfather, Lois wrote,

> "Nathan Clark Burnham, practiced law and medicine and was also a minister of the Swedenborgian Church in Lancaster [Pennsylvania]. He wrote a book, "Discrete Degrees," about the relation Swedenborg had found between the spiritual and natural life. The Swedenborgian religion, also called the New Church or Church of the New Jerusalem had recently come to America. [Lois's] Grandfather, wanting to be sure he was on firm ground, learned Hebrew in order to translate the Old Testament into English" (*Lois Remembers*, pp. 1-2).

Lois and Bill were married on January 24, 1918 with a"big church wedding" in Brooklyn (*Lois Remembers*, p. 22; *Bill W.: My First 40 Years*, p. 44; *Pass It On*, p. 58); and the marriage occurred in the "Swedenborgian Church in Brooklyn" (a fact that Bill recounted in the manuscript *W.G. Wilson Reflections*, p. 127, and in the manuscript titled *W.A. Wilson* [sic], at the Hotel Bedford, September 27, 1954, p. 101–both of which manuscripts were seen and copied by the author at Stepping Stones, and whose account has been *deleted* from works based on the manuscripts and since published as cited above).

Criticizing Bill's conversion to Christ at Calvary Rescue Mission, Lois commented, "As for me, I had never believed in emotional conversions. . ." (*Lois Remembers*, p. 88).

As for the First Century Christian Fellowship in which Bill had become involved, she said, "I felt no personal need for their teachings. . . . I did not think I needed the Oxford Group" (*Lois Remembers*, p. 91).

The theology of Swedenborgians, may well have given rise to some of Bill's interest in spiritualism, the spirit world, clairvoyance, New Thought, and psychic experiences. (See Braden, *These Also Believe*, pp.134-35, 321-22, 343-44, 472; *Varieties of American Religion*, pp. 201-14; Van Baalen, *The Chaos of Cults*, pp. 177-87).

Further, Bill had no biblical knowledge or beliefs to contribute at all until he met the Smiths:

"I learned a great deal from you people [T. Henry and Clarace Williams], from the Smiths themselves, and from Henrietta [Seiberling]. I hadn't looked in the Bible, up to this time, at all. You see, I had the [conversion] experience first and then this rushing around to help drunks and nothing happened" (Dick B., *The Akron Genesis of Alcoholics Anonymous*, p. 64).

And one of A.A.'s earliest teachers, Henrietta Seiberling, saw what appeared to her to be the inevitable and dire results of such diffusions. As to the talks of two speakers she heard at an A.A. dinner with over 3000 in attendance, she said:

"You would have thought they were giving you a description of psychiatrists work on them. . . . [The speakers had] no realization that they have lost their source of power" (Dick B., *The Akron Genesis of Alcoholics Anonymous*, p. 98).

At the last dinner she attended, Henrietta highlighted the problem:

> "And I spoke to Bill afterwards and I said there was no
> spirituality there or talk of what God had done in their lives.
> They were giving views, not news of what God had done"
> (John F. Seiberling, *Origins of Alcoholics Anonymous*,
> Employer Assistance Quarterly, p. 12).

Wilson later tried to give his own apology for altering the
original emphasis in order to suit all potential members and
observers:

> "The problem of the Steps has been to broaden and deepen
> them, both for newcomers and oldtimers. But the angles are so
> many, it's hard to shoot them rightly. We have to deal with
> atheists, agnostics, believers, depressives, paranoids,
> clergymen, psychiatrists, and all and sundry. How to widen the
> opening so it seems right and reasonable to enter there and at
> the same time avoid distractions, distortions, and the certain
> prejudices of all who may read, seems fairly much of an
> assignment" (*Pass It On*, p. 354).

The Admitted Failures in the East Coast Approach

First, the approach itself:

> "As far as I am concerned [said Lois Wilson in her later years],
> A.A. began in 1934 in my father's old house on Brooklyn
> Heights where Bill and I were living. When Bill came home to
> 182 Clinton St. from Towns Hospital in New York after his
> spiritual awakening, he began immediately bringing drunks to
> the house" (Dick B., *The Akron Genesis of Alcoholics
> Anonymous*, pp. 3-4).

Describing the results at Clinton Street, Bill wrote:

> "This is a fair sampling of the sort of people we had on Clinton Street for the ensuing three years, until 1939 to be exact. **Not a single one of them made a recovery in our house** but we learned a lot about drunks" (From Bill's "Fact Sheet," dated November 2, 1954, and found by the author at Stepping Stones. See Dick B., *Turning Point*, p. 110, emphasis added).

Of the early period when there was work with newcomers outside the Wilson home, Lois wrote:

> "It was an ecstatic time for us both. With Ebby and another alcoholic, Shep C., as our companions, we constantly went to Oxford Group meetings at Calvary Episcopal Church on Fourth Avenue. . . . Bill went back to Towns constantly to work on alcoholics there and often visited the Calvary Mission where Alec, the fisherman had taken residence. . . . **Although he had not permanently sobered up anyone in New York**, simply trying to help others had kept him from even thinking of drinking"(*Lois Remembers*, pp. 91, 95, emphasis added).

Bill said of his early efforts:

> "Then came still another vital realization. In working with other alcoholics for six months past, **there had been no success**" (From page four of a five-page memorandum by Bill which the author obtained from Stepping Stones. See Dick B., *Turning Point*, p. 112, emphasis added).

Bill soon began attributing his own lack of success to the Oxford Group and claimed:

> "Drunks could not seem to accept the rigor of the Oxford Groups program. They'd stay sober only briefly and then flop.

No success at all" (Bill's "Fact Sheet," *supra*. See Dick B., *Turning Point*, p. 111, emphasis added).

Then assigning failures to lack of prayer and meditation, Bill wrote:

> "Saving some of our Catholic members and a few others, we are, as a group, pretty deficient on the prayer and meditation side. Quite a number of older AAs run into a period of seeming spiritual bankruptcy, indeed, one might guess, by excessive activity not balanced by sufficient intake. Apparently it is possible to get very bad indigestion on a straight diet of 'good works'" (Letter from Wilson to Sam Shoemaker, dated January 15, 1945, at Episcopal Church Archives in Texas. See Dick B., *Turning Point*, p. 150).

At an even earlier date, Bill seemed to have had some real insight as to the mistaken New York *de-emphasis* of the biblical approach being taken Akron; for he wrote in January, 1940:

> "A few, who have worked ardently with other alcoholics on the philosophical, rather than the spiritual plane, now say of themselves: 'We believed that Faith without works is dead, but we have now conclusively proved that works without Faith is dead also'" (Kurtz and Ketcham, *The Spirituality of Imperfection*, p. 109).

And then came Bill's frank admission as to the power and success achieved through Akron's approach:

> "I explain this at some length because I want you to be successful with yourself and the people with whom you work. We used to pussyfoot on this spiritual business a great deal more out here [New York City] and the result was bad, for our record falls quite a lot short of the performance of Akron and Cleveland, where there are now about 350 alcoholics, many of them sober 2 or 3 years, with less than 20% ever having had

any relapse. Out there they have always emphasized the spiritual way of life as the core of our procedure and we have begun to follow suit **in New York for the simple reason that our record was only half as good**, most of the difficulties being directly attributable to temporizing over what it really takes to fix the drunks, i.e., the spiritual" (From Wilson's private correspondence. See Kurtz and Ketcham, *The Spirituality of Imperfection*, pp. 109-10, emphasis added).

Fitz M. (the Big Book's "Our Southern Friend"), a Notable, East Coast Exception!

There was an exception to the failures on the East Coast. And some of the glaring and specific failures were in Bill Wilson's immediate circle in the early New York days. Thus, Bill's own "sponsor" Ebby Thacher drank on for years and years, though Ebby finally did die sober, with the help of a different friend and sponsor in Texas. Also, Bill's partner in Works Publishing Company (publisher of the Big Book First Edition) was Hank Parkhurst–"the first New York alcoholic Bill had been able to sober up." Lois Wilson said: "Hank P., a dynamic, redheaded salesman just out of Towns Hospital, was the first of the men Bill worked with in New York who stayed sober any appreciable time–four years" (*Lois Remembers*, p. 101). But that sobriety was not to last very long. Parkhurst began drinking at or about the time his Big Book effort with Bill was launched in 1939 (*Pass It On*, p. 228). Parkhurst apparently died of alcoholism (Indicated in correspondence signed by Bill Wilson and found by the author in the Shoemaker papers at the Episcopal Church Archives in Texas). Sam Shoemaker had asked Bill to work with a professor of chemistry named Breithut, and this was right after Bill emerged from Towns Hospital. Bill worked with the professor quite avidly, but Lois reported: "Freddie didn't sober up completely for some time" (*Lois Remembers*, p. 94). The "atheist" objector Jim Burwell denounced God at meetings, stayed drunk for five years, and finally picked up a Bible in a hotel room and then did stay sober for many

Appendix 3

years. Bill told these facts to his distinguished audience at a lecture he conducted at Yale University.

But there was one who made it from beginning to end. The man was John Henry Fitzhugh Mayo, a resident of Cumberland, Maryland. Bill found Fitz at Towns Hospital. He may have been the second person, after Parkhurst, to get sober in New York. Fitz, his wife, and the Wilsons became close friends–with Bill and Lois virtually "commuting" to Fitz's home in Maryland and reciprocal visits by Fitz and his wife to the Wilsons in New York. Fitz attended some meetings at the Wilson home, and he joined Lois and Bill in attending Oxford Group meetings and "house-parties."

Fitz researched the availability of names for the new book (the first edition of A.A.'s basic text) at the Library of Congress. Fitz reported "The Way Out" had already been used many times. His sister Agnes loaned $1,000.00 to enable the Big Book to be printed. And Fitz endeavored to get A.A. under way in the Washington, D.C., area. Later he developed relationships with hospitals and gained A.A. access to the workhouse to which drunks were sent by DC courts.

In World War II, Fitz joined the Army, and was found to be suffering from cancer. He had an operation performed by Dr. Bob. He died October 4, 1943, eight years after he had stopped drinking and is buried on the grounds of Christ Episcopal Church at Owensville, Maryland where his father had once been rector.

There are several important points about Fitz. First, he was the son of an Episcopalian minister. Second, Fitz is the man described in the Big Book's basic text as having had a spiritual experience when he proclaimed: "Who are you to say there is no God," tumbled out of bed and to his knees, and found the peace and release from alcoholism he sought. Third, there are the unspoken and perhaps even suppressed facts about Fitz's Christian convictions and practices in the early A.A. arena on the East Coast. The author has tried to track down the facts, with the help of people in Maryland, but has run into a brick wall. Fourth, quite clearly, Fitz was well aware of the Christian roots of A.A. and wanted to retain them in the new textbook Bill had written. Fitz's valiant but unsuccessful attempts when the Big Book was being worked over on the East Coast have been described in several ways:

> Bill Wilson said, in *The Language of the Heart*:
>
> "The hassles as to what should go into our new book were terrific. For example, some wanted a purely psychological book which would draw in alcoholics without scaring them. We could tell them about the "God business" afterward. **A few, led by our wonderful southern friend, Fitz M., wanted a fairly religious book infused with some of the dogma we had picked up from the churches and missions which had tried to help us**" (p. 200, emphasis added).

And note the bias in Bill's references to "dogma," to what was "picked up" from churches and missions, and to the fact that these churches and missions had "tried to help." These were not the words Bill used in his more truthful, later references to how the Oxford Group message had saved his life and how Rev. Sam Shoemaker should properly be called a "co-founder" of A.A.

Bill's secretary of the early days, Ruth Hock, told the story more accurately:

> "Jimmy B. [the avowed atheist who stayed drunk for five years until he read the Bible] opposed the strong references to God, in both the steps and the rest of the early chapters. Hank wanted to soft-pedal them; but **Fitz insisted that the book should express Christian doctrines and use Biblical terms and expressions." Ruth remembered: "Fitz was for going all the way with 'God'. . ."** (*Pass It On*, p. 199, emphasis added).

Ruth Hock later related to A.A. historian Bill Pittman that hundreds of pages of the manuscript material, most containing

Christian subject matter, were tossed out before the final printing. The author tried, without success, further to document the following, seemingly related statements in *Pass It On*:

> Final editing of the book was done by Tom Uzzell, member of the faculty at New York University. Uzzell cut the book by at least a third (some say half–from 800 to 400 pages) and sharpened it in the process (*Pass It On,* p. 204).

Jimmy B. had a colorful description of this interchange [with the psychiatrist Dr. Howard]:

> "Dr. Howard read the manuscript and brought it back the next day," he recalled. "He said Bill was making a damn big mistake. 'This is the Oxford Group,' he said. 'You have to change the whole damn thing.'" We asked, 'Why? What is the matter with it? It is perfect.' "He said you have to take out the must. You have to take out the God–the complete God.' Did Bill go into a tizzy then! He almost blew his top. Here was his baby being torn apart by a screwball psychiatrist" (*Pass It On,* p. 204).

The author worked with two of the three authors of *Pass It On* (a third having died as that book was being written) and with the first and second archivists of A.A. to get the details on the foregoing editing. Not one of them could come up with the source material though all proclaimed it had to be valid and to have been validated. The author went to NYU to locate either Uzzell or the manuscripts, but nothing was to be found.

What a different A.A., different basic text, and different fellowship A.A. might have been had the views and efforts of the one early, successful, East Coast drunk, John Henry Fitzhugh Mayo, prevailed!

Observers' Comments on the Failures in Today's A.A.

Seemingly oblivious to the revolving doors in present-day A.A., some in our fellowship are at pains to deflect any analysis or criticism of success rates by stating that there are no "members" of A.A. (which is true). They say there are no reliable in-house surveys because of the fluid nature of A.A. attendance and the lack of faithful and identifiable allegiance to some particular home group by most "members" (a fact that A.A. membership surveys frankly acknowledge). They sometimes comment to the author directly at conferences and seminars and in correspondence that they have seen no failures in their groups; that there are no reliable scientific studies; and that mention of the problem constitutes disloyalty to the fellowship. They also have claimed the author's efforts involve unreliable research, a hidden agenda, and historical half-truths. In fact, though the visits to the author's website have been around 200 per day, a website for "history buffs" has recently banned any contributions from the author or those who quote his work.

To which the author himself often asks: Don't you attend meetings? Don't you see the dearth of old-timers? Don't you see the departures, drinking, and even deaths of those you came in with? Can't you see how many who are entering A.A. are compelled to go by the courts, compelled to go by their therapists and treatment centers, and compelled to attend by family and friends? Can't you see the lack of mention of God, the Bible, Jesus Christ, A.A. History, and the early program itself? Have you ever gone to A.A. count-downs at large conventions? Do you attend "chip" or "birthday" meetings where the number of those responding to sobriety calls diminishes markedly as calls are made for those with greater and greater sobriety and few answer those calls? Have you not seen the lack of interest in the meetings themselves, in helping newcomers, in staying with service commitments for any length of time? Have you even read A.A.'s own "Conference Approved" *DR. BOB and the Good Oldtimers,* or interviewed old-timers, or seen the early manuscript materials at A.A. General Services in New York, or at Bill's home at Stepping Stones, or at other important repositories?

Blindness is not a virtue when it comes to lack of observation concerning A.A.'s current state. As the publishing of books on A.A. (in and out of A.A.) grows, as the emphasis on "any god" or "no god" or "the group" or "meetings" increases, as the refusal to accept materials on early A.A. grows, and as the criticism of religion and church become ever more popular, one cannot fail to ask whether these things are detrimental. Whether they ignore the one important item–complete healing of alcoholism–and the foundational aim of enjoying a successful, serving relationship with our Creator. Early AAs shot for both. And they hit the mark. Today, whatever their reliability, the proofs of A.A.'s plummeting success rate are very very clear. They come from active AAs, from atheists on the outside, from Christians on the outside, from professionals in and out, and from statisticians in the United States and state governments and their agencies.

Here are the points they are making. More can be found in Dick B., *New Light on Alcoholism: God, Sam Shoemaker, and A.A.*, Appendix 12:

Charles Bufe

Charles Bufe candidly informed the author that he was an atheist, and it seems apparent he thinks A.A. is quite ineffective. His book is filled with statistics which he humbly concedes to be subject to further studies. Nonetheless, he makes these convincing points in *Alcoholics Anonymous: Cult or Cure?* 2d ed.:

> "The true success rate of AA is very probably somewhere between these two extremes (lifelong sobriety and five years' sobriety), depending, of course, on how one defines "success:" that is, **AA's success rate is probably somewhere between**

2.9% and 7% (of those who have attended AA)" (p.92, boldface added).

"When newcomers express doubts about the religiosity of the second step, they're normally told that their "Higher Power" can be anything they choose. Doorknobs, bedpans, and AA itself are often suggested as "Higher Powers" for atheist and agnostic newcomers. It doesn't seem to bother those making such suggestions that the very next step explicitly mentions 'God'" (p. 69).

"For now, the best evidence available suggests that AA is ineffective as a means of overcoming alcohol problems. . . . But the evidence is not conclusive, and until additional controlled studies are conducted, it will remain impossible to draw firm conclusions about AA's (in)effectiveness" (p. 101).

Dr. Stanton Peele

Stanton Peele told the author he was not a religious man, and he makes no effort to conceal his belief that A.A. is ineffective and that its "disease" theory is wrong.

"Several studies have shown that those who quit drinking via A.A. actually have higher relapse rates than those who quit on their own" ("Mr. Peele Responds," *Reason*, May, 1990, p. 12).

"In fact, research has not found AA to be an effective treatment for general populations of alcoholics. Consider the following summary by researchers at the Downstate (New York) Medical Center Department of Psychiatry: The general applicability of AA as a treatment method is much more limited than has been supposed in the past. Available data do not support AA's claims of much higher success rates than clinic treatment. Indeed, when population differences are taken into account, the reverse seems to be true" (Peele, *Diseasing of America*, pp. 56-67).

"Following the publication of *The Natural History of Alcoholism*, Dr. George Vaillant sent me additional data to those he reported in his book about alcoholics who were in remission. Of those who quit drinking on their own, none of the twenty-one men followed up since the end of the study were abusing alcohol. (Twelve had gone ten or more years without a drink, four had abstained for three to ten years, and five men drank less than once a month.) Of the twenty-two men Vaillant followed up who had relied on AA to abstain, only five had gone for ten or more years without a drink, six had gone for three to ten years, four had gone one to two years, two drank less than once a month, and five continued to abuse alcohol. Relapse was more common for the AA group: 81 percent of those who quit on their own either had abstained for ten or more years or drank infrequently, compared with the 32 percent of those who relied on AA who fall in these categories" (Peele, *Diseasing of America*, p. 194).

Ken Ragge

Ken Ragge's book, *The Real AA: Behind The Myth of 12-Step Recovery*, is so slanted toward criticism of A.A. and the Oxford Group, and so lacking in coverage of other A.A. roots such as the Bible, that its statistical presentations may seem to lack authority. Nonetheless, it presents these compelling facts:

"In a follow-up of 548 alcoholics at eight different AA-based treatment centers, the Rand researchers found that 18 percent of subjects had moderated their drinking and had become non-problem drinkers after treatment. Only 7 percent managed to abstain for the four-year follow up period" (p. 34).

"Of those who quit drinking on their own, none of the twenty-one men followed up since the end of the study were abusing alcohol. . . . Relapse was more common for the AA group: 81 percent of those who quit on their own either had abstained for ten or more years or drank infrequently, compared with the 32 percent of those who relied who fall in these categories" (p. 24).

"A most revealing study of the overall success of AA was done by Harvard psychiatrist and prominent authority on the 'disease' of alcoholism, George Vaillant. In one of the longest studies of its size and type, Vaillant followed 100 men for eight years. The men selected were the first 100 consecutive admissions for detoxification at an alcoholism clinic. They were followed up annually . . . It seemed perfectly clear. . . by turning to recovering alcoholics rather than to Ph.D.s for lessons in breaking self-detrimental and more or less involuntary habits, and by inexorably moving patients. . . into the treatment system of AA, I was working for the most exciting alcohol program in the world. But then came the rub. . . . After initial discharge, only 5 patients in the Clinic sample *never* relapsed to alcoholic drinking, and there is compelling evidence that the results of our treatment were no better than the natural history of the disease" (p. 23). In his more recent study, *The Natural History of Alcoholism Revisited* (1995), Vaillant appears to have modified his views. Whatever the facts, Vaillant has now joined the ranks of A.A. itself as a non-alcoholic trustee.

Jack Trimpey

Jack Trimpey has communicated with the author, and both agree that A.A. is still and truly "religious"–whatever one might call the religion. In his book, *Rational Recovery*, Trimpey writes:

"AA doesn't work. Abstinence rates for people in the recovery group movement are astonishingly low, under 10%" (p. 303).

William L. Playfair, M.D.

In his book, *The Useful Lie*, Dr. Playfair writes from the perspective of a Christian physician, but his conclusions about A.A. are not based on a full knowledge or accurate presentation of the facts about A.A.'s roots in the Bible. Nonetheless, he makes some solid arguments concerning the present-day failures of A.A.

> "Not one study has ever found AA or its derivatives to be better than not receiving any help at all" (p. 66).

> "Some have pointed to the Oxford Group Movement and AA's ties to it as proof of the Christian origin of AA and its views. There are a number of problems with this thesis. While the founder of the Oxford Group Movement was no doubt a real Christian, many of his views–especially those that impressed Bill W. and Dr. Bob–are highly questionable from a Christian perspective. . . . But what influence the Oxford Group had on AA seems to have been forgotten and overshadowed by other not-so-Christian influences" (pp. 97-98).

> "Through official AA publications and the publications of spinoff groups–reflecting the views of most of the recovery industry–the sin concept is discounted. Even if one could prove that AA founders were Christians and that AA and the Twelve Steps were based on Biblical principles, that would not change the fact that the recovery industry as a whole is about as non-Christian as it can get" (p. 98).

Martin and Diedre Bobgan

In *12 Steps to Destruction* [quoting William Miller and Reid Hester], these Christian writers said:

"Given the absence of a single controlled evaluation supporting the effectiveness of A.A., and the presence of these negative findings, however, we must conclude that at the present time the alleged effectiveness of A.A. remains unproved" (p. 191).

Enoch Gordis, M.D.

Dr. Enoch Gordis, Director of NIAAA, sent the present author (Dick B.) a letter containing A.A.'s 1989 membership survey which stated:

"Only half of those coming to A.A. for the first time remain more than three months; twenty-nine percent have been sober over five years; those with 10 to 15 years of sobriety amount to 6.8%; and those with more than twenty-five years of sobriety represent less than one-half of one percent"

Scott Tonigan, Ph.D.

Dr. Tonigan, Deputy Director of the Research Division, Center on Alcoholism in New Mexico, wrote:

"It is an axiom in the field that about 75% of those who turn to AA drop out by the end of the first year" (*Akron Beacon Journal*, Friday, June 9, 1995).

Joan Matthews-Larson, Ph.D.

Dr. Joan Matthews-Larson wrote:

"Relapse among treated alcoholics is so prevalent that professional journals label one-year follow-up studies of treatment outcome as 'long term.' The extent of the relapse problem was demonstrated in 1980 in the Rand Report, the results of a federally funded four-year study of 922 alcoholic men who had been treated in several hospitals.

. . . After four years, only 7 percent remained abstinent. My educated guess is that the abstinent 7 percent have spent most of their four years involved with support or therapy groups, using AA or psychotherapy to 'adjust' their attitudes and 'manage' their unstable emotions" (*Seven Weeks to Sobriety: The Proven Program to Fight Alcoholism through Nutrition*, p. 21).

Professor Herbert Fingarette

In his title, *Heavy Drinking*, Professor Fingarette wrote:

"[A]mong A.A. members 'slipping is a normal and frequent activity'. . . there is no evidence that the particular way of life advocated by A.A. is the only, or even the most effective application of this theme."

Susan Powter

In her book, *Sober . . . and Staying That Way: The Missing Link in the Cure for Alcoholism*, Susan Powter wrote:

"*One day at a time*, fine, but please, experts contend that AA has a 12 percent recovery rate. What happens to the other 88 percent of us" (p. 15)?

What Will Be the Success Rates of A.A. in the Future?

Let's be candid: Who knows! But there are some emerging factors that can be seen today. First, A.A. has stopped growing in the United States. Second, some of its present sources such as court-mandated attendance may very well dry up because of prohibitions against compulsory religious programs in the First and Fourteenth Amendments to the United States Constitution. Four courts have already ruled against compulsory attendance on constitutional grounds. Third, the literature now being published by A.A. as "Conference Approved" is more and more soliciting and including diverse contributions from just about anyone, rather than contributions by those who have established their recoveries by the power of God, as the early AAs did. Fourth, there is no particular sign as yet that the present-day Christian bashing in meetings will abate. Fifth, there has not yet been any evidence that A.A. as an organization is at all interested in publishing any more facts about the early A.A. Christian fellowship, the ideas it borrowed from the Bible, the "old-fashioned prayer meetings" it held, the surrenders to Jesus Christ that were mandatory, or the early emphasis on return to religion and church that was favored by most early AAs.

If the power of the Creator continues to be diminished as the *sine qua non* of healing, just what "power" can still suffering alcoholics expect to get from a bed pan, a light bulb, a group, or "something" or "nothing at all?" If the Bible continues to be ignored as a source for A.A.'s basic ideas, just what religious or medical or therapeutic or treatment program will provide new basic standards for recovery? If prayer, seeking God's guidance, study of religious literature, and other sources of "Divine help" are tossed out, are the Twelve Steps (which mention God) to be supplanted by private interpretations that rely on "any god," "not-god," no "god," or no belief at all?

If the number of "anonymous" and "12-Step" and "self-help" groups continues to rise, will there be a corresponding dilution of the still-existing, widespread approval of A.A.? If the number of "Christ-centered" or Christian 12 Step programs continues to rise, will such programs continue to draw religiously inclined people away from A.A. as they are doing today? If the statistics as to A.A.'s ineffectiveness continue to be disseminated as widely as they are, will people gravitate more to "rational recovery," "secular sobriety," nutritional programs, religious programs, government programs, or "moderation management" ideas?

For some time, A.A. has fostered the notion that it is somewhat immune from dilution or extinction because it has its "Twelve Traditions." Most frequently cited as proof of what dilutes and extinguishes are "The Washingtonians" and even the Oxford Group from which A.A. sprang. But A.A. is no more immune from extinction or from substantial modification than the many movements which preceded it–the Washingtonians, the Women's Christian Temperance Union, the Anti-Saloon League, the Salvation Army, Christian Endeavor, the Young Men's Christian Association, the Prohibition experiment, and Moral Re-Armament.

It is therefore impractical to predict success rates for the future. It seems almost certain A.A. will not return to the Bible, to Protestant religious ideas, to Christianity, or to God Almighty as the acknowledged source of its success. It seems almost certain also that the influx of new religions, new ethnic groups, New Age, and new language problems will outpace even A.A.'s own efforts to "universalize" its program to mollify new groups or movements and suit any and all comers. It also seems likely that medicine, government, religion, and non-profit agencies will not continue to sit idly by and watch a decline, to send people to A.A., and to measure its failures without themselves producing new programs, ideas, and solutions. And not necessarily good ones!

There is one thing that can occur, but it cannot be predicted for A.A. as a whole. Christian fellowships can be still be formed *within* A.A. Bible study groups can again be, and now are being, held *within* A.A. Early A.A.'s spiritual history, principles, and practices can be disseminated far more widely. The information age will demystify some of the prevalent thinking in the 12 Step Fellowships, absurd though it has been, that it pays to be quiet, to be unthinking, and to be stupid. Computers, internet sites, television, videos, audios, and books will bring the facts to the fore so quickly in the next few years that many options for obtaining more information will become available.

Perhaps the most important possibility can be a hungering return by individual AAs and groups of AAs to the power of the Creator, to the importance of His Son Jesus Christ, to the truths in His Word, to communication with and from Almighty God, to learning and knowing and understanding more about Him, and to receiving the deliverance and forgiveness and healing He promises.

The author believes the statement: "There are no atheists in fox holes." There may not be fox holes as such in today's spiritual battle. But there certainly is a formidable foe. There are the "wiles of the devil" and the "principalities . . . powers . . . rulers of the darkness of this world . . . spiritual wickedness in high *places*" which the brethren must withstand and against which the brethren must stand and wrestle (See Eph. 6:10-18, as well as Sam Shoemaker's discussion in *God's Control*, 1939). As Dr. Carl G. Jung apparently told Rowland Hazard and later stated to Bill Wilson, the spiritual battle can be won by "union with God." The battle was between God (Spirit) and the devil spirit (alcohol) or alcoholism. Jung tried to explain to Bill:

> Alcohol in Latin is *spiritus*, and you use the same word for the highest religious experiences as well as for the most depraving poison. The helpful formula therefore is: *spiritus contra spiritum* (See *Pass It On*, p. 384).

Whether one chooses to put on the whole armor of God and fight a spiritual battle with spiritual power–the power of God Almighty–is, of course, an individual matter. But when alcoholism, addiction, treatment, punishment, fellowships, and prohibition continue to grow more and more out of control, the individual can look to the successes of early A.A. The individual suffering soldier or athlete can look to what A.A. had when it relied on *Yahweh*, the one, true, living God–the Creator who is described with great particularity in the Good Book.

Some Recent Statistics for Believers–to Show Them They have Company

The Anglican Digest issue, Advent AD 2000, titled "Gallup Surveys A Day In The Spiritual Life of America," p. 40, begins with this statement: "100 people were asked: In the last 24 hours - that is, between this time yesterday and this time today - did you happen to do any of the following?" And we have selected the following from the answers given:

- 55%   Prayed at a meal
- 51%   Talked to someone about God or some aspect of your faith or spirituality
- 44%   Shared faith
- 36%   Read the Bible
- 24%   Watched/listened to religious radio/TV
- 15%   Attended a prayer service or Bible study or worship group

A survey by George H. Gallup, Jr., and Robert Bezilla (issued by the Princeton Religious Research Center), which appeared in *The Maui News* on September 16, 1994, was as follows:

[The headline read:] "Bible still best seller, but lessons being lost."

[The article began:] "It never appears on the best seller lists, but the Bible is the nation's perennial best-selling book"

It's safe to say that things were no different in the 1930's. In fact, they were probably much better! And why not today, as well! It's time again to try God! More important, to seek His care and protection before you get in trouble. He's in the prayer answering business. And you can get instructions from His best seller!

Bibliography

Publications by or about Samuel Moor Shoemaker, Jr.

Shoemaker, Samuel Moor, Jr., "A 'Christian Program.'" In *Groups That Work: The Key to Renewal . . . for Churches, Communities, and Individuals*. Compiled by Walden Howard and the Editors of Faith At Work. Michigan: Zondervan, 1967.

———. "Act As If." *Christian Herald*. October, 1954.

———. "A First Century Christian Fellowship: A Defense of So-called Buchmanism by One of Its Leaders." Reprinted from the *Churchman*, circa 1928.

———. "And So from My Heart I Say . . ." *The A.A. Grapevine*. New York: The A.A. Grapevine, Inc., September, 1948.

———. . . . *And Thy Neighbor*. Waco, Texas: Word Books, 1967.

———. *A Young Man's View of the Ministry*. New York: Association Press, 1923.

———. *Beginning Your Ministry*. New York: Harper & Row Publishers, 1963.

———. *By the Power of God*. New York: Harper & Brothers, 1954.

———. *Calvary Church Yesterday and Today*. New York: Fleming H. Revell, 1936.

———. *Children of the Second Birth*. New York: Fleming H. Revell, 1927.

———. *Christ and This Crisis*. New York: Fleming H. Revell, 1943.

———. *Christ's Words from the Cross*. New York: Fleming H. Revell, 1933.

———. *Confident Faith*. New York: Fleming H. Revell, 1932.

———. *Extraordinary Living for Ordinary Men*. Michigan: Zondervan, 1965.

———. *Faith at Work*. A symposium edited by Samuel Moor Shoemaker. Hawthorne Books, 1958.

———. *Freedom and Faith*. New York: Fleming H. Revell, 1949.

———. *God and America*. New York: Book Stall, 61 Gramercy Park North, New York, n.d.

———. *God's Control*. New York: Fleming H. Revell, 1939.

———. *How to Become a Christian*. New York: Harper & Brothers, 1953.

———. "How to Find God." *The Calvary Evangel*. July, 1957, pp. 1-24.

———. *How to Help People*. Cincinnati: Forward Movement Publications, 1976.

———. *How You Can Find Happiness*. New York: E. P. Dutton & Co., 1947.

———. *How You Can Help Other People*. New York: E. P. Dutton & Co., 1946.

295

————. *If I Be Lifted Up.* New York: Fleming H. Revell, 1931.

————. *In Memoriam: The Service of Remembrance.* Princeton: The Graduate Council, Princeton University, June 10, 1956.

————. *Living Your Life Today.* New York: Fleming H. Revell, 1947.

————. "Lord, Teach Us to Pray." *Creative Help for Daily Living* (Foundation for Christian Living, Pawling, New York) 28, no. 2 (1977), Part ii.

————. *Morning Radio Talk No. 1, by Reverend Samuel M. Shoemaker,* American Broadcasting Co., 1 page transcript of program for October 4, 1945.

————. *My Life-Work and My Will.* Pamphlet, Christian ministry conference, Concord, N.H., circa 1930.

————. *National Awakening.* New York: Harper & Brothers, 1936.

————. *One Boy's Influence.* New York: Association Press, 1925.

————. "Power to Become." *The Calvary Evangel.* December, 1944.

————. *Realizing Religion.* New York: Association Press, 1923.

————. *Religion That Works.* New York: Fleming H. Revell, 1928.

————. *Revive Thy Church.* New York: Harper & Brothers, 1948.

————. *Sam Shoemaker at His Best.* New York: Faith At Work, 1964.

————. *So I Stand by the Door and Other Verses.* Pittsburgh: Calvary Rectory, 1958.

————. *Steps of a Modern Disciple.* Atlanta, GA: Lay Renewal Publications, 1972.

————. *The Breadth and Narrowness of the Gospel.* New York: Fleming H. Revell, 1929.

————. *The Calvary Evangel, monthly articles in.* New York. Calvary Episcopal Church.

————. *The Church Alive.* New York: E. P. Dutton & Co., Inc., 1951.

————. *The Church Can Save the World.* New York: Harper & Brothers, 1938.

————. *The Conversion of the Church.* New York: Fleming H. Revell, 1932.

————. "The Crisis of Self-Surrender." *Guideposts.* November, 1955.

————. *The Experiment of Faith.* New York: Harper & Brothers. 1957.

————. *The Gospel According to You.* New York: Fleming H. Revell, 1934.

————. *The James Houston Eccleston Day-Book: Containing a Short Account of His Life and Readings for Every Day in the Year Chosen from His Sermons.* Compiled by Samuel M. Shoemaker, Jr. New York: Longmans, Green & Co., 1915.

————. "The Spiritual Angle." *The A.A. Grapevine.* New York: The A.A. Grapevine, Inc., October, 1955.

————. "The Way to Find God." *The Calvary Evangel* (August, 1935).

————. *They're on the Way.* New York: E. P. Dutton, 1951.

————. "Creative Relationships." In *Together.* New York: Abingdon Cokesbury Press, 1946.

————. "The Twelve Steps of A.A.: What They Can Mean to the Rest of Us." *The Calvary Evangel.* New York: The Evangel, 1953.

————. "Those Twelve Steps As I Understand Them." *Best of the Grapevine: Volume II.* New York: The A.A. Grapevine, Inc., 1986.

————. "12 Steps to Power." *Faith At Work News.* Reprint. 1983.

————. *Twice-Born Ministers.* New York: Fleming H. Revell, 1929.

————. *Under New Management.* Grand Rapids: Zondervan Publishing House., 1966.

———. *What the Church Has to Learn from Alcoholics Anonymous.* Reprint of 1956 sermon. Available at A.A. Archives, New York.

———. *With the Holy Spirit and with Fire.* New York: Harper & Brothers, 1960.

A Guide to Calvary Episcopal Church: 125th Anniversary 1855-1980. Pittsburgh: Calvary Episcopal Church, 1980.

"Buchman Religion Explained to 1,000." *New York Times.* May 27, 1931.

"Calvary Mission." Pamphlet. New York: Calvary Episcopal Church, n.d.

"Campus Calls by Dr. Shoemaker Foster Chain of Religious Cells." *New York Tribune.* February 25, 1951.

Centennial History: Calvary Episcopal Church, 1855-1955. Pittsburgh: Calvary Episcopal Church, 1955.

"Church Ejects Buchman Group." *New York Times.* November 8, 1941.

"Crusaders of Reform." *Princeton Alumni Weekly.* June 2, 1993.

Cuyler, John Potter, Jr. *Calvary Church in Action.* New York: Fleming H. Revell, 1934.

Day, Sherwood S. "Always Ready: S.M.S. As a Friend." *The Evangel* (New York: Calvary Church, July-August, 1950).

Get Changed; Get Together; Get Going: A History of the Pittsburgh Experiment. Pittsburgh: The Pittsburgh Experiment, n.d.

Harris, Irving. *The Breeze of the Spirit.* New York: The Seabury Press, 1978.

———. "S.M.S.—Man of God for Our Time." *Faith At Work* (January-February, 1964).

"Houseparties Across the Continent." *The Christian Century.* August 23, 1933.

Knippel, Charles Taylor. *Samuel M. Shoemaker's Theological Influence on William G. Wilson's Twelve Step Spiritual Program of Recovery (Alcoholics Anonymous).* Dissertation. St. Louis University, 1987.

"Listening to God Held Daily Need." *New York Times.* December 4, 1939.

Norton-Taylor, Duncan. "Businessmen on Their Knees." *Fortune.* October, 1953.

Olsson, Karl A. "The History of Faith at Work" (five parts). *Faith at Work News.* 1982-1983.

Peale, Norman Vincent. "The Unforgettable Sam Shoemaker." *Faith At Work.* January, 1964.

———. "The Human Touch: The Estimate of a Fellow Clergyman and Personal Friend." *The Evangel* (New York: Calvary Church, July-August, 1950).

Pitt, Louis W. "New Life, New Reality: A Brief Picture of S.M.S.'s Influence in the Diocese of New York." *Faith at Work*, July-August, 1950.

"Pittsburgh Man of the Year." *Pittsburgh Post Gazette.* January 12, 1956.

Sack, David Edward. *Sam Shoemaker and the "Happy Ethical Pagans."* Princeton, New Jersey: paper prepared in the Department of Religion, Princeton University, June, 1993.

"Sam Shoemaker and Faith at Work." Pamphlet on file at Faith At Work, Inc., 150 S. Washington St., Suite 204, Falls Church, VA 22046.

Schwartz, Robert. "Laymen and Clergy to Join Salute to Dr. S. M. Shoemaker." *Pittsburgh Press.* December 10, 1961.

Shoemaker, Helen Smith. *I Stand by the Door.* New York: Harper & Row, 1967.

"Sees Great Revival Near." *New York Times.* September 8, 1930.

Sider, Michael J. *Taking the Gospel to the Point: Evangelicals in Pittsburgh and the Origins of the Pittsburgh Leadership Foundation*. Pittsburgh: Pittsburgh Leadership Foundation, n.d.

"Soul Clinic Depicted By Pastor in Book." *New York Times*. August 5, 1927.

"Ten of the Greatest American Preachers." *Newsweek*. March 28, 1955.

The Pittsburgh Experiment's Groups. Pittsburgh: The Pittsburgh Experiment, n.d.

Tools for Christian Living. Pittsburgh: The Pittsburgh Experiment, n.d.

"Urges Church Aid Oxford Group." *New York Times*. January 2, 1933, p. 26.

Wilson, Bill. "I Stand by the Door." *The A.A. Grapevine*. New York: The A.A. Grapevine, Inc., February, 1967.

Woolverton, John F. "Evangelical Protestantism and Alcoholism 1933-1962: Episcopalian Samuel Shoemaker, The Oxford Group and Alcoholics Anonymous." *Historical Magazine of the Protestant Episcopal Church* 52 (March, 1983).

Alcoholics Anonymous

Publications About

Alcoholics Anonymous. (multilith volume). New Jersey: Works Publishing Co., 1939.

Alcoholics Anonymous: The Story of How More Than 100 Men Have Recovered from Alcoholism. New York City: Works Publishing Company, 1939.

B., Dick. *Anne Smith's Journal, 1933-1939: A.A.'s Principles of Success*. 3rd ed. Kihei, HI: Paradise Research Publications, Inc., 1998.

———. *The Oxford Group & Alcoholics Anonymous: A Design for Living That Works*. 3ʳᵈ ed., Kihei, HI: Paradise Research Publications, 1998.

———. *Dr. Bob and His Library: A Major A.A. Spiritual Source*. 3rd ed. Kihei, HI: Paradise Research Publications, Inc. 1998.

———. *New Light on Alcoholism: God, Sam Shoemaker, and A.A.*, 2d ed., Kihei, HI: Paradise Research Publications, Inc., 1999..

———. *That Amazing Grace: The Role of Clarence and Grace S. in Alcoholics Anonymous*. San Rafael, CA: Paradise Research Publications, 1996.

———. *The Akron Genesis of Alcoholics Anonymous*. 3rd ed. Kihei, HI: Paradise Research Publications, Inc., 1998.

———. *The Books Early AAs Read for Spiritual Growth*. 7th ed., Kihei, HI, CA: Paradise Research Publications, Inc., 1998.

———. *The Good Book and The Big Book: A.A.'s Roots in the Bible*. 2d ed., Kihei, HI: Paradise Research Publications, Inc., 1997.

———, and Bill Pittman. *Courage to Change: The Christian Roots of the 12-Step Movement*. Grand Rapids, MI: Fleming H. Revell, 1994.

———. *Turning Point: A History of Early A.A.'s Spiritual Roots and Successes*. Kihei, HI: Paradise Research Publications, Inc., 1997.

———. *Good Morning! Quiet Time, Morning Watch, Meditation, and Early A.A.*. 2d ed. Kihei, HI: Paradise Research Publications, Inc., 1998.

———. *Utilizing Early A.A.'s Spiritual Roots for Recovery Today*. Kihei, HI: Paradise Research Publications, 1998.

_____. *The Golden Text of A.A.: God, The Pioneers, and Real Spirituality*. Kihei, HI: Paradise Research Publications, 1999.

_____. *By the Power of God: A Guide to Early A.A. Groups & Forming Similar Groups Today*. Kihei, HI: Paradise Research Publications, 2000.

B., Jim. *Evolution of Alcoholics Anonymous*. New York: A.A. Archives.

Bishop, Charles, Jr. *The Washingtonians & Alcoholics Anonymous*. WV: The Bishop of Books, 1992.

C., Stewart. *A Reference Guide to the Big Book of Alcoholics Anonymous*. Seattle: Recovery Press, 1986.

Clapp, Charles, Jr. *Drinking's Not the Problem*. New York: Thomas Y. Crowell, 1949.

Conrad, Barnaby. *Time Is All We Have*. New York: Dell Publishing, 1986.

Darrah, Mary C. *Sister Ignatia: Angel of Alcoholics Anonymous*. Chicago: Loyola University Press, 1992.

E., Bob. *Handwritten note to Lois Wilson on pamphlet entitled "Four Absolutes."* (copy made available to the author at Founders Day Archives Room in Akron, Ohio, in June, 1991).

———. Letter from Bob E. to Nell Wing. Stepping Stones Archives.

First Steps: Al-Anon . . . 35 Years of Beginnings. New York: Al-Anon Family Group Headquarters, 1986.

Fitzgerald, Robert. *The Soul of Sponsorship: The Friendship of Father Ed Dowling, S.J., and Bill Wilson in Letters*. Center City, Minn.: Hazelden, 1995.

Ford, Betty, with Chris Chase. *The Times of My Life*. New York: Harper and Row, 1978.

Ford, John C. *Depth Psychology, Morality and Alcoholism*. Massachusetts: Weston College, 1951.

Gray, Jerry. *The Third Strike*. Minnesota: Hazelden, 1949.

Hunter, Willard, with assistance from M. D. B. *A.A.'s Roots in the Oxford Group*. New York: A.A. Archives, 1988.

Knippel, Charles T. *Samuel M. Shoemaker's Theological Influence on William G. Wilson's Twelve Step Spiritual Program of Recovery*. Ph. D. dissertation. St. Louis University, 1987.

Kurtz, Ernest. *Not-God: A History of Alcoholics Anonymous*. Exp. ed. Minnesota: Hazelden, 1991.

———. *Shame and Guilt: Characteristics of the Dependency Cycle*. Minnesota: Hazelden, 1981.

Liberty Magazine, September, 1939.

Morreim, Dennis C. *Changed Lives: The Story of Alcoholics Anonymous*. Minneapolis: Augsburg Fortress, 1991.

Morse, Robert M, M.D., and Daniel K. Flavin, M.D. "The Definition of Alcoholism." *The Journal of the American Medical Association*. August 26, 1992, pp. 1012-14.

P., Wally. *But, for the Grace of God . . .: How Intergroups & Central Offices Carried the Message of Alcoholics Anonymous in the 1940s*. West Virginia: The Bishop of Books, 1995.

Peale, Norman Vincent. *The Positive Power of Jesus Christ*. Pauling, NY: The Foundation for Christian Living, 1980.

Pittman, Bill. *AA The Way It Began*. Seattle: Glen Abbey Books, 1988.

Poe, Stephen E. and Frances E. *A Concordance to Alcoholics Anonymous*. Nevada: Purple Salamander Press, 1990.

Robertson, Nan. *Getting Better Inside Alcoholics Anonymous*. New York: William Morrow & Co., 1988.

S., Clarence. *Going through the Steps*. 2d ed. Altamonte Springs, FL: Stephen Foreman, 1985.

————. *My Higher Power—The Lightbulb*. 2d ed. Altamonte Springs, FL: Stephen Foreman, 1985.

Seiberling, John F. *Origins of Alcoholics Anonymous*. (A transcript of remarks by Henrietta B. Seiberling: transcript prepared by Congressman John F. Seiberling of a telephone conversation with his mother, Henrietta in the spring of 1971): Employee Assistance Quarterly. 1985; (1); pp. 8-12.

Sikorsky, Igor I., Jr. *AA's Godparents*. Minnesota: CompCare Publishers, 1990.

Smith, Bob and Sue Smith Windows. *Children of the Healer*. Illinois: Parkside Publishing Corporation, 1992.

The Tidings. Los Angeles, CA: Roman Catholic Newspaper, March 26, 1943.

Thomsen, Robert. *Bill W*. New York: Harper & Row, 1975.

Walker, Richmond. *For Drunks Only*. Minnesota: Hazelden, n.d.

————. *The 7 Points of Alcoholics Anonymous*. Seattle: Glen Abbey Books, 1989.

Webb, Terry. *Tree of Renewed Life: Spiritual Renewal of the Church through the Twelve-Step Program*. New York: Crossroad, 1992.

Wilson, Bill. *How The Big Book Was Put Together*. New York: A.A. General Services Archives, Transcript of Bill Wilson Speech delivered in Fort Worth, Texas, 1954.

————. *Bill Wilson's Original Story*. Bedford Hills, New York: Stepping Stones Archives, n.d., a manuscript whose individual lines are numbered 1 to 1180.

————. "Outline and first two chapters" written by Bill and assembled by Frank Amos. Bedford Hills, NY: Stepping Stones Archives.

————. "Main Events: Alcoholics Anonymous Fact Sheet by Bill." November 1, 1954. Stepping Stones Archives. Bedford Hills, New York.

————. "The Fellowship of Alcoholics Anonymous." *Quarterly Journal of Studies on Alcohol*. Yale University, 1945, pp. 461-73.

————. *W. G. Wilson Recollections*. Bedford Hills, New York: Stepping Stones Archives, September 1, 1954 transcript of Bill's dictations to Ed B.

————. *Bill W. My First 40 Years: An Autobiography*. Center City, MN: Hazelden, 2000.

Wilson, Jan R., and Judith A. Wilson. *Addictionary: A Primer of Recovery Terms and Concepts from Abstinence to Withdrawal*. New York: Simon and Schuster, 1992.

Wilson, Lois. *Lois Remembers*. New York: Al-Anon Family Group Headquarters, 1987.

Windows, Sue Smith. (daughter of A.A.'s Co-Founder, Dr. Bob). Typewritten Memorandum entitled, *Henrietta and early Oxford Group Friends, by Sue Smith Windows*. Delivered to the author of this book by Sue Smith Windows at Akron, June, 1991.

Wing, Nell. *Grateful to Have Been There: My 42 Years with Bill and Lois, and the Evolution of Alcoholics Anonymous.* Illinois: Parkside Publishing Corporation, 1992. *Yale Quarterly Journal of Studies on Alcohol,* 1945.

Publications Approved by Alcoholics Anonymous

Alcoholics Anonymous. 3rd ed. New York: Alcoholics Anonymous World Services, Inc., 1976.

Alcoholics Anonymous. 2d ed. New York: Alcoholics Anonymous, 1955.

Alcoholics Anonymous. 1st ed. New Jersey: Works Publishing, 1939.

Alcoholics Anonymous Comes of Age. New York: Alcoholics Anonymous World Services, Inc., 1957.

A Newcomer Asks . . . York, England: A.A. Sterling Area Services, n.d.

As Bill Sees It: The A.A. Way of Life . . . *selected writings of A.A.'s Co-Founder.* New York: Alcoholics Anonymous World Services, Inc., 1967.

Best of the Grapevine. New York: The A.A. Grapevine, Inc., 1985.

Best of the Grapevine, Volume II. New York: The A.A. Grapevine, Inc., 1986.

Came to Believe. New York: Alcoholics Anonymous World Services, Inc., 1973.

Daily Reflections. New York: Alcoholics Anonymous World Services, Inc., 1991.

DR. BOB and the Good Oldtimers. New York: Alcoholics Anonymous World Services, Inc., 1980.

44 Questions. New York: Works Publishing, Inc., 1952.

Members of the Clergy Ask about Alcoholics Anonymous. New York: Alcoholics Anonymous World Services, 1961, 1979-revised 1992, according to 1989 Conference Advisory Action.

Pass It On. New York: Alcoholics Anonymous World Services, Inc., 1984.

Questions & Answers on Sponsorship. New York: Alcoholics Anonymous World Services, Inc., 1976.

The A.A. Grapevine: "RHS"—issue dedicated to the memory of the Co-Founder of Alcoholics Anonymous, DR. BOB. New York: A.A. Grapevine, Inc., 1951.

The A.A. Service Manual. New York: Alcoholics Anonymous World Services, Inc., 1990-1991.

The Co-Founders of Alcoholics Anonymous. New York: Alcoholics Anonymous World Services, Inc., 1972.

The Language of the Heart. Bill W.'s Grapevine Writings. New York: The A.A. Grapevine, Inc., 1988.

This is A.A. . . . *An Introduction to the A.A. Recovery Program.* New York: Alcoholics Anonymous World Services, Inc., 1984.

Twelve Steps and Twelve Traditions. New York: Alcoholics Anonymous World Services, Inc., 1953.

Pamphlets Circulated in Early A.A.

A.A. God's Instrument. Chicago: Chicago Area Alcoholics Anonymous Service Office, 1954.

A. A. Sponsorship: Its Opportunities and Its Responsibilities. Cleveland: Cleveland Ohio District Office, 1944.

A Guide to the Twelve Steps of Alcoholics Anonymous. Akron: AA of Akron, n.d.

A Guide to Serenity. Cleveland: The Cleveland District Office of Alcoholics Anonymous, n.d.

Alcoholics Anonymous: An Interpretation of our Twelve Steps. Washington, D.C.: Paragon Creative Printers, 1944.

A Manual for Alcoholics Anonymous. Akron: AA of Akron, n.d.

Central Bulletin, Volumes I - III. Cleveland Central Committee, October, 1942 - December, 1945.

Delahanty, Edward J., M.D. *The Therapeutic Value of the Twelve Steps of A.A.* Salt Lake City, UT: Alcoholism Foundations, n.d.

G., Clyde. *My Quiet Time.* Cleveland: Alcoholics Anonymous, n.d.

Handles and Hodge Podge, comp. a member of Alcoholics Anonymous. Cleveland: The Cleveland District Office of Alcoholics Anonymous, n.d.

Handles for Sobriety, comp. A Member of Alcoholics Anonymous. Cleveland: The Cleveland District Office of Alcoholics Anonymous, n.d.

"It's All in the Mind" Chicago: Chicago Area Alcoholics Anonymous Service Office, n.d.

Second Reader for Alcoholics Anonymous. Akron: AA of Akron, n.d.

Smith, Roy. *Emergency Rations.* Cleveland: The Cleveland District Office of Alcoholics Anonymous, n.d.

Spiritual Milestones in Alcoholics Anonymous. Akron: A.A. of Akron, n.d.

The New Way of Life: A.A. Cleveland: The Cleveland District Office of Alcoholics Anonymous, n.d.

T., John. *A.A.: God's Instrument.* Chicago: Chicago Area Alcoholics Anonymous Service Office, n.d.

The Devil and A.A. Chicago: Chicago Area Alcoholics Anonymous Service Office, 1948.

The Four Absolutes. Cleveland: Cleveland Central Committee of A.A., n.d.

The New Way of Life: A.A. Cleveland: The Cleveland District Office of Alcoholics Anonymous, n.d.

Twelve Steps of AA and The Bible. From the collection of Clancy U., n.d.

What Others Think of A.A. Akron: Friday Forum Luncheon Club, circa 1941.

Wood, Charles L. *Prayers for Alcoholics.* Cincinnati: Foreword Movement Publications, n.d. From a Midwest Intergroup Office.

Alcoholics Anonymous: Pro, Con, and Evaluated

A Program for You: A Guide to the Big Book's Design for Living. Hazelden Foundation, 1991.

B., Mel. *New Wine: The Spiritual Roots of the Twelve Step Miracle.* Hazelden Foundation, 1991.

Bartosch, Bob and Pauline. *A Bridge to Recovery.* La Habra, CA: Overcomers Outreach, Inc., 1994.

Bishop, Charlie, Jr. and Pittman, Bill. *To Be Continued...The Alcoholics Anonymous World Biography 1935-1994.* Wheeling, WV: The Bishop of Books, 1994.

Bobgan, Martin and Deidre. *12 Steps to Destruction: Codependency Recovery Heresies.* Santa Barbara, CA: EastGate Publishers,   1991.

Bufe, Charles. *Alcoholics Anonymous: Cult or Cure? 2d ed.,* Tucson, AZ: Sharp Press, 1998.

Burns, Dr. Cathy. *Alcoholics Anonymous Unmasked: Deception and Deliverance.* Mt. Carmel, PA: Sharing, 1991.

Burns, Robert E., C.S.P. *The Catholic Church and Alcoholics Anonymous.* Columbia, 31: 15-16, May, 1952.

C., Chuck. *A New Pair of Glasses.* Irvine, CA: New-Look Publishing Company, 1984.

Chambers, Cal. *Two Tracks-One Goal: How Alcoholics Anonymous Relates to Christianity.* Langley, B.C., Canada: Credo Publishing Corporation, 1992.

Clinebell, Howard. *Understanding and Counseling Persons with Alcohol, Drug, and Behavioral Addictions.* Rev. and enl. ed. Nashville: Abingdon Press, 1998.

Costantino, Frank. *Holes in Time: The Autobiography of a Gangster.* 2d ed. Dallas, TX: Acclaimed Books, 1986.

Cunningham, Loren. *Is That Really You, God?: Hearing the Voice of God.* Seattle, WA: YWAM Publishing, 1984.

Davis, Martin M. *The Gospel and the Twelve Steps: Developing a Closer Relationship with Jesus.* San Diego, CA: Recovery Publications, Inc., 1993.

Dowling, The Reverend Edward, S.J. *Catholic Asceticism and the Twelve Steps.* St. Louis, MO, The Queen's Work, Brooklyn, 1953.

Doyle, Paul Barton. *In Step with God: A Scriptural Guide for Practicing 12 Step Programs.* Brentwood, TN: New Directions, 1989.

Dunn, Jerry G. *God is for the Alcoholic.* Chicago: Moody Press, 1965.

Fingarette, Herbert. *Heavy Drinking: The Myth of Alcoholism as a Disease.* Berkeley, CA: University of California Press, 1988.

Fitzgerald, Robert. *The Soul of Sponsorship: The Friendship of Fr. Ed Dowling, S.J. and Bill Wilson in Letters.* Hazelden, 1995.

Hemfelt, Robert and Fowler, Richard. *Serenity: A Companion for Twelve Step Recovery.* Nashville, TN: Thomas Nelson Publishers, 1990.

Jellinek, E. M. *The Disease Concept of Alcoholism.* New Haven, CN: College and University Press, 1960.

Kessel, Joseph. *The Road Back: A Report on Alcoholics Anonymous.* New York: Alfred A. Knopf, 1962.

Kurtz, Ernest and Ketcham, Katherine. *The Spirituality of Imperfection: Modern Wisdom from Classic Stories.* New York: Bantam Books, 1992.

Landry, Mim J. *Overview of Addiction Treatment Effectiveness.* Rev. ed., 1997. U.S. Department of Health and Human Services.

Larson, Joan Mathews. *Seven Weeks to Sobriety: The Proven Program to Fight Alcoholism Through Nutrition.* New York: Fawcett Columbine, 1992

McQ., Joe. *The Steps We Took.* Little Rock, AR: August House Publishers, Inc., 1990.

Miller, J. Keith. *A Hunger for Healing: The Twelve Steps as a Classic Model for Christian Spiritual Growth.* San Francisco: HarperSanFrancisco, 1991.

O., Dr. Paul. *There's more to Quitting Drinking than Quitting Drinking.* Laguna Niguel, CA: Sabrina Publishing, 1995.

P., Wally. *Back to Basics: The Alcoholics Anonymous Beginners' Classes. Take all 12 Steps in Four One-Hour Sessions*. Tucson, AZ: Faith With Works Publishing Company, 1997.

Parham, A. Philip. *Letting God: Christian Meditations for Recovering Persons*. San Francisco: Harper & Row, 1987.

Peale, Norman Vincent. *The Positive Power of Jesus Christ: Life-Changing Adventures in Faith*. Pauling, NY: Foundation for Christian Living, 1980.

———. *The Power of Positive Thinking*. Pauling, NY: Peale Center for Christian Living, 1978.

Peele, Stanton. *The Diseasing of America: Addiction Treatment out of Control. Lexington*, MA: Lexington Books, 1989.

Playfair, William L. *The Useful Lie*. Wheaton, IL: Crossway Books, 1991.

Ragge, Ken. *More Revealed: A Critical Analysis of Alcoholics Anonymous and the Twelve Steps*. Henderson, NV: Alert! Publishing, 1991.

_____. *The Real A.A.: Behind the Myth of 12-Step Recovery*. Tucson, AZ: Sharp Press, 1998.

Life Recovery Bible, The: The Living Bible. Wheaton, IL: Tyndale House Publishers, Inc., 1992.

Seiden, Jerry. *Divine or Distorted?: God As We Understand God*. San Diego, CA: Recovery Publications, Inc., 1993.

Self-Help Sourcebook, The: Your Guide to Community and Online Support Groups. 6th.ed. compiled and edited by Barbara J. White and Edward J. Madara. Denville, NJ: American Self-Help Clearinghouse, 1994.

Shoemaker, Samuel M., Jr. *Revive Thy Church Beginning with Me*. New York: Harper & Brothers, 1948.

———. *The Church Alive*. New York: E. P. Dutton, 1951.

Stafford, Tim. *The Hidden Gospel of the 12 Steps. Christianity Today*, July 22, 1991.

Trimpey, Jack. *Rational Recovery: The New Cure for Substance Addiction*. New York: Pocket Books, 1996.

———. *Revolutionary Alternative for Overcoming Alcohol and Drug Dependence, A: The Small Book*. Rev. ed. NY: Delacorte Press, 1992.

U.S. Department of Health and Human Services. Substance Abuse and Mental Health Services Administration. *National Household Survey on Drug Abuse: Main Findings 1996*. Rockville, MD: SAMHSA, Office of Applied Studies, 1998.

Vaillant, George E. *The Natural History of Alcoholism Revisited*. Cambridge, MA: Harvard University Press, 1995.

Way Home, The: A Spiritual Approach to Recovery. Orlando, FL: Bridge Builders, Inc., 1996.

White, William L. *Slaying The Dragon: The History of Addiction Treatment and Recovery in America*. Bloomington, IL: Chestnut Health Systems/Lighthouse Institute, 1998

Wing, Nell. *Grateful to have Been There: My 42 Years with Bill and Lois and the Evolution of Alcoholics Anonymous*. Park Ridge, IL: Parkside Publishing Corporation, 1992.

The Bible—Versions of and Books About

Abegg, Martin, Jr. and Flint, Peter and Ulrich, Eugene. *The Dead Sea Scrolls Bible: The Oldest Known Bible Translated for the First Time into English*. HarperSanFrancisco, 1999.

Authorized King James Version. New York: Thomas Nelson, 1984.

Benson, Clarence H. *A Popular History of Christian Education*. Chicago: Moody Press.

Birdsall, J. N. *The New Bible Dictionary* (Language of the New Testament), 1975.

Boman, Thorlief. *Hebrew Thought Compared with Greek*, 1960.

Bruce, F. F. *The Gospel of John*, 1983.

Bullinger, Ethelbert W. *A Critical Lexicon and Concordance to the English and Greek New Testament*. Michigan: Zondervan, 1981.

———. *Figures of Speech Used in the Bible*. Grand Rapids: MI: Baker Book House, 1968.

Burns, Kenneth Charles. "The Rhetoric of Christology." Master's thesis, San Francisco State University, 1991.

Codex Alexandrinus (British Museum, London).

Codex Sinaiticus (British Museum, London).

Codex Vaticanus (Vatican, Rome).

Comparative Study Bible, New International Version, Amplified Version, King James Version, Updated New American Standard Bible. Grand Rapids, MI: Zondervan Publishing House, 1999.

Contemporary English Version (no other data available to author).

Every Catholic's Guide to the Sacred Scriptures. Nashville: Thomas Nelson, 1990.

"Gideon" Bible (Authorized King James Version)

Gray, James M. Synthetic Bible Studies: Containing an Outline Study of Every Book of the Bible, With Suggestions for Sermons, Addresses and Bible Expositions. New York: Fleming H. Revell Company.

Harnack, Adolph. *The Expansion of Christianity in the First Three Centuries*. New York: G. P. Putnam's Sons, Volume I, 1904; Volume II, 1905.

Jukes, Andrew. *The Names of GOD in Holy Scripture*. Michigan: Kregel Publications, 1967.

Kohlenberger, John R., III, gen. ed. *The Contemporary Parallel New Testament*. New York: Oxford University Press, 1997.

___. *The Interlinear NIV Hebrew-English Old Testament*. Grand Rapids, MI: Zondervan Publishing House, 1987.

___ and Swanson, James A., *The Hebrew English Concordance To The Old Testament With The New International Version*, Grand Rapids, MI: Zondervan Publishing House, 1998.

Lamsa, George M. *Idioms in the Bible Explained and A Key to the Original Gospels*. HarperSanFrancisco, 1985.

Lightfoot, John. *A Commentary on the New Testament from the Talmud and Hebraica*, Volume III, 1989.

Mau, Charles P. *James M. Gray As a Christian Educator*. Master's thesis, Fuller Theological Seminary, 1963.

Megivern, James J. *Official Catholic Teachings: Bible Interpretation*. North Carolina: McGrath Publishing Company, 1978.
Moffatt, James. *A New Translation of the Bible*. New York: Harper & Brothers, 1954.
New Bible Dictionary. 2d ed. Wheaton, Illinois: Tyndale House Publishers, 1987.
On, J. Edwin. *Full Surrender*. London: Marshall, Morgan & Scott, 1951.
Phillips, J. B. *The New Testament in Modern English*. New York: The Macmillan Company, 1958.
Puskas, Charles B. *An Introduction to the New Testament*. Mass.: Hendrickson Publishers, 1989.
Recovery Devotional Bible. Grand Rapids, MI: Zondervan Publishing House, 1993.
Revised Standard Version. New York: Thomas Nelson, 1952. New York: Schocken Books, 1995.
Ryrie, Charles C. *Basic Theology: A Popular Systematic Guide to Understanding Biblical Truth*. Chicago: Moody Press, 1999.
Serenity: A Companion for Twelve Step Recovery. Nashville: Thomas Nelson, 1990.
Sharpe, John and Van Kampen, Kimberly. *The Bible as Book: The Manuscript Tradition*. London: The British Library and Oak Knoll Press, 1998.
Schaff, Philip. *History of the Christian Church*. Grand Rapids, MI: Wm. B. Eerdmans, Volume II, 1956.
Stern, David H., *Complete Jewish Bible*, Clarksville, MD: Jewish New Testament Publications, Inc., 1998.
Strong, James. *The Exhaustive Concordance of the Bible*. Iowa: Riverside Book and Bible House, n.d.
The Abingdon Bible Commentary. New York: Abingdon Press, 1929.
The Companion Bible. Michigan: Zondervan Bible Publishers, 1964.
The Jerusalem Bible, Reader's ed., New York, Doubleday, 1968.
The Life Recovery Bible. Wheaton, IL: Tyndale House Publishers, 1992.
The Revised English Bible. Oxford: Oxford University Press, 1989.
The Schocken Bible: Volume I, The Five Books of Moses
The Word Study Concordance. Pasadena, CA: Tyndale House Publishers, Inc., 1978.
The Word Study New Testament. Pasadena, CA: Tyndale House Publishers, Inc., 1978.
Vine, W. E. *Vine's Expository Dictionary of Old and New Testament Words*. New York: Fleming H. Revell, 1981.
Young's Analytical Concordance to the Bible. New York: Thomas Nelson, 1982.
Zodhiates, Spiros. *The Hebrew-Greek Key Study Bible*. 6th ed. AMG Publishers, 1991.

Bible Devotionals

Chambers, Oswald. *My Utmost for His Highest*. London: Simpkin Marshall, Ltd., 1927.
Clark, Glenn, *I Will Lift Up Mine Eyes*. New York: Harper & Brothers, 1937.
Dunnington, Lewis L. *Handles of Power*. New York: Abingdon-Cokesbury Press, 1942.
Fosdick, Harry Emerson. *The Meaning of Prayer*. New York: Association Press, 1915.
Holm, Nora Smith. *The Runner's Bible*. New York: Houghton Mifflin Company, 1915.
Jones, E. Stanley. *Abundant Living*. New York: Abingdon-Cokesbury Press, 1942.
———. *Victorious Living*. New York: Abingdon Press, 1936.

Parham, A. Philip. *Letting God: Christian Meditations for Recovering Persons.* New York: Harper & Row, 1987.

Prescott, D. M. *A New Day: Daily Readings for Our Time.* New ed. London: Grosvenor Books, 1979.

The Upper Room: Daily Devotions for Family and Individual Use. Quarterly. 1st issue: April, May, June, 1935. Edited by Grover Carlton Emmons. Nashville: General Committee on Evangelism through the Department of Home Missions, Evangelism, Hospitals, Board of Missions, Methodist Episcopal Church, South.

The Two Listeners. *God Calling.* Edited by A. J. Russell. Australia: DAYSTAR, 1953.

Tileston, Mary W. *Daily Strength for Daily Needs.* Boston: Roberts Brothers, 1893.

Publications by or about the Oxford Group & Oxford Group People

A Day in Pennsylvania Honoring Frank Nathan Daniel Buchman in Pennsburg and Allentown. Oregon: Grosvenor Books, 1992.

Allen, Geoffrey Francis. *He That Cometh.* New York: The Macmillan Company, 1933.

Almond, Harry J. *Foundations for Faith.* 2d ed. London: Grosvenor Books, 1980.

————. *Iraqi Statesman: A Portrait of Mohammed Fadhel Jamali.* Salem, OR: Grosvenor Books, 1993.

Austin, H. W. "Bunny". *Frank Buchman As I Knew Him.* London: Grosvenor Books, 1975.

————. *Moral Re-Armament: The Battle for Peace.* London: William Heinemann, 1938.

Batterson, John E. *How to Listen to God.* N.p., n.d.

Bayless, W. N. *The Oxford Group: A Way of Life*, n.d.

Becker, Mrs. George. "Quiet Time in the Home." N.p., n.d.

Begbie, Harold. *Life Changers.* New York: G. P. Putnam's Sons, 1927.

————. *Souls in Action.* New York: Hodder & Stoughton, 1911.

————. *Twice-Born Men.* New York: Fleming H. Revell, 1909.

Belden, David C. *The Origins and Development of the Oxford Group (Moral Re-Armament).* D. Phil. Dissertation, Oxford University, 1976.

Belden, Kenneth D. *Beyond The Satellites: Is God is Speaking-Are We Listening?* London: Grosvenor Books, 1987.

————. *Meeting Moral Re-Armament.* London: Grosvenor Books, 1979.

————. *Reflections on Moral Re-Armament.* London: Grosvenor Books, 1983.

————. *The Hour of the Helicopter.* Somerset, England: Linden Hall, 1992.

Bennett, John C. *Social Salvation.* New York: Charles Scribner's Sons, 1935.

Benson, Clarence Irving. *The Eight Points of the Oxford Group.* London: Humphrey Milford, Oxford University Press, 1936.

Blair, David. *For Tomorrow-Yes!* Compiled and edited from David Blair's Notebook by Jane Mullen Blair & Friends. New York: Exposition Press, 1981.

Blair, Emily Newell. "The Oxford Group Challenges America." *Good Housekeeping*, October, 1936.

Blake, Howard C. *Way to Go: Adventures in Search of God's Will.* Burbank, CA: Pooh Stix Press, 1992.

Braden, Charles Samuel. *These Also Believe*. New York: The Macmillan Company, 1951.
_____. *Varieties of American Religion*. New York: Willett, Clark & Company, 1936.
Brown, Philip Marshall. *The Venture of Belief*. New York: Fleming H. Revell, 1935.
Buchman, Frank N. D. *Remaking the World*. London: Blandford Press, 1961.
———, and Sherwood Eddy. *Ten Suggestions for Personal Work* (not located).
———. *The Revolutionary Path: Moral Re-Armament in the thinking of Frank Buchman*. London: Grosvenor, 1975.
———. *Where Personal Work Begins*. Extracts and notes from talks given at the Lily Valley Conference near Kuling, China 1-13 August, 1918. London: Grosvenor Books, 1984.
Frank Buchman-80. Compiled by His Friends. London: Blandford Press, 1958.
Bundy, David D. *Keswick: A Bibliographic Introduction to the Higher Life Movements*. Wilmore, Kentucky: B. L. Fisher Library of Asbury Theological Seminary, 1975.
———. "Keswick and the Experience of Evangelical Piety." Chap. 7 in *Modern Christian Revivals*. Urbana, IL: University of Illinois Press, 1992.
Campbell, Paul. *The Art of Remaking Men*. Bombay: Himmat Publications, 1970.
———. *The Strategy of St. Paul*. London: Grosvenor Books, 1956.
———, and Peter Howard. *Remaking Men*. New York: Arrowhead Books, 1954.
Cantrill, Hadley. *The Psychology of Social Movements*. New York: John Wiley & Sons, Inc., 1941.
Carey, Walter, Bishop of Bloemfontein. *The Group System and the Catholic Church*. Archives of the Episcopal Church, Austin, Texas, n.d.
Chesteron, G. K. *The Well and The Shallows*, circa 1935, pp. 435-39.
Clapp, Charles, Jr. *The Big Bender*. New York: Harper & Row, 1938.
———. *Drinking's Not the Problem*. New York: Thomas Y. Crowell, 1949.
Clark, Walter Houston. *The Oxford Group: Its History and Significance*. New York: Bookman Associates, 1951.
Cook, Sydney and Garth Lean. *The Black and White Book: A Handbook of Revolution*. London: Blandford Press, 1972.
Crossman, R. H. S. *Oxford and the Groups*. Oxford: Basil Blackwell, 1934.
Crothers, Susan. *Susan and God*. New York: Harper & Brothers, 1939.
Day, Sherwood Sunderland. *The Principles of the Group*. Oxford: University Press, n.d.
Dayton, Donald W., ed. *The Higher Christian Life: Sources for the Study of the Holiness, Pentecostal and Keswick Movements*. New York: Garland Publishing, 1984.
Dinger, Clair M. *Moral Re-Armament: A Study of Its Technical and Religious Nature in the Light of Catholic Teaching*. Washington, D.C.: The Catholic University of America Press, 1961.
"Discord in Oxford Group: Buchmanites Ousted by Disciple from N.Y. Parish House." *Newsweek*. November 24, 1941.
Dorsey, Theodore H. *From a Far Country: The Conversion Story of a Campaigner for Christ*. Huntington, Indiana: Our Sunday Visitor Press, n.d.
Drakeford, John W. *People to People Therapy*. New York: Harper & Row, 1978.
Driberg, Tom. *The Mystery of Moral Re-Armament: A Study of Frank Buchman and His Movement*. New York: Alfred A. Knopf, 1965.
du Maurier, Daphne. *Come Wind, Come Weather*. London: William Heinemann, 1941.

Entwistle, Basil, and John McCook Roots. *Moral Re-Armament: What Is It?* Pace Publications, 1967.

Eister, Allan W. *Drawing Room Conversion.* Durham: Duke University Press, 1950.

Ferguson, Charles W. *The Confusion of Tongues.* Garden City: Doubleday, Doran Company, Inc., 1940.

Foot, Stephen. *Life Began Yesterday.* New York: Harper & Brothers, 1935.

Ford, John C., S.J. *Moral Re-Armament and Alcoholics Anonymous.* NCCA "Blue Book," Vol 10, 1968.

Forde, Eleanor Napier. *Guidance: What It Is and How to Get It.* Paper presented by Eleanor Napier Forde at Minnewaska, NY, September, 1927.

———. *The Guidance of God.* London: The Oxford Group, 1927.

Gordon, Anne Wolrige. *Peter Howard, Life and Letters.* London: Hodder & Stoughton, 1969.

Gray, Betty. *Watersheds: Journey to a faith.* London: Grosvenor, 1986.

Grensted, L. W. *The Person of Christ.* New York: Harper & Brothers, 1933.

Grogan, William. *John Riffe of the Steelworkers.* New York: Coward—McCann, 1959.

Hadden, Richard M. "Christ's Program for World-Reconstruction: Studies in the Sermon on the Mount." *The Calvary Evangel*, 1934-35, pp. 11-14, 44-49, 73-77, 104-07, 133-36.

Hamilton, A. S. Loudon. *MRA: How It All Began.* London: Moral Re-Armament, 1968.

———. *Some Basic Principles of Christian Work.* The Oxford Group, n.d.

———. "Description of the First Century Christian Fellowship." Vol. 2, *The Messenger*, June, 1923.

Hamlin, Bryan T. *Moral Re-Armament and Forgiveness in International Affairs.* London: Grosvenor, 1992.

Harris, Irving. *An Outline of the Life of Christ.* New York: The Oxford Group, 1935.

———. *Out in Front: Forerunners of Christ. A Study of the Lives of Eight Great Men.* New York: The Calvary Evangel, 1942.

———. *The Breeze of the Spirit.* New York: The Seabury Press, 1978.

Harrison, Marjorie. *Saints Run Mad.* London: John Lane, Ltd., 1934.

Henderson, Michael. *A Different Accent.* Richmond, VA: Grosvenor Books USA, 1985.

———. *All Her Paths Are Peace: Women Pioneers in Peacemaking.* CT: Kumerian Press, 1994.

———. *Hope for a Change: Commentaries by an Optimistic Realist.* Salem, OR: Grosvenor Books, 1991.

———. *On History's Coattails: Commentaries by an English Journalist in America.* Richmond, VA: Grosvenor USA, 1988.

Henson, Herbert Hensley. *The Oxford Group Movement.* London: Oxford University Press, 1933.

Hicks, Roger. *How Augustine Found Faith: Told in his own words from F. J. Sheed's translation of The Confessions of St. Augustine.* N.p., 1956.

———. *How to Read the Bible.* London: Moral Re-Armament, 1940.

———. *Letters to Parsi.* London: Blandford Press, 1960.

———. *The Endless Adventure.* London: Blandford Press, 1964.

———. *The Lord's Prayer and Modern Man.* London: Blandford Press, 1967.

Hofmeyr, Bremer. *How to Change*. New York: Moral Re-Armament, n.d.
———. *How to Listen*. London: The Oxford Group, 1941.
Holme, Reginald. *A Journalist for God: The memoirs of Reginald Holme*. London: A Bridge Builders Publication, 1995.
Holmes-Walker, Wilfrid. *The New Enlistment*. London: The Oxford Group, circa 1937.
Howard, Peter. *Frank Buchman's Secret*. Garden City: New York: Doubleday & Company, Inc., 1961.
———. *Fighters Ever*. London: William Heinemann, 1941
———. *Innocent Men*. London: William Heinemann, 1941.
———. *Ideas Have Legs*. London: Muller, 1945.
———. *That Man Frank Buchman*. London: Blandford Press, 1946.
———. *The World Rebuilt*. New York. Duell, Sloan & Pearce, 1951.
Hunter, T. Willard, with assistance from M.D.B. *A.A.'s Roots in the Oxford Group*. New York: A.A. Archives, 1988.
———. *Press Release*. Buchman Events/Pennsylvania, October 19, 1991.
———. *"It Started Right There" Behind the Twelve Steps and the Self-help Movement*. Oregon: Grosvenor Books, 1994.
———. *The Spirit of Charles Lindbergh: Another Dimension*. Lanham, MD: Madison Books, 1993.
———. *Uncommon Friends' Uncommon Friend*. A tribute to James Draper Newton, on the occasion of his eighty-fifth birthday. (Pamphlet, March 30, 1990).
———. *World Changing Through Life Changing*. Thesis, Newton Center, Mass: Andover-Newton Theological School, 1977.
Hutchinson, Michael. *A Christian Approach to Other Faiths*. London: Grosvenor Books, 1991.
———. *The Confessions*. (privately published study of St. Augustine's *Confessions*).
Jaeger, Clara. *Philadelphia Rebel: The Education of a Bourgeoise*. Virginia: Grosvenor, 1988.
Jones, Olive M. *Inspired Children*. New York: Harper & Brothers, 1933.
———. *Inspired Youth*. New York: Harper & Brothers, 1938.
Kitchen, V. C. *I Was a Pagan*. New York: Harper & Brothers, 1934.
Kestne, Eugene. *The Lord of History*. Boston: Daughters of St. Paul, 1980.
Koenig, His Eminence Franz Cardinal. *True Dialogue*. Oregon: Grosvenor USA, 1986.
Laun, Ferdinand. *Unter Gottes Fuhring*. The Oxford Group, n.d.
Lean, Garth. *Cast Out Your Nets*. London: Grosvenor, 1990.
———. *Frank Buchman: A Life*. London: Constable, 1985.
———. *Good God, It Works*. London: Blandford Press, 1974.
———. *Joyful Remembrance*. London: Executors of Garth D. Lean, 1994.
———. *On the Tail of a Comet: The Life of Frank Buchman*. Colorado Springs: Helmers & Howard, 1988.
———, and Morris Martin. *New Leadership*. London: William Heinemann, 1936.
Leon, Philip. *A Philosopher's Quiet Time*. N.p., n.d.
———. *The Philosophy of Courage or the Oxford Group Way*. New York: Oxford University Press, 1939.
"Less Buchmanism." *Time*, November 24, 1941.

Letter 7, The: The South African Adventure. A Miracle Working God Abroad. Oxford: The Groups, A First Century Christian Fellowship, 1930.

Macintosh, Douglas C. *Personal Religion*. New York: Charles Scribner's Sons, 1942.

Mackay, Malcom George. *More than Coincidence*. Edinburgh: The Saint Andrew Press, 1979.

Macmillan, Ebenezer. *Seeking and Finding*. New York: Harper & Brothers, 1933.

Margetson, The Very Reverend Provost. *The South African Adventure*. The Oxford Group, n.d.

Martin, Morris H. *The Thunder and the Sunshine*. Washington D.C.: MRA, n.d.

———. *Born to Live in the Future*. n.l.: Up With People, 1991.

McAll, Dr. Frances. *So what's the alternative?* London: Moral Re-Armament, 1974.

Molony, John N. *Moral Re-Armament*. Melbourne: The Australian Catholic Truth Society Record, June 10, 1956.

Mottu, Philippe. *The Story of Caux*. London: Grosvenor, 1970.

Mowat, R. C. *Modern Prophetic Voices: From Kierkegaard to Buchman*. Oxford: New Cherwel Press, 1994.

———. *The Message of Frank Buchman*. London: Blandford Press, n.d.

———. *Report on Moral Re-Armament*. London: Blandford Press, 1955.

———. *Creating the European Community*. London, 1973.

———. *Decline and Renewal: Europe Ancient and Modern*. Oxford: New Cherwel Press, 1991.

Moyes, John S. *American Journey*. Sydney: Clarendon Publishing Co., n. d.

Murray, Robert H. *Group Movements Throughout the Ages*. New York: Harper & Brothers. 1935.

Newton, Eleanor Forde. *I Always Wanted Adventure*. London: Grosvenor, 1992.

———. *Echoes From The Heart*. Fort Myers Beach, Florida, 1986.

Newton, James Draper. *Uncommon Friends: Life with Thomas Edison, Henry Ford, Harvey Firestone, Alexis Carrel, & Charles Lindbergh*. New York: Harcourt Brace, 1987.

Nichols, Beverley. *The Fool Hath Said*. Garden City: Doubleday, Doran & Company, 1936.

Orglmeister, Peter. *An Ideology for Today*. Pamphlet, 1965.

Perry, Edward T. *God Can Be Real*. Moral Re-Armament, Inc., 1969.

Petrocokino, Paul. *The New Man for the New World*. Cheshire: Paul Petrocokino, n.d.

———. *The Right Direction*. Great Britain: The City Press of Chester, Ltd., n.d.

———. *An Experiment: Try This For a Fortnight*. Privately published pamphlet, n.d.

Phillimore, Miles. *Just for Today*. Privately published pamphlet, 1940.

Prescott, D. M. *A New Day: Daily Readings for Our Time*. New ed. London: Grosvenor Book, 1979.

Raynor, Frank D., and Leslie D. Weatherhead. *The Finger of God*. London: Group Publications, Ltd., 1934.

Reynolds, Amelia S. *New Lives for Old*. New York. Fleming H. Revell, 1929.

Roots, The Right Reverend Herbert, Bishop of Hankow, China. *The Two Options*. The Oxford Group, 1934.

Roots, John McCook. *An Apostle to Youth*. Oxford, The Oxford Group, 1928.

Rose, Cecil. *When Man Listens*. New York: Oxford University Press, 1937.

Rose, Howard J. *The Quiet Time*. New York: Oxford Group at 61 Gramercy Park, North, 1937.

Russell, Arthur J. *For Sinners Only*. London: Hodder & Stoughton, 1932.

———. *One Thing I Know*. New York: Harper & Brothers, 1933.

Sangster, W. E. *God Does Guide Us*. New York: The Abingdon Press, 1934.

Sherry, Frank H. and Mahlon H. Hellerich. *The Formative Years of Frank N. D. Buchman*. (Reprint of article at Frank Buchman home in Allentown, Pennsylvania).

Spencer, F. A. M. *The Meaning of the Groups*. London: Methuen & Co., Ltd., 1934.

Spoerri, Theophil. *Dynamic out of Silence: Frank Buchman's Relevance Today*. Translated by John Morrison. London: Grosvenor Books, 1976.

Streeter, Burnett Hillman. *The God Who Speaks*. London: Macmillan & Co., Ltd., 1936.

———. *Reality*. London, 1943.

Suenens, Rt. Rev. Msgr. *The Right View of Moral Re-Armament*. London: Burns and Oates, 1952.

The Bishop of Leicester, Chancellor R. J. Campbell and the Editor of the "Church of England Newspaper." *Stories of our Oxford House Party.*, July 17, 1931.

The Groups in South Africa 1930. South Africa: The Groups, 1930.

The Layman with a Notebook. *What Is the Oxford Group?* London: Oxford University Press, 1933.

Thornhill, Alan. *One Fight More*. London: Frederick Muller, 1943.

———. *The Significance of the Life of Frank Buchman*. London: Moral Re-Armament, 1952.

———. *Best of Friends: A Life of Enriching Friendships*. United Kingdom, Marshall Pickering, 1986.

Thornton-Duesbury, Julian P. *Sharing*. The Oxford Group. n.d.

———. *The Oxford Group: A Brief Account of its Principles and Growth*. London: The Oxford Group, 1947.

———. *The Open Secret of MRA*. London: Blandford, 1964.

———. *A Visit to Caux: First-hand experience of Moral Re-Armament in action*. London: The Oxford Group, 1960.

"Calvary's Eviction of Buchman." *Time Magazine*, November 24, 1941.

Twitchell, Kenaston. *Do You Have to Be Selfish*. New York: Moral Re-Armament, n.d.

———. *How Do You Make Up Your Mind*. New York: Moral Re-Armament, n.d.

———. *Regeneration in the Ruhr*. Princeton: Princeton University Press, 1981.

———. *Supposing Your Were Absolutely Honest*. New York: Moral Re-Armament, n.d.

———. *The Strength of a Nation: Absolute Purity*. New York: Moral Re-Armament, n.d.

Van Baalen, *The Chaos of Cults: A Study in Present-Day Isms*, 4th rev. ed. Grand Rapids: Wm. B. Eerdmans, 1967.

Van Dusen, Henry P. "Apostle to the Twentieth Century: Frank N. D. Buchman." *The Atlantic Monthly*, Vol. 154, pp. 1-16 (July 1934).

———. "The Oxford Group Movement: An Appraisal." *The Atlantic Monthly*. Vol. 154, pp. 230-252 (August 1934).

Viney, Hallen. *How Do I Begin?* The Oxford Group, 61 Gramercy Park, New York., 1937.

Vrooman, Lee. *The Faith That Built America*. New York: Arrowhead Books, Inc., 1955.

Waddy, Charis. *The Skills of Discernment*. London: Grosvenor Books, 1977.

Walter, Howard A. *Soul Surgery: Some Thoughts On Incisive Personal Work*. Oxford: The Oxford Group, 1928.

Watt, Frederick B. *Great Bear: A Journey Remembered*. Yellowknife, Northwest Territories, Canada: The Northern Publishers, 1980.

Weatherhead, Leslie D. *Discipleship*. London: Student Christian Movement Press, 1934.

———. *How Can I Find God?* London: Fleming H. Revell, 1934.

———. *Psychology and Life*. New York: Abingdon Press, 1935.

West, The Right Rev. George. *The World That Works*. London: Blandford, 1945.

Williamson, Geoffrey. *Inside Buchmanism*. New York: Philosophical Library, Inc., 1955.

Winslow, Jack C. *Church in Action* (no data available to author).

———. *Vital Touch with God: How to Carry on Adequate Devotional Life*. The Evangel, 8 East 40th St., New York, n.d.

———. *When I Awake*. London: Hodder & Stoughton, 1938.

———. *Why I Believe in the Oxford Group*. London: Hodder & Stoughton, 1934.

Books by or about the Oxford Group and A.A.'s Christian Mentors

Bushnell, Horace. *The New Life*. London: Strahan & Co., 1868.

Chapman, J. Wilbur. *Life and Work of Dwight L. Moody*. Philadelphia, 1900.

Cheney, Mary B. *Life and Letters of Horace Bushnell*. New York: Harper & Brothers, 1890.

Drummond, Henry. *Essays and Addresses*. New York: James Potts & Company, 1904.

———. *Natural Law in the Spiritual World*. Potts Edition.

———. *The Changed Life*. New York: James Potts & Company, 1891.

———. *The Greatest Thing in the World and Other Addresses*. London: Collins, 1953.

———. *The Ideal Life*. London: Hodder & Stoughton, 1897.

———. *The New Evangelism and Other Papers*. London: Hodder & Stoughton, 1899.

Edwards, Robert L. *Of Singular Genius, of Singular Grace: A Biography of Horace Bushnell*. Cleveland: The Pilgrim Press, 1992.

Findlay, James F., Jr. *Dwight L. Moody American Evangelist*. Chicago, University of Chicago Press, 1969.

Fitt, Emma Moody, *Day by Day with D. L. Moody*. Chicago: Moody Press, n.d.

Goodspeed, Edgar J. *The Wonderful Career of Moody and Sankey in Great Britain and America*. New York: Henry S. Goodspeed & Co., 1876.

Guldseth, Mark O. *Streams*. Alaska: Fritz Creek Studios, 1982.

Hopkins, C. Howard. *John R. Mott, a Biography*. Grand Rapids: William B. Erdmans Publishing Company, 1979.

James, William. *The Varieties of Religious Experience*. New York: First Vintage Books/The Library of America, 1990.

Meyer, F. B. *Five Musts*. Chicago: Moody Press, 1927.

———. *The Secret of Guidance*. New York: Fleming H. Revell, 1896.

Moody, Paul D. *My Father: An Intimate Portrait of Dwight Moody*. Boston: Little Brown, 1938.

Moody, William R. *The Life of D. L. Moody*. New York: Fleming H. Revell, 1900.
Mott, John R. *The Evangelization of the World in This Generation*. London, 1901.
————. *Addresses and Papers* (no further data at this time).
————. *Five Decades and a Forward View*. 4th ed. New York: Harper & Brothers, 1939.
Pollock, J. C. *Moody: A Biographical Portrait of the Pacesetter in Modern Mass Evangelism*. New York: Macmillan, 1963.
Smith, George Adam. *The Life of Henry Drummond*. New York: McClure, Phillips & Co., 1901.
Speer, Robert E. *Studies of the Man Christ Jesus*. New York: Fleming H. Revell, 1896.
————. *The Marks of a Man*. New York: Hodder & Stoughton, 1907.
————. *The Principles of Jesus*. New York: Fleming H. Revell Company, 1902.
Stewart, George, Jr. *Life of Henry B. Wright*. New York: Association Press, 1925.
Wright, Henry B. *The Will of God and a Man's Lifework*. New York: The Young Men's Christian Association Press, 1909.

Spiritual Literature-Non-Oxford Group

[Almost all of these books were owned, studied, recommended, and loaned to others by Dr. Bob and h is wife, Anne.]

Allen, James. *As a Man Thinketh*. New York: Peter Pauper Press, n.d.
————. *Heavenly Life*. New York: Grosset & Dunlap, n.d.
Barton, George A. *Jesus of Nazareth*. New York: The Macmillan Company, 1922.
Bode, Carl, ed. *The Portable Emerson*. New ed. New York: Penguin Books, 1981.
Brother Lawrence. *The Practice of the Presence of God*. Pennsylvania: Whitaker House, 1982.
Browne, Lewis. *This Believing World: A Simple Account of the Great Religions of Mankind*. New York: The Macmillan Co., 1935.
Carruthers, Donald W. *How to Find Reality in Your Morning Devotions*. Pennsylvania: State College, n.d.
Chambers, Oswald. *Studies in the Sermon on the Mount*. London: Simpkin, Marshall, Ltd., n.d.
Clark, Francis E. *Christian Endeavor in All Lands*. N.p.: The United Society of Christian Endeavor, 1906.
Clark, Glenn. *Clear Horizons*. Vol 2. Minnesota: Macalester Park Publishing, 1941.
————. *Fishers of Men*. Boston: Little, Brown, 1928.
————. *God's Reach*. Minnesota: Macalester Park Publishing, 1951.
————. *How to Find Health through Prayer*. New York: Harper & Brothers, 1940.
————. *I Will Lift Up Mine Eyes*. New York: Harper & Brothers, 1937.
————. *Stepping Heavenward: The Spiritual Journal of Louise Miles Clark*. Minnesota: Macalester Park Publishing, 1940.
————. *The Lord's Prayer and Other Talks on Prayer from The Camps Farthest Out*. Minnesota: Macalester Publishing Co., 1932.
————. *The Man Who Talks with Flowers*. Minnesota: Macalester Park Publishing, 1939.
————. *The Soul's Sincere Desire*. Boston: Little, Brown, 1925.

————. *Touchdowns for the Lord. The Story of "Dad" A. J. Elliott*. Minnesota: Macalester Park Publishing Co., 1947.

————. *Two or Three Gathered Together*. New York: Harper & Brothers, 1942.

Daily, Starr. *Recovery*. Minnesota: Macalester Park Publishing, 1948.

Eddy, Mary Baker. *Science and Health with Key to the Scriptures*. Boston: Published by the Trustees under the Will of Mary Baker G. Eddy, 1916.

Fillmore, Charles. *Christian Healing*. Kansas City: Unity School of Christianity, 1936.

————, and Cora Fillmore. *Teach Us to Pray*. Lee's Summit, Missouri: Unity School of Christianity, 1950.

Fosdick, Harry Emerson. *A Great Time to Be Alive*. New York: Harper & Brothers, 1944.

————. *As I See Religion*. New York: Grosset & Dunlap, 1932.

————. *On Being a Real Person*. New York: Harper & Brothers, 1943.

————. *The Man from Nazareth*. New York: Harper & Brothers, 1949.

————. *The Manhood of the Master*. London: Student Christian Association, 1924.

————. *The Meaning of Faith*. New York: The Abingdon Press, 1917.

————. *The Meaning of Prayer*. New York: Association Press, 1915.

————. *The Meaning of Service*. London: Student Christian Movement, 1921.

Fox, Emmet. *Alter Your Life*. New York: Harper & Brothers, 1950.

————. *Find and Use Your Inner Power*. New York: Harper & Brothers, 1937.

————. *Power through Constructive Thinking*. New York: Harper & Brothers, 1932.

————. *Sparks of Truth*. New York: Grosset & Dunlap, 1941.

————. *The Sermon on the Mount*. New York: Harper & Row, 1934.

————. Pamphlets: *Getting Results by Prayer* (1933); *The Great Adventure* (1937); *You Must Be Born Again* (1936).

Glover, T. R. *The Jesus of History*. New York: Association Press, 1930.

Gordon, S. D. *The Quiet Time*. London: Fleming, n.d.

Heard, Gerald. *A Preface to Prayer*. New York: Harper & Brothers, 1944.

Herman, E. *Creative Prayer*. London: James Clarke & Co., circa 1921.

Hickson, James Moore. *Heal the Sick*. London: Methuen & Co., 1925.

James, William. *The Varieties of Religious Experience*. New York: First Vintage Press/The Library of America Edition, 1990.

Jones, E. Stanley. *Abundant Living*. New York: Cokesbury Press, 1942.

————. *Along the Indian Road*. New York: Abingdon Press, 1939.

————. *Christ and Human Suffering*. New York: Abingdon Press, 1930.

————. *Christ at the Round Table*. New York: Abingdon Press, 1928.

————. *The Choice Before Us*. New York: Abingdon Press, 1937.

————. *The Christ of Every Road*. New York: Abingdon Press, 1930.

————. *The Christ of the American Road*. New York: Abingdon-Cokesbury Press, 1944.

————. *The Christ of the Indian Road*. New York: Abingdon Press, 1925.

————. *The Christ of the Mount*: A Working Philosophy of Life. New York: Abingdon Press, 1931.

————. *Victorious Living*. New York: Abingdon Press, 1936.

————. *Way to Power and Poise*. New York: Abingdon Press, 1949.

Jung, Dr. Carl G. *Modern Man in Search of a Soul*. New York: Harcourt Brace Jovanovich, 1933.

Kagawa, Toyohiko. *Love: The Law of Life*. Philadelphia: The John C. Winston Company, 1929.

Kempis, Thomas à. *The Imitation of Christ*. Georgia: Mercer University Press, 1989.

Laubach, Frank. *Prayer (Mightiest Force in the World)*. New York: Fleming H. Revell, 1946.

Layman, Charles M. *A Primer of Prayer*. Nashville: Tidings, 1949.

Lieb, Frederick G. *Sight Unseen*. New York: Harper & Brothers, 1939.

Ligon, Ernest M. *Psychology of a Christian Personality*. New York: Macmillan, 1935.

Link, Dr. Henry C. *The Rediscovery of Man*. New York: Macmillan, 1939.

Lupton, Dilworth. *Religion Says You Can*. Boston: The Beacon Press, 1938.

Moseley, J. Rufus. *Perfect Everything*. Minnesota: Macalester Publishing Co., 1949.

Oursler, Fulton. *Happy Grotto*. Declan and McMullen, 1948.

———. *The Greatest Story Ever Told*. New York: Doubleday, 1949.

Parker, William R., and Elaine St. Johns. *Prayer Can Change Your Life*. New ed. New York: Prentice Hall, 1957.

Peale, Norman Vincent. *The Art of Living*. New York: Abingdon-Cokesbury Press, 1937.

Rawson, F. L. *The Nature of True Prayer*. Chicago: The Marlowe Company, n.d.

Sheean, Vincent. *Lead Kindly Light*. New York: Random House, 1949.

Sheen, Fulton J. *Peace of Soul*. New York: McGraw Hill, 1949.

Sheldon, Charles M. *In His Steps*. Nashville, Broadman Press, 1935.

Silkey, Charles Whitney. *Jesus and Our Generation*. Chicago: University of Chicago Press, 1925.

Speer, Robert E.. *Studies of the Man Christ Jesus*. New York: Fleming H. Revell, 1896.

Stalker, James. *The Life of Jesus Christ*. New York: Fleming H. Revell, 1891.

The Confessions of St. Augustine. Translated by E. B. Pusey. A Cardinal Edition. New York: Pocket Books, 1952.

The Fathers of the Church. New York: CIMA Publishing, 1947.

Trine, Ralph Waldo. *In Tune with the Infinite*. New York: Thomas H. Crowell, 1897.

———. *The Man Who Knew*. New York: Bobbs Merrill, 1936.

Troward, Thomas. *The Edinburgh Lectures on Mental Science*. N.p., n.d.

Uspenskii, Peter D. *Tertium Organum*. New York: A.A. Knopf, 1922.

Weatherhead, Leslie D. *Discipleship*. New York: Abingdon Press, 1934.

———. *How Can I Find God?* New York: Fleming H. Revell, 1934.

———. *Psychology and Life*. New York: Abingdon Press, 1935.

Wells, Amos R. *Expert Endeavor: A Text-book of Christian Endeavor Methods and Principles*. Boston: United Society of Christian Endeavor, 1911.

Werber, Eva Bell. *Quiet Talks with the Master*. L.A.: De Vorss & Co., 1942.

Williams, R. Llewelen, *God's Great Plan, a Guide to the Bible*. Hoverhill Destiny Publishers, n.d.

Willitts, Ethel R. *Healing in Jesus Name*. Chicago: Ethel R. Willitts Evangelists, 1931.

Worcester, Elwood, Samuel McComb, and Isador H. Coriat. *Religion and Medicine: The Moral Control of Nervous Disorders*. New York: Moffat, Yard & Company, 1908.

Dick B.'s Historical Titles on Early A.A.'s Spiritual Roots and Successes

Dr. Bob and His Library: A Major A.A. Spiritual Source　　　　(3rd Edition)
Fwd. by Ernest Kurtz, Ph.D., Author, *Not-God: A History of Alcoholics Anonymous.*
A study of the immense spiritual reading of the Bible, Christian literature, and Oxford
Group books done and recommended by A.A. co-founder, Dr. Robert H. Smith. Paradise
Research Pub., Inc.; 156 pp.; 6 x 9; perfect bound; $15.95; 1998; ISBN 1-885803-25-7.
Anne Smith's Journal, 1933-1939　　　　(3rd Edition)
Fwd. by Robert R. Smith, son of Dr. Bob & Anne; co-author, *Children of the Healer.*
Dr. Bob's wife, Anne, kept a journal in the 1930's from which she shared with early AAs
and their families ideas from the Bible and the Oxford Group. Her ideas substantially
influenced A.A.'s program. Paradise Research Publications, Inc.; 180 pp.; 6 x 9; perfect
bound; 1998; $16.95; ISBN 1-885803-24-9.
The Oxford Group & Alcoholics Anonymous　　　　(Second Edition)
Foreword by Rev. T. Willard Hunter; author, columnist, Oxford Group activist.
A comprehensive history of the origins, principles, practices, and contributions to A.A. of
"A First Century Christian Fellowship" (also known as the Oxford Group) of which A.A.
was an integral part in the developmental period between 1931 and 1939. Paradise Research
Publications, Inc.; 432 pp.; 6 x 9; perfect bound; 1998; $17.95; ISBN 1-885803-19-2.
(Previous title: *Design for Living*).
The Akron Genesis of Alcoholics Anonymous　　　　(Newton Edition)
Foreword by former U.S. Congressman John F. Seiberling of Akron, Ohio.
The story of A.A.'s birth at Dr. Bob's Home in Akron on June 10, 1935. Tells what early
AAs did in their meetings, homes, and hospital visits; what they read; how their ideas
developed from the Bible, Oxford Group, and Christian literature. Depicts roles of A.A.
founders and their wives; Henrietta Seiberling; and T. Henry Williams. Paradise Research
Publications, Inc.; 400 pp., 6 x 9; perfect bound; 1998; $17.95; ISBN 1-885803-17-6.
The Books Early AAs Read for Spiritual Growth　　　　(7th Edition)
Foreword by former U.S. Congressman John F. Seiberling of Akron, Ohio.
The most exhaustive bibliography (with brief summaries) of all the books known to have
been read and recommended for spiritual growth by early AAs in Akron and on the East
Coast. Paradise Research Publications, Inc.; 126 pp.; 6 x 9; perfect bound; 1998; $15.95;
ISBN 1-885803-26-5.
New Light on Alcoholism: God, Sam Shoemaker, and A.A.　　　　(Second Edition)
Forewords by Nickie Shoemaker Haggart, daughter of Sam Shoemaker; Julia Harris;
and Karen Plavan, Ph.D.
A comprehensive history and analysis of the all-but-forgotten specific contributions to A.A.
spiritual principles and practices by New York's famous Episcopal preacher, the Rev. Dr.
Samuel M. Shoemaker, Jr.—dubbed by Bill W. a "co-founder" of A.A. and credited by Bill
as the well-spring of A.A.'s spiritual recovery ideas. Paradise Research Pub., Inc.; approx.
672 pp.; 6 x 9; perfect bound; 1999; $24.95; ISBN 1-885803-27-3.
The Good Book and The Big Book: A.A.'s Roots in the Bible　　　　(Second Edition)
Fwd. by Robert R. Smith, son of Dr. Bob & Anne; co-author, *Children of the Healer.*
The author shows conclusively that A.A.'s program of recovery came primarily from the
Bible. This is a history of A.A.'s biblical roots as they can be seen in A.A.'s Big Book,
Twelve Steps, and Fellowship. Paradise Research Publications, Inc.; 264 pp.; 6 x 9; perfect
bound; 1997; $17.95; ISBN 1-885803-16-8.

That Amazing Grace: The Role of Clarence and Grace S. in Alcoholics Anonymous
Foreword by Harold E. Hughes, former U.S. Senator from, and Governor of, Iowa. Precise details of early A.A.'s spiritual practices—from the recollections of Grace S., widow of A.A. pioneer, Clarence S. Paradise Research Pub; 160 pp.; 6 x 9; perfect bound; 1996; $16.95; ISBN 1-885803-06-0.

Good Morning!: Quiet Time, Morning Watch, Meditation, and Early A.A.   (2d Ed.)
A practical guide to Quiet Time—considered a "must" in early A.A. Also discusses biblical roots, history, helpful books, and how to. Paradise Research Pub; 154 pp.; 6 x 9; perfect bound; 1998; $16.95; ISBN: 1-885803-22-2.

Turning Point: A History of Early A.A.'s Spiritual Roots and Successes
Fwd. by Paul Wood, Ph.D., Pres., Nat. Council on Alcoholism and Drug Dependence. *Turning Point* is a comprehensive history of early A.A.'s spiritual roots and successes. It is the culmination of six years of research, traveling, and interviews. Dick B.'s latest title shows specifically what the Twelve Step pioneers borrowed from: (1) The Bible; (2) The Rev. Sam Shoemaker's teachings; (3) The Oxford Group; (4) Anne Smith's Journal; and (5) meditation periodicals and books, such as *The Upper Room*. Paradise Research Publications, Inc.; 776 pp.; 6 x 9; perfect bound; 1997; $29.95; ISBN: 1-885803-07-9.

Utilizing Early A.A.'s Spiritual Roots for Recovery Today
This booklet is the first of a series containing the remarks of Dick B. at his annual seminars at The Wilson House—birthplace of A.A. co-founder Bill Wilson. It is intended as a guide for study groups who wish to apply today the highly successful program and principles of early A.A.. Paradise Research Publications, Inc.; 106 pp.; 6 x 9; perfect bound; 2000; $14.95; ISBN 1-885803-28-1.

The Golden Text of A.A.: God, the Pioneers, and Real Spirituality
This booklet is the second of a series containing the remarks of Dick B. at his annual seminars at The Wilson House. The booklet contains the sincere and surprising credit that Bill Wilson and Bill Dotson (A.A. #3) gave to God for curing them of the disease of alcoholism.; 94pp; 6 x 9; perfect bound; 2000; $14.95; ISBN 1-885803-29-X.

By the Power of God: A Guide to Early A.A. Groups & Forming Similar Groups Today
Fwd. by Ozzie Lepper, Pres./Managing Dir., The Wilson House, East Dorset, VT. Precise details of early A.A.'s spiritual practices—from the recollections of Grace S., widow of A.A. pioneer, Clarence S. Paradise Research Pub; 260 pp.; 6 x 9; perfect bound; 2000; $16.95; ISBN 1-885803-30-3.

Why Early A.A. Succeeded: The Good Book in Alcoholics Anonymous Yesterday and Today
Foreword by Jeffrey H. Boyd, M.D., M. Div., M.P.H.; Chairman of Psychiatry, Waterbury Hospital, Waterbury, CT; Ordained Episcopal Minister; Chairman of the New England Evangelical Theological Society.
Paradise Research Pub; approx 330 pp.; 6 x 9; perfect bound; 2001; $17.95; ISBN 1-885803-31-1.

About the Author

Dick B. writes books on the spiritual roots of Alcoholics Anonymous. They show how the basic and highly successful biblical ideas used by early AAs can be valuable tools for success in today's A.A. His research can also help the religious and recovery communities work more effectively with alcoholics, addicts, and others involved in Twelve Step programs.

The author is an active, recovered member of A.A.; a retired attorney; and a Bible student. He has sponsored more than eighty men in their recovery from alcoholism. Consistent with A.A.'s traditions of anonymity, he uses the pseudonym "Dick B."

He has had fifteen titles published: *Dr. Bob and His Library*; *Anne Smith's Journal, 1933-1939*; *The Oxford Group & Alcoholics Anonymous: A Design for Living That Works*; *The Akron Genesis of Alcoholics Anonymous*; *The Books Early AAs Read for Spiritual Growth*; *New Light on Alcoholism: God, Sam Shoemaker, and A.A.*; *Courage to Change* (with Bill Pittman); *The Good Book and The Big Book: A.A.'s Roots in the Bible*; *That Amazing Grace: The Role of Clarence and Grace S. in Alcoholics Anonymous*; *Good Morning!: Quiet Time, Morning Watch, Meditation, and Early A.A.*; *Turning Point: A History of Early A.A.'s Spiritual Roots and Successes*, *Hope!: The Story of Geraldine D., Alina Lodge & Recovery*, *Utilizing Early A.A.'s Spiritual Roots for Recovery Today*, *The Golden Text of A.A.*, and *By the Power of God: A Guide to Early A.A. Groups & Forming Similar Groups Today*. The books have been the subject of newspaper articles, and have been reviewed in *Library Journal, Bookstore Journal, For a Change, The Living Church, Faith at Work, Sober Times, Episcopal Life, Recovery News, Ohioana Quarterly, The PHOENIX, MRA Newsletter*, and the *Saint Louis University Theology Digest*.

Dick is the father of two married sons (Ken and Don) and a grandfather. As a young man, he did a stint as a newspaper reporter. He attended the University of California, Berkeley, where he received his A.A. degree, majored in economics, and was elected to Phi Beta Kappa in his Junior year. In the United States Army, he was an Information-Education Specialist. He received his A.B. and J.D. degrees from Stanford University, and was Case Editor of the Stanford Law Review. Dick became interested in Bible study in his childhood Sunday School and was much inspired by his mother's almost daily study of Scripture. He joined, and was president of, a Community Church affiliated with the United Church of Christ. By 1972, he was studying the origins of the Bible and began traveling abroad in pursuit of that subject. In 1979, he became much involved in a Biblical research, teaching, and fellowship ministry. In his community life, he was president of a merchants' council, Chamber of Commerce, church retirement center, and homeowners' association. He served on a public district board and was active in a service club.

In 1986, he was felled by alcoholism, gave up his law practice, and began recovery as a member of Alcoholics Anonymous. In 1990, his interest in A.A.'s Christian roots was sparked by his attendance at A.A.'s International Convention in Seattle. He has traveled widely; researched at archives, and at public and seminary libraries; interviewed scholars, historians, clergy, A.A. "old-timers" and survivors; and participated in programs on A.A.'s roots.

The author owns Good Book Publishing Co. and has several works in progress. Much of his research and writing is done in collaboration with his older son, Ken, who holds B.A., B.Th., and M.A. degrees. Ken has been a lecturer in New Testament Greek at a Bible college and a lecturer in Fundamentals of Oral Communication at San Francisco State University.

Dick belongs to the American Historical Association, Maui Writers Guild, Christian Association for Psychological Studies, Alcohol and Temperance History Group, The Authors' Guild. He is available for conferences, panels, seminars, and interviews.

How to Order Dick B.'s Historical Titles on Early A.A.

Order Form

Qty.

Send:

____	*Anne Smith's Journal, 1933-1939*	@ $16.95 ea.	$_____
____	*By the Power of God* (early A.A. groups today)	@ $16.95 ea.	$_____
____	*Dr. Bob and His Library*	@ $15.95 ea.	$_____
____	*Good Morning!* (Quiet Time, etc.)	@ $16.95 ea.	$_____
____	*New Light on Alcoholism* (Sam Shoemaker)	@ $24.95 ea.	$_____
____	*The Akron Genesis of Alcoholics Anonymous*	@ $17.95 ea.	$_____
____	*The Books Early AAs Read for Spiritual Growth*	@ $15.95 ea.	$_____
____	*The Golden Text of A.A.*	@ $14.95 ea.	$_____
____	*The Good Book and The Big Book* (Bible roots)	@ $17.95 ea.	$_____
____	*The Oxford Group & Alcoholics Anonymous*	@ $17.95 ea.	$_____
____	*That Amazing Grace* (Clarence and Grace S.)	@ $16.95 ea.	$_____
____	*Turning Point* (a comprehensive history)	@ $29.95 ea.	$_____
____	*Utilizing Early A.A.'s Spiritual Roots ... Today*	@ $14.95 ea.	$_____
____	*Why Early A.A. Succeeded*	@ $17.95 ea.	$_____

[For 14 vol. Set, put $199.95 in "Subtotal" & $25.00 in S&H]   Subtotal $_____

Shipping and Handling (within the U.S.)**   Shipping and Handling (S&H) $_____
    Add 10% of retail price (minimum $4.50)
** Please contact us for S&H charges for non-U.S. orders   Total Enclosed $_____

Name: _____ (as it appears on your credit card, if using one)

Address: _____ E-mail: _____

City: _____ State: ____ Zip: _____

CC #: _____ MC VISA AMEX DISC Exp. _____

Tel.: _____ Signature _____

Special Value. Get the Set!

If purchased separately, Dick B.'s 14 titles would normally sell for US$256.30, plus Shipping and Handling (S&H). Using this Order Form, you may purchase sets of all 14 titles for **only US$199.95 per set**, plus US$25.00 for S&H (USPS Priority Mail).

Please mail this Order Form, along with your check or money order, to: Dick B., c/o Good Book Publishing Co., P.O. Box 837, Kihei, HI 96753-0837. Please make your check or money order payable to "**Dick B.**" in U.S. dollars drawn on a U.S. bank.